THE WORLD OF ADOLESCENCE

Literature and psychoanalysis are different media for exploring the world of the mind, and in this finely crafted book BETA COPLEY gives equal weight to literary, psychotherapeutic and social perspectives on adolescence.

Inspired by the writings of Klein, Bion and Meltzer on groups and on mental states, she is also mindful of the problems associated with treating literary works as case histories. She addresses three celebrated literary works with adolescence in mind: Shakespeare's *Romeo and Juliet* and *Much Ado about Nothing*, and Pushkin's *Eugene Onegin*. For the reader these will evoke their own memories of love, conflict and growing up, and set the stage for the clinical material in the second half of the book.

She also returns to the oft-studied theme of adolescent development and the social framework; and gives rich examples of problems of young people in areas such as leaving home, developing sexuality, and social conflict. These will illuminate not only the therapeutic work, but something of the basic struggles of adolescence itself.

Beta Copley illustrates the core approach of intensive one-to-one work with adolescents. This is neither widely available nor always appropriate. She looks at other forms of intervention derived from it, which may also be of inestimable benefit for young people in need: the work of a counselling service for young people, psychoanalytic family therapy, and psycho-analytic group therapy for adolescents. The development of these wider approaches to work with adolescents is based in long-term workshops at the Tavistock Clinic, London.

THE WORLD OF ADOLESCENCE

PHOENIX PUBLIC LIBRARY

OCT 2 0 1994

LITERATURE, SOCIETY AND PSYCHOANALYTIC PSYCHOTHERAPY

BETA COPLEY

'an association in which the free development of
each is the condition of the free development of all'

Free Association Books / London / 1993

3 1730 01975 4311

Published in Great Britain in 1993 by
Free Association Books Ltd
26 Freegrove Road
London N7 9QR

© Beta Copley 1993

A CIP catalogue record for this book is available from the British Library

ISBN 1-85343-310-1

The right of Beta Copley to be identified as author of this work has been asserted
by her in accordance with the Copyright, Designs and Patents Act 1988

Typeset from author's discs by Archetype
Printed in the EC by T.J. Press

CONTENTS

ACKNOWLEDGEMENTS

Many people have helped to make the writing of this book possible. I want to thank my husband for his help, encouragement and patience with the project as a whole. I also thank Sally Box for reading and discussing the manuscript from its inception, although this, of course, does not commit her to agreement with its contents.

I am grateful to Dr Leslie Sohn for my personal psychoanalysis. I am also grateful for my training in intensive psychoanalytic psychotherapy at the Tavistock Clinic, and to my multidisciplinary colleagues in the Adolescent Department for the shared endeavours in the application of psychoanalytic thought to brief, family and group work. I also want to thank the many people, too numerous to name individually, who have taken part with me in workshops and seminars at the Tavistock Clinic, and in related courses in Birmingham and Rome, for contributions which provide an essential background to the writing of this book.

I am also grateful to those who, in the past and in the present, have given me various kinds of valuable individual help: in supervision; by the provision of stimulating opportunities for learning, work and teaching; as co-therapists; by allowing me to make use of clinical material; by reading individual chapters of the book, and also by discussion and encouragement. These include Esther Bick; Richard Bird; Mary Boston; Anna Dartington; Barbara Forryan; Ros Jamieson; Robert Gosling; Martha Harris; Bianca Iaccarino; Donald Meltzer; Isabel Menzies Lyth; Luiz Meyer; Roger Money-Kyrle; Anton Obholzer; Elizabeth Oliver-Bellasis; Judith Powell; Sheila Simpson; Ronald Strom; Rolene Szur; Jorge Thomas; Paul Upson; Arthur Hyatt Williams; Gianna Williams; Linda Winkley and Isca Wittenberg. I also acknowledge my appreciation of those who have worked with my colleagues and myself. Changes to protect confidentiality have, of course, been made, so that no account is recognizable except, perhaps, by those who have been directly involved. I hope that if anyone in this position should come across this book, they will not mind the inclusion of something that has taken place in the context of an adolescence which for them has passed, and is now referred to with the purpose of helping others in their development to adulthood.

I also thank my editor, Ann Scott, for her patient support, and my copy-editor, Gillian Beaumont, for her helpful attention to the text.

Shakespeare citations are from the Arden Edition Shakespeare: *Romeo and Juliet*, edited by Brian Gibbons, London: Methuen, 1980 and *Much Ado about Nothing*, edited by A.R. Humphreys, London: Methuen, 1981. Lines from *Eugene Onegin* by Alexander Pushkin, translated by Charles Johnston (Penguin Classics 1977, Revised edition 1979) copyright © Charles Johnston, 1977, 1979, are reproduced by permission of Penguin Books Ltd. I am also grateful to the Health Education Authority for permission to quote from *Today's Young Adults - 16–19 Year Olds Look at Diet, Alcohol, Smoking, Drugs and Sexual Behaviour*, London: HEA, 1992.

INTRODUCTION

Thou canst not speak of that thou dost not feel.
(*Romeo and Juliet*, III.iii.64)

This book is about the complex experience of adolescence, both as a developmental process and as a state of mind. The approach is psychoanalytic. Much of it relates to problems of adolescence, and to therapy with those in emotional difficulties. It starts with the discussion of two Shakespeare plays, *Romeo and Juliet* and *Much Ado about Nothing*, and of a verse novel, *Eugene Onegin* by Pushkin. This is followed by a review of adolescent development and a discussion of problematic issues regarding young people in contemporary society. The last section addresses different ways of engaging therapeutically with adolescents.

Literature, as Freud recognized, predates psychoanalysis in its perception of the depth of human emotions, both within the individual and in relationship with others. *Romeo and Juliet* remains a source of information about adolescent interaction. In the Messina of *Much Ado about Nothing*, deception, self-idealization, and an inability to look inside oneself and inside society impede the growth of an ability to 'suffer love' among the young people. Problems relating to emotional growth in adolescence come to life within the characters and events of *Eugene Onegin,* and we are shown how the failure to recognize emotional truth leads to developmental disaster. The contents of these works are the subject matter of both literature and psychoanalysis, which are themselves, as M.H. Williams and Waddell (1991) say, different media for exploring the world of the mind.

Our own response to what is conveyed to us is relevant to both literature and psychoanalysis. In the theatre, as we watch *Much Ado about Nothing,* we may sense within ourselves something of the underlying lovingness existing between Beatrice and Benedick early on in the play, although the words and gestures may often depict something different. This has something in common with our attempt to evaluate our own response to what is communicated to us in a therapeutic setting.

I have adolescence particularly in mind as I follow some of the experience which is conveyed to us in the works discussed here, but also think about their general content. Literary criticism, however, is not intended, nor do I attempt to relate to the wider literary, historical or national aspects of the writing. I quote as extensively as possible from the literature, hoping to keep in touch with its atmosphere and beauty and to encourage further reference to the original. It must be recognized that there is a degree of crudeness, or even ugliness, in laying theories and everyday descriptions alongside such works of art, even though this is justified by the help it may give us in noticing and trying to make use of understanding derived from what we read. On the other hand, it is possible that our theories may acquire some added liveliness and potential in our minds from being able to function meaningfully in relationship with such literature, and in conse-quence become more richly available to us for further application.

Pushkin has a particular facility for being both close to and distant from his characters; he not only presents us with varying perspectives of adolescent change, but puts us in touch with our own responses to them. According to Dryden (1668), when Shakespeare 'describes any thing, you more than see it, you feel it too'. Coleridge (1812) tells us that Shakespeare 'has availed himself of his psychological genius to develop all the minutiae of the human heart: showing us the thing that, to common observers, he seems solely intent upon, he makes visible what we would not otherwise have seen'. Shakespeare helps us to see, feel and use the findings of our senses in conjunction with each other. He shows us emotionality from different points of view – or what Bion, avoiding the specifically visual element denoted by that term, calls 'vertices'. This is also the work of psychoanalysis. Keats (1817a) deeply admires what he calls Shakespeare's quality of *'Negative Capability*, that is when a man is capable of being in uncertainties, Mysteries, doubts, without any irritable reaching after fact & reason' [original emphasis]. The paradoxical quality of being able to bear not knowing and not understanding, while fundamentally wanting to know and understand, is central to the capacity to bear and think about the emotionality discussed in this book, and is one which we therapists need to try to tolerate (Bion, 1970).

A psychoanalytic approach can help us to notice and think about what is conveyed, such as the nature of anxieties apparent in the represented emotionality of some of the characters in *Much Ado about Nothing*. Writers making use of psychoanalytic understanding are, however, sometimes criticized, at times with some justification, for treating a work of literature as a 'case history' or attempting to derive a specific meaning from it or impose one on it. When one reads plays such as *Romeo and Juliet* and *Much Ado about Nothing*, one probably cannot help having the experience of the characters as people: people who feel 'real', people who may come to assume an individual personal identity in our minds, and can be discussed in such terms. This is just one aspect of the greatness of the writing. In *Eugene Onegin* Pushkin himself writes of 'my Onegin', 'my Tatyana', and at times he treats them as if they were actual separate human beings! The depth and complexity of meaning evoked in such work, however, are, of course, not only – nor necessarily – expressed through the characters as 'people', or their direct interactions, but by what Wilson Knight (1961) calls a play's 'atmosphere', and Skura (1981, pp. 55–6) refers to as 'the more general tension between characters as characters, and characters as part of a state of mind which pervades the work'. Recent developments in psychoanalysis which relate to the need to learn from experience (Bion, 1962a) support the kind of psychoanalytic appreciation that helps us to follow and learn from a work of literature.[1]

The 'object-relations' approach within psychoanalytic theory followed here, to which Klein, Fairbairn, Winnicott, Balint and others have all made their own particular contributions, furthers

the interest arising out of Freud's work regarding the development
of mental and emotional experience. Despite its stark and
impersonal-sounding name, it is essentially concerned with
relationships between people, although admittedly at times it
makes use of somewhat unappealing language. In the context of a
wider psychoanalytic framework, I draw largely on the work of
Klein and those who follow her, in particular Bion and Meltzer, and
make frequent reference to Winnicott's rich understanding of
adolescence. Klein (1946) contrasts 'paranoid-schizoid' states of
mind which are primarily egocentric with those of the 'depressive
position', within which loving concern for those we love is
experienced. Such understanding, as further developed, particularly by Bion and Meltzer, underlines both a concept of value in
psychoanalysis and the need to understand and to use one's own
emotional experience. According to Bion, failure to do the latter
can be as disastrous for the development of the personality as failure
to eat, drink or breathe is for life itself (Bion, 1962a). This, of course,
makes links with the kind of understanding developed in literature,
such as in Shakespeare's study of King Lear, one who 'hath ever but
slenderly known himself' (*King Lear*, I.i.292–3).

I hope that the discussion of the plays and verse novel in the early
part of the book may evoke contact for the reader with what, for
him or her, is a relevant personal background for thinking about
adolescence. I also hope that the imagery and illumination within
the literature will contribute to thinking about the changes of
puberty and adolescence and the strivings towards adulthood,
which we move on to address in the second part of the book.
Relevant theoretical issues are presented here, although concepts
which are useful in thinking about the literature, but unlikely to be
familiar to all readers, are introduced earlier and clarified as
necessary as they arise.

The examples in the clinical part of the book have been chosen
with the hope of illuminating not only the therapeutic work, but
something of the basic struggles of adolescence itself. I have
described some of the interaction in considerable detail, hoping to
convey something of the quality of the live experiences that
contribute to the therapy. I start with an illustration and discussion
of intensive individual psychoanalytic psychotherapy. This method

of work can address an adolescent's problems in considerable depth, and provides the core experience for the application of psychoanalytic understanding to therapy with adolescents. Unfortunately, however, what can be a very rewarding engagement is not sufficiently available for those who need it and could use it. On the other hand, experience has indicated that some adolescents may benefit from different forms of intervention which may be particularly appropriate to their needs. Difficulties that arise in the process of adolescent change may sometimes respond to quite brief contact; family involvements may call for a family approach, at least in the first instance, and for some young people therapeutic adolescent group therapy is the treatment of choice. Increased understanding of processes such as splitting, and the way we, as therapists, try to bear and think about what is invoked in us as we work, have supported the development of these different forms of therapy, which can make psychoanalytic understanding more widely available to adolescents, and in some instances also to their families, in a form that they can use. I explore these ways of working and the indications for their use by means of clinical material. The therapeutic relationship, based on the understanding derived from individual psychoanalytic psychotherapy, remains central to them all, but needs to operate within a clear framework of thought which has regard to the nature of the contact.

The development of these wider aproaches to work with adolescents discussed here is based in, and indebted to, the understanding arising out of long-term workshops at the Tavistock Clinic, London. Responsibility for selection and presentation of the clinical work in this book, which was carried out in a variety of locations by colleagues and myself, is, however, mine.

PART ONE:
STUDIES IN LITERATURE WITH ADOLESCENCE IN MIND

1 A Plague on All Our Houses: A Discussion of Shakespeare's Play *Romeo and Juliet*

The play opens with strife between the rival houses of Capulet and Montague. The Capulet servants, Gregory and Sampson, are engaged in talk of a sexual and aggressive kind, directed against those of the rival house of Montague whom they are expecting to appear. Sampson boasts that he will show himself to be 'a tyrant: when I have fought with the men I will be civil with the maids, I will cut off their heads . . . Ay, the heads of the maids or their maidenheads; take it in what sense thou wilt.' He claims to be 'a pretty piece of flesh', and says to Gregory, as a Montague approaches: 'My naked weapon is out. Quarrel. I will back thee.' Gregory quibbles about the meaning: 'How, turn thy back and run?' When the Montague servants appear, Sampson seeks to provoke them to start a fight: 'Let us take the law of our sides: let them begin.' He then 'bites his thumb' (making a noise with the thumb against the upper teeth) at the Montagues, 'which is a disgrace to them if they bear it', and a fight soon starts (I.i.1–60). The scene for the dynamics of the play is set. The extent of the antagonism between the two houses is clear; it is also apparent how pleasure can be found in the indulgence of polarization and provocation.

A 'world' associated with puberty and the onset of adolescence is brilliantly evoked in this first scene. (We are later told that Juliet's age is thirteen.) Underlying the general sexual banter and the chauvinistic talk, the meaning of some of the quibbles is clear; the reference to 'maidenheads' implies genitality, but of a kind related to an aggressive, raping potency, seeking to possess a maiden rather than to love her. Nowadays we can also link some of the activity and talk, such as the provocative thumb-biting or turning of the back and running, with sadistic oral and anal phantasies of childhood and the infantile sexuality described by Freud (1905a) and Abraham (1924), and vividly portrayed in the actual context of psychoanalysis of children by Klein (1932). This scene graphically represents the way in which aggressive phantasies with an infantile origin may accompany the physical genital developments of puberty in circumstances where there is as yet no actual potentially modifying experience of genital love. This aspect of early adolescence is discussed in Chapter 4.

The scene also helps us to think about the complexities of group mentality and behaviour, which are highly relevant to adolescence. When the Capulet servants meet up with those of the Montagues, a tacit belief is conveyed that a fight will take place; indeed it seems that the purpose of the meeting will be to fight. The exchanges here are strongly suggestive of what Bion (1961, p. 152) has called 'fight/flight basic assumption group' behaviour, portraying a common state of mind that the purpose of the group is inevitably to fight something or to run away from it. Bion considers any group to be subject to apparently obscure emotional drives which lead it to act as if it had certain basic assumptions about its aims. He instances three such 'basic assumptions', which he sees as operating at different times and displacing each other. One is of 'fight/flight', which we encounter here. The other two are of 'dependence', implying extreme dependent expectations of being sustained by a 'leader', which can be seen in the context of a psychotherapy group (see below, p. 250), and of 'pairing', with the implication that the purpose of the group is to produce an unborn 'saviour', an example of which occurs later in this chapter (see below, p. 23). The language of a basic assumption group 'is degenerate and debased' (ibid., p.186), and instead of developing thought, 'the group uses an existing language as a mode of action'. We see here how the Capulet servants use their debased talk as an entry to the action of the fight, making the fight itself even more inevitable.

Bion distinguishes such basic assumption groups from a 'work group', the function of which 'consists essentially of the translation of thoughts and feelings into behaviour which is adapted to reality' (1961, p. 157) with characteristics 'similar to those attributed by Freud (1911) to the ego' (ibid., p. 143). A work group takes cognizance of factors which basic assumption mentality does not, such as attention to task and to time, and has the capacity to learn from experience. Work group activity is essentially pervaded by emotions of one of the basic assumption groupings (ibid., p. 97), by which it is sometimes hindered and occasionally furthered (ibid., p. 188); students, for example, can be supported by an underlying attitude of healthy dependence when they want help from their teacher in a learning activity, but can also become passively dependent, expecting to be spoon-fed.

We know from our own experience how co-operation calling for a work group mentality in which issues are thought about, and where members seek to empathize with different points of view and yet stick to a task, can be difficult to sustain. An atmosphere of reasoned, forceful argument may further a satisfactory 'work group' outcome of the task of a committee; on the other hand, however, members can become polarized into actual fight/flight basic assumption mentality. In this instance rival viewpoints are fought over, often with the emergence of victors and losers; thoughtfulness is certainly lost.[1]

When they are pervaded by a fight/flight basic assumption frame of mind, neither Montagues nor Capulets are capable of recognizing each other as fellow citizens with individual needs. Benvolio, a Montague and Romeo's cousin – not only well-meaning, as his name suggests, but in a state of mind that encompasses a wider range of human relationships than that of fighting or fleeing – arrives and draws his sword to try to stop the fighting: 'Part, fools, put up your swords, you know not what you do' (I.i.61–2). Tybalt, a Capulet and Juliet's cousin, also, however, comes on the scene, and reinforces the fight/flight activity:

Tybalt   What, drawn, and talk of peace? I hate the word,
As I hate hell, all Montagues, and thee:
Have at thee, coward. (*They fight.*)

Enter three or four Citizens with clubs . . .

Citizens   . . . Strike! Beat them down! Down with the Capulets!
Down with the Montagues!

Enter old Capulet in his [night]*gown, and Lady Capulet.*

Capulet   What noise is this? Give me my long sword, ho!
Lady Capulet   A crutch, a crutch! Why call you for a sword?

Enter Old Montague and Lady Montague.

Capulet   My sword I say! Old Montague is come,
and flourishes his blade in spite of me.
Montague   Thou villain Capulet! Hold me not! let me go!
Lady Montague   Thou shalt not stir one foot to seek a foe.

                                                        (I.i.67–78)

Prince Escalus then enters, and in his stern judgement declares:

Three civil brawls bred of an airy word
By thee, old Capulet, and Montague,
Have thrice disturb'd the quiet of our streets . . .

                                                        (I.i.87–9)

If ever you disturb our streets again
Your lives shall pay the forfeit of the peace.

                                                        (I.i.94–5)

Capulet next appears in a non-confrontational situation, and
maintains:

But Montague is bound as well as I,
In penalty alike, and 'tis not hard I think
For men so old as we to keep the peace.

                                                        (I.ii.1–3)

Can such fighting be stopped, and if so, at what cost? Can the peace
be kept, and if so, by what means? This fight finally stops after the
arrival of the Prince, under pain of torture (I.i.84). The earlier
attempts failed: Benvolio was outnumbered; the cries of 'Beat them
down! Down with the Capulets! Down with the Montagues!' from
the intervening citizens suggest that they were facing not only the

risk of death or injury, but also of contamination with fight/flight mentality. Such an affray clearly has links with group confrontations in our society, which will be discussed in Chapter 5.

Attempts to allocate blame to 'the others' stand in the way of any mutual resolution of conflict. Responsibility for starting it can be projected on to the other side, as Sampson the servant does initially: 'Let them begin'. Responsibility for continuation can also be perceived as being in 'the other': Capulet experiences the menace as being in Montague; and Montague experiences the villainy as being in Capulet. By means of 'projective identification', parts of oneself can be separated from the self and actually felt to be relocated in someone else; neither Montague nor Capulet experiences any aggressive intent in himself, but only in the other. (I shall use the term 'projective identification' in a variety of contexts in this part of the book, and hope that by this means it will become clearer to those who are not familiar with it, before I discuss it more fully in Chapter 4 (see pp. 97–103 below). The double-edged interventions of Lady Capulet and Lady Montague, uttered amidst the fray, may also add fuel to the fire. We see as the play progresses how Prince Escalus's 'deterrent' of the death penalty proves to be of no avail as a long-term measure. Capulet's belief that he and Montague can now keep the peace as old men denies the presence of conflict, both within the younger generation and among the servants, as evidenced by the recent affray, without even the overt stimulation of an 'airy word' by either of them on that occasion. Thinking about the emotional conflict is avoided, and the continuation of fight/flight basic assumption emotionality may be unconsciously condoned.

We are in touch with a 'world' where the 'source' of fear and 'cause' of hate tend to be experienced as located outside the self or the group or subgroup to which one may belong, and the degree of enmity may be variously experienced as very great, or even totally denied. The importance to social life of denials and projections of feelings and thoughts by individuals and their expression elsewhere in a social system, addressed in papers by Jaques (1955) and Menzies Lyth (1959), is apparent here, as it is in our own society.

Romeo, whose sighs and withdrawn behaviour have already
been commented on with concern by his parents, arrives after the
affray and talks to Benvolio:

> Where shall we dine? O me! What fray was here?
> Yet tell me not, for I have heard it all.
> Here's much to do with hate, but more with love.
> Why then, O brawling love, O loving hate,
> O anything of nothing first create!
> O heavy lightness, serious vanity,
> Misshapen chaos of well-seeming forms!
> Feather of lead, bright smoke, cold fire, sick health,
> Still-waking sleep that is not what it is!
> This love feel I that feel no love in this.
>
> (I.i.171–80)

> Tut, I have lost myself, I am not here.
> This is not Romeo, he's some other where.
>
> (I.i.195–6)

Romeo turns from the evidence of the affray to his own struggles
with some new experience of puzzling, contradictory, identity-con-
fusing, chaotic adolescent feelings to do with a perception of love
arising within himself, yet no longer feeling totally himself. He finds
that Benvolio's expression of sympathy for him 'Doth add more
grief to too much of mine own' (I.i.187) and, claiming to be a sick
man, confesses: 'In sadness, cousin, I do love a woman' (I.i.202). It
emerges that Romeo's 'love', later called mere 'doting' by Friar
Lawrence (II.iii.78), is for Rosaline, a Capulet, who has sworn to
live in chastity, and remains unrequited. Benvolio suggests that the
way to forget is to 'Examine other beauties' (I.i.226). This is, of
course, what does happen when Romeo and his friends – Benvolio,
a Montague, and Mercutio, a kinsman of the Prince – succeed, by a
mixture of chance and subterfuge, in obtaining invitations to the
Capulet feast from the latter's servant, and Romeo and Juliet fall in
love.

The active involvement of a Capulet servant with his master's
cause is again apparent in the giving of invitations to Romeo and
his friends to come 'to our house' (I.ii.77) for the forthcoming
Capulet party: 'My master is the great rich Capulet, and if you be

not of the house of Montague, I pray come and crush a cup of wine.
Rest you merry' (I.ii.80–3). The smug self-satisfied gratification in
lauding one's own affiliation (here Capulet) and labelling membership of another group (here Montague) as automatically beyond the
pale is apparent. This, of course, lends emotional support to the
maintenance of the feuding status quo. Individuals such as the 'fiery
Tybalt', who professes to hate peace, the Montagues and hell
equally, are willing contributors to such a culture, basking in
'heavenly' self-idealization and prejudice. At the Capulet party
Tybalt recognizes the masked Romeo's voice as that of a Montague
(I.v.53), and immediately sends for his rapier. The divide in his mind
between Capulets and Montagues, together with his accompanying
prejudice, is so absolute that a parallel could even be drawn with
racism: Tybalt feels that the 'sound colour' of Romeo's voice is
sufficient justification to designate and take action against an
enemy.

> *Capulet*   Content thee, gentle coz, let him alone,
> A* bears him like a portly gentleman;
> And, to say truth, Verona brags of him
> To be a virtuous and well-govern'd youth.
> I would not for the wealth of all this town
> Here in my house do him disparagement.
>
> (I.v.63–9)

> *Tybalt*   I'll not endure him.
> *Capulet*   He shall be endur'd.
> What, goodman boy! I say he shall! Go to.
> Am I the master here or you?
>
> (I.v.74–7)

The polarized splitting between the two houses, portrayed here by
Tybalt, whereby idealized aspects of people (here felt to belong to
one's own house) are kept widely apart from those which are felt
to be bad (and attributed to the other), is characteristic of what
Klein called the paranoid-schizoid position (Klein, 1946). This
contrasts with the state of mind she described as the depressive
position, in which emotionality is more integrated and an individual

---

* A: he (Chambers, 1977).

can be aware of responding with conflicting feelings of love or hatred to the same person, but with those of loving concern for that person being paramount. 'Depressive anxiety is the crucial element of mature relationships, the source of generous and altruistic feelings that are devoted to the well-being of the object' (Hinshelwood, 1991, p. 138). These states of mind, which originate in infancy, will be discussed in greater detail in Chapter 4. The change in Capulet from how he was in the affray to how he is here in the role of host speaks to a current depressive frame of mind linked with his introjective identification – that is, his feeling of closeness to a loved internal image of Verona. The Verona he has in his mind is pleased with its citizens in their own right, irrespective of membership of one or other of the polarized houses that exist externally within it. In such a state of mind Capulet successfully opposes the splitting and projections of Tybalt, and on this occasion is able keep the peace.

Here we also see something of the to-and-fro of the adolescent life of Romeo and his small group of friends. The relationships are clearly very different from those instanced at the beginning of the play in a group dominated by basic assumption fight/flight group mentality. The purpose of this – mainly Montague – adolescent gatecrashing of the Capulet party is not to fight the Capulets but to 'examine other beauties'. It is, however, a violation of both parental and current mores of Verona, and is obviously dangerous in such a polarized setting. The friends have their own characters: Benvolio is clearly sensible about social issues, and is often seen as avoiding unnecessary conflict; Mercutio is mercurial, witty, bawdy, imaginative and also a dreamer of dreams (I.iv.53–103). But, as is common among adolescents, Romeo and his friends are at times out of touch with aspects of themselves. Romeo says after the affray that he has 'lost himself', implicitly in a state of mind concerned with Rosaline. Sometimes, however, losing currently troublesome aspects of oneself can be a piece of purposeful, unconscious mental activity. When Romeo has left Mercutio and Benvolio after the Capulet feast to woo Juliet (although they still believe that it is Rosaline whom he seeks), Mercutio calls after him: 'Romeo! Humours! Madman! Passion! Lover!' (II.i.7). He also attributes certain wishes to Romeo:

O Romeo, that she were, O that she were
An open-arse and thou a poperin pear!
Romeo, good night. I'll to my truckle-bed
This field-bed is too cold for me to sleep.

(II.i.37–40)

The sexuality which is active in Mercutio's mind is unequivocally
felt to exist in Romeo, but clearly untinged with Romeo's actual
delicate longings. Mercutio, although he is full of his customary
bawdy sexual quibbles, appears to locate a phantasy concerning
sexual involvement, or perhaps the risk of feeling left out in the
cold by exclusion from it, in Romeo, and retires to his 'truckle-bed',
a small mobile bed suitable for a child. Here we are graphically
shown how it is possible for one person to disembarrass his own
mind of certain feelings and, as far as he is concerned, locate them
in that of another by projective identification. Romeo, having gone
to seek Juliet, presumably does not even hear Mercutio and, in any
case, is unlikely to be affected by what Mercutio conveys, as the
contents also form part of a joking camaraderie. The response,
however, to the actual receipt of a projective identification can, of
course, vary according to the recipient and his or her state of mind;
we saw the violent consequences of mutually projected aggression
among the protagonists of the affray.

Active 'splitting off' by projective identification of currently
unmanageable emotions into other members of an adolescent
group of friends of the kind glimpsed here often plays an important
part in the life of young people as they adjust to their developing
and changing sense of themselves. As we turn to Romeo and Juliet's
love, we are painfully aware, however, that they cannot divest
themselves of their Montague or Capulet identities, however much
they wish to do so.

Romeo's love for the rejecting Rosaline has been quickly replaced
by that for Juliet, 'Alike bewitched by the charms of looks' (II.i.6).
It is love at first sight, expressed initially in terms of a gentle and
pure pilgrimage (I.v.94), but soon to be lent power by passion
(III.ii.5–7). The anxieties surrounding their 'bud of love' (II.ii.121)

are apparent even before they meet. As Romeo and his adolescent friends gatecrash the Capulet party, Romeo fears that he is too early:

> for my mind misgives
> Some consequence yet hanging in the stars . . .
>
> (I.iv.106–7)

> some vile forfeit of untimely death.
>
> (I.iv.111)

Juliet, too, after their first meeting fears: 'my grave is like to be my wedding bed' (I.v.134) and later has painful thoughts that her love is for a 'loathed enemy' (I.v.140). At their next meeting later that night ('the balcony scene'), the beautiful poetry describes the deepening of their love, but with fear in the background. They both struggle with their respective Montague and Capulet identities, at moments psychically discarding them. Thus Juliet:

> Be but sworn my love
> And I'll no longer be a Capulet.
>
> (II.ii.35–6)

> O be some other name!
> What's in a name? That which we call a rose
> By any other word would smell as sweet.
>
> (II.ii.42–4)

And Romeo:

> Call me but love, and I'll be new baptiz'd:
> Henceforth I never will be Romeo.
>
> (II.ii.50–1)

We are thus aware that they feel the need to split off intrinsic aspects of themselves – who they are, their names, their identities – in response to their feelings of mutual love arising in the context of the feud between their families. Juliet voices fears about their haste:

> I have no joy in this contract tonight:
> It is too rash, too unadvised, too sudden,
> Too like the lighning, which does cease to be
> Ere one can say 'It lightens'.
>
> (II.ii.117–20)

Despite her awareness of the dangers of such haste, however, she presses Romeo to arrange marriage, and he goes to Friar Lawrence the next morning to do so.

Fear of revenge based on family enmity, and the action taken in spite of it, are clearly relevant to forebodings of 'some consequence yet hanging in the stars' and 'this contract' that is 'too sudden'. We learn from the Prologue that the lovers are 'star-cross'd' and 'death-mark'd' on account of their 'parents' rage'. Shakespeare makes us aware of their anxieties with 'star-cross'd' impact, based in the poetic, thematic depth of the drama, but also from a more ordinary adolescent level. Freud's (1936) view that an expectation of being badly treated by 'Fate' represents a materialization of our own punitive conscience of childhood may be relevant to the latter. We, the audience, may experience both the fear of impending doom for the 'star-cross'd' lovers consequent on their 'death-mark'd love', where the fault is felt to lie in their houses, but also – as with Cassius in *Julius Caesar* – possibly in themselves, as they seek with great haste to marry against their parents' wishes and their families' culture.

Romeo comes to the Friar as the latter is gathering 'baleful weeds and precious-juicèd flowers' (II.iii.4):

> For nought so vile, that on the earth doth live,
> But to the earth some special good doth give;
> Nor ought so good but, strained from that fair use,
> Revolts from true birth, stumbling on abuse.
> Virtue itself turns vice, being misapplied,
> And vice sometime's by action dignified.
> Within the infant rind of this weak flower
> Poison has residence, and medicine power . . .
>
> (II.iii.13–20)

> Two such opposèd kings encamp them still
> In man as well as herbs: grace and rude will;
> And where the worser is predominant,
> Full soon the canker death eats up that plant.
>
> (II.iii.23–6)

The Friar is aware of the danger of death if 'worser is predominant'. But the innocent simplicity with which he finds some special goodness in that which is vile and the potential dignification of vice may leave one puzzled about the degree of firmness and clarity in his perception of goodness, despite his apparently sincere commitment to promote it. At Romeo's request to be married that day to Juliet, he exclaims:

> Holy Saint Francis! what a change is here!
> Is Rosaline, that thou didst love so dear,
> So soon forsaken?
>
> (II.iii.61–3)

Although he chides Romeo, and seems unimpressed by the latter's contention that Juliet 'Doth grace for grace and love for love allow' (II.iii.82), he does agree to carry out the marriage:

> In one respect I'll thy assistant be.
> For this alliance may so happy prove
> To turn your households' rancour to pure love.
>
> (II.iii.86–8)

He responds to Romeo's 'O let us hence, I stand on sudden haste' (II.iii.89) with 'Wisely and slow, they stumble that run fast' (II.iii.90), although in fact he marries them that afternoon. The 'virtue' of wishing to extend love may lead him to the 'vice' of secret collusive action with adolescent haste, thus belying his own beliefs.

Just an hour (III.i.114–15) after what the Friar only finally, after the deaths of Romeo and Juliet, calls the 'stolen marriage' (V.iii.232), a further Capulet/Montague affray occurs, despite Benvolio's thoughtful attempt to avoid it:

> I pray thee, good Mercutio, let's retire:
> The day is hot, the Capels are abroad,
> And if we meet we shall not 'scape a brawl,
> For now these hot days is the mad blood stirring.
>
> (III.i.1–4)

Romeo is challenged by Tybalt. Unknown to Tybalt, Romeo and he are now related by marriage. Romeo, in his identification with Juliet, extends good feelings to Tybalt and holds back from fighting.

The suddenness and secrecy of the marriage, however, do not allow
Romeo to substantiate his claim to a Capulet-related identity, even
among his friends, and he makes what in that setting must seem an
outrageous claim to Tybalt, as if he indeed were no longer Romeo
and a Montague:

> And so, good Capulet, which name I tender
> As dearly as mine own, be satisfied.
>
> (III.i.70–1)

Mercutio, understandably, sees this as a 'calm, dishonourable, vile
submission' (III.i.72) and takes up Tybalt's challenge. As Romeo
tries to stop the fight, Mercutio is killed, calling: 'A plague o' both
your houses!' (III.i.108). Romeo, deeply moved by Mercutio's death
on his behalf, and feeling that his reputation is stained, is now
driven by emotions related to his masculinity and his identity as a
Montague, exclaiming:

> O sweet Juliet,
> Thy beauty hath made me effeminate
> And in my temper soften'd valour's steel . . .
>
> (III.i.115 – 17)

> . . . fire-ey'd fury be my conduct now!
>
> (III.i.126)

Romeo now fights and kills Tybalt, then flees to the Friar from
whom he learns that the Prince has decreed his immediate
banishment. He threatens suicide if he has to be apart from Juliet.
After the Friar has rebuked him as a 'fond mad man' (III.iii.52) and
for 'womanish' tears, 'wild acts' and 'the unreasonable fury of a
beast' (III.iii.109–10), Romeo is finally persuaded to accept his exile
in Mantua:

> Where thou shalt live till we can find a time
> To blaze your marriage, reconcile your friends,
> Beg pardon of the Prince.
>
> (III.iii.149–51)

After the marriage, Juliet's sexual longings for Romeo and the
increasing passion of her love are apparent as she secretly awaits
him:

                        Come, civil night,
     Thou sober-suited matron, all in black,
     And learn me how to lose a winning match
     Play'd for a pair of stainless maidenhoods.
     Hood my unmann'd blood, bating in my cheeks,
     With thy black mantle, till strange love grow bold,
     Think true love acted simple modesty.

                                            (III.ii.10–16)

Hearing from her Nurse that Romeo has killed Tybalt, Juliet rails
briefly against him as inwardly deceitful:

     Was ever book containing such vile matter
     So fairly bound?

                                            (III.ii.83–4)

but quickly relents. With the contrivance of the Nurse, they spend
one night together before the banished Romeo must leave. They
finally part in sorrow and fear:

     Juliet   I have an ill-divining soul! . . .

                                            (III.v.54)

     Romeo   Dry sorrow drinks our blood. Adieu, adieu.

                                            (III.v.59)

The action of the play itself takes place in less than a week, and the
issue of speed frequently recurs. In Verona, against the background
of enmity between the houses of Montague and Capulet, the issues
of time, the greedy, speedy promotion of 'pure love' and the
ignoring of potential catastrophe are central. There is an absence
of any capacity to respond to what might be the disastrous outcome
of a sudden marriage between two members of the opposing
houses in that society.

Bion's concept of containment (Bion, 1962a,b), which will be
elaborated on in Chapter 4 (see below, pp. 84–6), relates, among
other things, to the need in personal and social development for
some thoughtful space in which anxieties, undeveloped thoughts
and new ideas can be reflected upon, and their meaning can be
attended to. What we see here is a failure to contain.

Both Romeo and Juliet have some awareness of the rashness of
their haste, yet seek immediate marriage. As adolescents they

complain of the slowness of adults, whom they appear to see as a differently endowed category of people: Romeo contends that the Friar, not being 'as young as I' (III.iii.65), has no capacity to grasp his feelings. Juliet castigates her Nurse's slowness as a go-between as due to lack of 'affections and warm youthful blood' (II.v.12). The Nurse openly colludes in bypassing Juliet's parents. The Friar, despite his quasi-parental relationship with Romeo, does not open his mind to the possible, realistic presence in the lovers of anxieties (which, we know, include the fear of death), or reflect on the possible consequences of hasty adolescent action. Despite his professed belief in 'wisely and slow', he goes along with the young people's demands in the hope that their alliance may turn their 'households' rancour to pure love' (II.iii.88). We can again surmise the presence of some group mentality that impedes thoughtfulness and an ability to contain. The Friar's capacity to think reflectively appears to fall away into the debased action language of what could be a basic assumption 'pairing' group state of mind with the young lovers, so that he becomes joined with them in their adolescent haste and marries them immediately. This would imply the emergence of a kind of hope (which Bion calls 'Messianic') that an idea or person, as yet unborn, 'will save the group from feelings of hatred, destructiveness and despair'. This kind of 'basically assumed' hope has a quality of magic; it is not the result of – nor subjected to – thought or work, but is treated by rationalization as if it were actually effective, and thus displaces the existence of time (Bion, 1961, p. 151). In this instance the hope would be that the alliance between the potentially productive heirs of the opposing Montague and Capulet houses, Romeo and Juliet, will turn their households' hatred to shared love. Such a powerful emotion, accepted as operating immediately, 'at a stroke', rules out any thoughtful activity that would be necessary to bring a more prosaic form of hopefulness to fruition. Despite the Friar's protestations on behalf of wisdom and lack of speed, he does not take account of the possible consequences arising from the real state of affairs, in particular the actual hatred prevailing between the two households.

Early in the play we learn that Paris seeks to marry Juliet. Capulet then says:

Let two more summers wither in their pride
Ere we may think her ripe to be a bride . . .

(I.ii.10–11)

But woo her, gentle Paris, get her heart,
My will to her consent is but a part . . .

(I.ii.16–17)

When Lady Capulet broaches the subject of this marriage, Juliet responds: 'It is an honour that I dream not of' (I.iii.66). In answer to her mother's praises of Paris and the question 'Can you love the gentleman?' (I.iii.79), she replies: 'I'll look to like' (I.iii.97). The formal relationships between Juliet and her mother suggest the expectation of obedience together with some possibility of a degree of concern for each other's point of view. They also, perhaps, convey the presence of some remaining aspect of latency – 'a period of emotional quiescence between the dramas and turmoil of childhood and adolescence' (Rycroft, 1968). Juliet is more warmly intimate with her comic, loquacious Nurse, who later becomes an active go-between in the secret arrangements surrounding her marriage to Romeo. The Nurse, however, with her somewhat callow and sexualized references to painful past events such as the deaths of her own husband and child, and also to Juliet's weaning in childhood (I.iii.48), alerts us to an absence of emotional depth which becomes more apparent in the context of future losses in the play. Relationships in the Capulet household are manifestly very different after Tybalt's death. Capulet – unaware, of course, of Juliet's marriage to Romeo – now declares that she will be ruled by him, and decrees her immediate marriage to Paris (III.iv.21).

Juliet is the only surviving Capulet child (I.ii.15). The escalating, manic sense of urgency for her to be married to Paris is evocative of the haste accompanying her marriage to Romeo, which culminates in his banishment and the deaths of Tybalt and Mercutio. The present haste may represent a drive for an heir by Capulet and a guarantee of family survival in a desperate contest with death which cannot be sustained in thought. It seems that some of the pain occasioned by Tybalt's death is to be palliated by Juliet's marriage to Paris. As an audience we are also aware of the loss occasioned by the death of Mercutio, who may have symbolically represented a more realistic hopefulness about any resolution of conflict within this society: he was a kinsman of the Prince, outside the membership of the houses whose enmity led to his death. He was also represented as an imaginative dreamer (I.iv.53–103), who might have had some capacity to encompass a wider emotionality than that of oppositional strife. Lady Capulet tells Juliet of the 'joyful tidings' of the planned marriage to Paris 'to put thee from thy heaviness' (III.v.108), although Juliet's continuous tears, overtly for her cousin Tybalt's death, are secretly for the banishment of her actual husband, Romeo, who killed him (V.iii.235). Her evasiveness and 'chopp'd logic' (III.v.149) about the decreed marriage to Paris breach Capulet's sufferance. He treats her as his disobedient possession, and threatens to disown her:

> But fettle your fine joints 'gainst Thursday next
> To go with Paris to Saint Peter's Church,
> Or I will drag thee on a hurdle thither.
> Out . . . !
>
> (III.v.153–6)

Juliet pleads in vain to her mother:

> Is there no pity sitting in the clouds
> That sees into the bottom of my grief?
> O sweet my mother, cast me not away,
>
> (III.v.196–8)

She turns to her Nurse, who is unable to offer any emotional comfort or recognition of her plight, and now advises her to marry Paris (bigamously): 'O, he's a lovely gentleman. Romeo's a dishclout to him' (III.v.219). Juliet, cursing the Nurse's perfidy – 'Ancient damnation! O most wicked fiend' (III.v.235) – and voicing thoughts of suicide as an alternative, seeks some way out from Friar Lawrence (IV.i.84). He gives her his 'distilling liquor' (IV.i.94), a drug to simulate death on her wedding day, with the secret underlying plan to arrange her rescue by Romeo from the Capulet vault when she awakes. Juliet now tells her parents that she will marry Paris; Capulet brings the wedding forward by a day, and indulges in manic preparations for it. Juliet fearfully takes the potion. Her parents are left to discover their 'dead' daughter. Capulet now experiences

Juliet's apparent death and his lack of an heir: 'Death is my son-in-law, Death is my heir' (IV.v.38). The Friar, who arrives to perform the marriage of Juliet and Paris, hypocritically asks: 'Come, is the bride ready to go to church?' (IV.v.33) and, being told of Juliet's 'death', goes on to berate the family for their grief, asserting: 'now Heaven hath all' (IV.v.67).

The rash 'stolen marriage' in itself brought forebodings of death to the couple. Lies and hypocrisy are generated in consequence of it, and go on to penetrate the fragility of the adult Capulet world. Any capacity for thoughtfulness is lost. Neither the formal relationship between Juliet and her mother nor the superficiality of the Nurse's response to her mental pain provides containment of her anxieties. Some of the events in the Capulet household can be seen as a container of limited capacity fragmenting in response to the enormity of what it is asked to contain. Drugs are then turned to, and further mask the truth. Catastrophe ensues.

We are now in touch with a world where the vagaries of time and communications have important and urgent significance for life and death, with implications of incipient disaster: Capulet has brought the time of the wedding, and hence of Juliet's awakening, further forward, and the Friar's communication to alert the banished Romeo, who was to welcome the 'dead' Juliet back to life at the precise time of her awakening, miscarries.

The banished Romeo, with no news from the Friar, hears of Juliet's apparent death, and his immediate intent becomes to lie with her that night by taking 'soon-speeding' (V.i.60) poison. Speed remains important to the end, although the urgency is now for death:

As violently as hasty powder fir'd
Doth hurry from the fatal cannon's womb.

(V.ii.64–5)

The poison is obtained from a poor apothecary who risks his life in the illegal transaction. He – together with his shop, with its dead stuffed animals and musty seeds – brings to mind a deathly shadow of the originally optimistic Friar Lawrence. Romeo declares:

Come, cordial and not poison, go with me
To Juliet's grave, for there must I use thee.

(V.i.85-6)

At the Capulet tomb, Paris, mourning Juliet, apprehends Romeo, whom he recognizes as the murderer of Tybalt and believes to be about to shame the dead bodies (V.iii.53). Paris challenges Romeo, and is killed by him. At times Romeo doubts his own sanity (V.iii.80), and is unable to trust his observation of the 'dead' Juliet:

Beauty's ensign yet
Is crimson in thy lips and in thy cheeks,
And Death's pale flag is not advanced there.

(V.iii.94-6)

Sometimes his intended death has different meanings for him, other than actually dying, such as that of preserving Juliet from his fear that she is being held as Death's 'paramour' (V.iii.105). Finally declaring: 'Thus with a kiss I die' (V.iii.120), Romeo poisons himself just before Juliet's awakening. Juliet now kills herself with Romeo's dagger (V.iii.169). The Friar's initially expressed anxiety about the spreading of poison has become only too apparent, and the sterile 'canker death' (II.iii.26) has set in.

Bion (1970) discusses the concept of catastrophic change: how change that is necessary for growth can be both dreaded and disruptive to the group, as the coming together in Verona of a Capulet and a Montague are here. Change in the relations between the two houses is necessary for a safer and more stable Verona to flourish, but what happens is that not only Romeo and Juliet, but also Tybalt, Mercutio and Paris die violently, and Lady Montague dies of grief. Bion suggests that it is the function of some form of governing body – which he calls an 'establishment', meaning an aspect of the group that can exercise power and thoughtful responsibility on behalf of it – both to contain a new idea of what he calls 'Messianic' significance and to make it available for the group, without the group being 'exploded' by the impetus of the new idea, or the idea denuded: 'The recurrent configuration is of an explosive force with a restraining framework. For example . . .

the new idea constrained within a formulation not intended to express it' (1970, p. 79). In other words, the idea necessary for change needs to be made available for use without implementation of the accompanying sense of catastrophe arising from the dynamic disruptive impact of the new alongside the old. The Friar, however, can be seen as falling into a basic assumption pairing state of mind with the lovers, and omnipotently and secretly enacting the new idea of love on behalf of the establishment of Verona, rather than attempting to contain it, and to be indirectly aided in this by the Nurse, who is unable to think about it. Conflict with the temporal establishment of the apparently implacable Prince and his governmental style, involving torture and threats of death, is not faced (III.iii.151). The potential explosiveness of bringing this new and out-of-focus idea of the love felt by Romeo and Juliet into focus with the divided world of mutually projected hatred normally maintained by their houses is not recognized, and no change occurs in the polarized, revengeful pattern. The group is disrupted by deaths.

In the final reckoning in Verona, we hear:

Prince   Where be these enemies? Capulet, Montague?
See what a scourge is laid upon your hate,
That heaven finds means to kill your joys with love;
And I for winking at your discords too,
Have lost a brace of kinsmen. All are punished.
Capulet   O brother Montague, give me thy hand.
This is my daughter's jointure, for no more
Can I demand.
Montague   But I can give thee more,
For I will raise her statue in pure gold,
That while Verona by that name is known,
There shall no figure at such rate be set
As that of true and faithful Juliet.
Capulet   As rich shall Romeo's by his lady's lie,
Poor sacrifices of our enmity.
Prince   A glooming peace this morning with it brings:
The sun for sorrow will not show his head.
Go hence to have more talk of these sad things.
Some shall be pardon'd, and some punished,

> For never was a story of more woe
> Than this of Juliet and her Romeo.
>
> (V.iii.290–309)

Will the deaths of Romeo and Juliet themselves presage an enduring move towards depressive concern and reconciliation by Capulet and Montague based on shared love and mourning, and, if so, will this extend to members of both their houses? Can a feud in society – widely spread among its protagonists, each side smugly claiming virtue for itself – be healed by protestations of love and material offerings, any more than by princely decree accompanied by the force of would-be deterrent penalties, or by omnipotent action operating in conjunction with adolescent love and pressure? Verona has been catastrophically disrupted by violent deaths, including those of the heirs of both the Capulet and Montague houses. Will the feelings and imagery surrounding their deaths become vested in concrete epitaphs, or can they be symbolically transformed to enable love arising out of 'the misshapen chaos' (I.i.177) of that society to be viable? Without any real recognition of the hatred spread within society, is it possible for Capulet and Montague to create any space within which the beauty of the disruptive idea of Capulet/Montague love can develop, or will it be buried with the lovers? A governing body or 'establishment' can evade its task by seeming to promote it (Bion, 1970, p. 78). Romeo considered the gold with which he bought his poison to be 'poison to men's souls' (V.ii.80). The epitaph in the form of the golden statues of Romeo and Juliet could – following Bion – serve to demonstrate that the idea of 'love' between the two houses was 'Loaded with honours and sank without a trace' (Bion, 1970, p. 78). We may be left wondering if the outward portrayal of love in such golden splendour will also be a spur to thoughtful work based on 'more talk of these sad things' (V.iii.306), necessary for true reconciliation and the foundation of a living and meaningful memorial to love.[2,3]

2 ACHIEVING ADULTHOOD IN A WORLD OF DECEPTION: A DISCUSSION OF SHAKESPEARE'S PLAY *MUCH ADO ABOUT NOTHING*

Much Ado about Nothing is probably best known and widely enjoyed for the 'merry war' and 'skirmish of wit' between Beatrice and Benedick. From the beginning, underlying the merriment, we are aware of both the presence of pain, as shown in the biting sharpness of their repartee, and a sense of some lovingness between them, which is often evoked in the audience. The love between Claudio and Hero nearly ends in tragedy. Specific reference is made to Claudio's youth, but a sense of unfulfilled adolescence accompanies all four young people, who appear to have difficulties in bringing potentially loving experiences to fulfilment, and moving forward into adulthood. We shall see how the problems which beset them seem to be influenced both by the nature and membership of the courtly society of Messina, and by anxieties which affect the quality and ongoing development of relationships in adolescence.

It may be useful briefly to recall the outline of the plot. *Much Ado about Nothing* is set in Messina, in and around the house of Leonato, the Governor, where he lives with his daughter Hero, his niece Beatrice, and his brother Antonio. Don Pedro, Prince of Aragon, and his companions Benedick, a young lord of Padua, and Claudio, a young lord of Florence, arrive there on their way back from a war. Don Pedro's bastard brother, Don John, also accompanies them. Claudio soon speaks of his feelings for Hero, and an early marriage is arranged. Don Pedro leads a merry deception designed to get Beatrice and Benedick to believe independently that the one pines for the other, so that they too should marry.

A more sombre aspect of the plot runs alongside: the envious and spoiling Don John leads a malicious deception slandering Hero's chastity, in consequence of which Claudio spurns and shames her at what was to have been their wedding. It is given out that Hero has died from the shock, while she is in fact kept in hiding by Friar Francis, who was to have performed the ceremony. It is through his offices, the observations and actions of the comic watch of Dogberry and Verges, and the now serious interventions of Beatrice and Benedick, that the situation is restored. The play ends with the weddings of the two young couples.

In the first scene a messenger responds to Leonato's question as to 'how many gentlemen' had been lost in the war with 'But few of any sort, and none of name' (I.i.6). Don Pedro, a member of the ruling power at the time of the play, is mentioned as having bestowed much honour on Claudio, who 'hath borne himself beyond the promise of his age, doing, in the figure of a lamb, the feats of a lion' (I.i.13–14). The emphasis on position and name as the major factors relevant to loss of life and the significance given to honour are relevant to the appraisal of the courtly aspects of the society we are to experience in the play.

Claudio questions his friend Benedick on his liking for Hero: 'Is she not a modest young lady?' (I.i.153). Benedick asks if he wants to buy her, since he enquires after her (I.i.167), and the conversation continues:

Claudio   Can the world buy such a jewel?
Benedick   Yea, and a case to put it into.

(I.i.168–9)

This interchange may lead us to wonder how much market valuation, costly display, masculine possessiveness and the opinion of others may form part of the values of this society, into which Benedick appears to have some insight. When Don Pedro joins them, Claudio soon speaks somewhat haltingly of his feelings for Hero: 'If my passion change not shortly . . .' (I.i.202); 'That I love her, I feel' (I.i.211). When Benedick has gone, he speaks more eloquently:

Claudio   Hath Leonato any son, my lord?
Don Pedro   No child but Hero, she's his only heir.
Dost thou affect her, Claudio?
Claudio   O my lord,
When you went onward on this ended action,
I look'd upon her with a soldier's eye,
That lik'd, but had a rougher task in hand
Than to drive liking to the name of love:
But now I am return'd, and that war-thoughts
Have left their places vacant, in their rooms
Come thronging soft and delicate desires,
All prompting me how fair young Hero is,
Saying I lik'd her ere I went to wars.

                                                        (I.i.274–85)

Here we can glimpse a move from a latency frame of mind, focused on the single-sex peer-group activity of the recent campaign in the external world, to a space to be filled by something softer. Benedick has already spoken of his 'being a professed tyrant' (I.i.155–6) to women, and of how he will remain a bachelor, free from mistrust (I.i.228). Later he deliberates over the change in Claudio and his own possible vulnerability to what he seems to regard as the illness of love, providing us with a beautiful account of what appears to be a move from latency to a more adolescent state of mind:

I do much wonder that one man, seeing how much another man is a fool when he dedicates his behaviours to love, will, after he hath laughed at such shallow follies in others, become the argument of his own scorn by falling in love: and such a man is Claudio. I have known when there was no music with him but the drum and the fife, and now had he rather hear the tabor and the pipe. I have known when he would have walked ten mile afoot to see a good armour, and now will he lie ten nights awake carving the fashion of a new doublet. He was wont to speak plain to the purpose, like an honest man and a soldier, and now he is turned orthography – his words are a very fantastical banquet, just so many strange dishes. May I be so converted and see with these eyes? I cannot tell; I think not ... One woman is fair, yet I am well; another is wise, yet I am well; another virtuous, yet I am well; but till all graces be in one woman, one woman shall not come in my grace.

                                                        (II.iii.4–30)

Claudio is anxious that 'his liking could seem too sudden' (I.i.294). For him, as for Romeo and Juliet, there is an emphasis on speed, as there is so often in adolescence, but in this case it seems that there is to be some social disguise to make his desire for Hero acceptable, or perhaps respectable. Don Pedro assures Claudio that he will be 'like a lover presently' (I.i.286), and offers a 'remedy' (I.i.299) in order that Claudio shall 'have her' (I.i.290): disguised in the evening's masked revels, he, Don Pedro, will – claiming to Hero to be Claudio – woo and win her, and then, making use of his own rank, obtain her father's consent to the couple's marriage; and in fact he does so. It appears that neither waiting for love nor doubts about its nature are to be suffered, and that the would-be lover is to have an early, albeit somewhat second-hand, remedy for his desire as the outcome of a masked wooing by another on his behalf. This conversation is overheard, and various second-hand versions of it circulate.

Don John has recently been reconciled to Don Pedro, and is invited to partake of Leonato's hospitality as a member of his brother's entourage (I.i.144), but largely excludes himself from such society. He accepts that he is both melancholy and a 'plain-dealing villain'. He complains to his followers, Borachio and Conrade, that he is 'trusted with a muzzle' but will not sing in his cage, claiming: 'If I had my mouth I would bite; if I had my liberty I would do my liking.' He prefers to be a canker (wild rose) in a hedge rather than a rose in his brother's grace (I.iii.25–35) and, full of envy, appears to enjoy nursing his grievances. An account from Borachio, Don John's eavesdropping follower, that Don Pedro intends to woo Hero for himself and then give her to Claudio, gives Don John food for displeasure; Claudio 'had all the glory' of his earlier overthrow, and he intends to cross Claudio in any way he can (I.iii.54–63). Don John goes on to use this account as a basis for stirring up trouble in the course of the evening's revels, during which the wooing takes place.

A different version of the proposed wooing of Hero reaches Leonato from his brother, Antonio, who has himself heard it from a servant; that Don Pedro tells Claudio that he himself loves Hero, and will court her himself. Antonio comments that the tidings 'show well outward'. While Leonato plans to let Hero know what may be expected, he seeks to hold such news 'as a dream' until the outcome is known (I.ii.4–21). This contrasts with the frequent acceptance in this society of an 'outward' view.

The revels themselves, in which most of the company take part, abound with deceptions both of identity and of information. The wearing of masks is accompanied by denials of recognition, connivance with false recognition, and the passing on of deceptions and innuendos by 'incognito' personalities (II.i.103–57). Don John, correctly recognizing the masked Claudio, asks him if he is Benedick, to which Claudio replies that he is; Don John then tells Claudio that the Prince woos Hero for himself (II.i.152). Claudio is immediately convinced that Don Pedro has abused his trust:

> 'Tis certain so; the Prince woos for himself.
> Friendship is constant in all other things
> Save in the office and affairs of love:
> Therefore all hearts in love use their own tongues;
> Let every eye negotiate for itself,
> And trust no agent; for beauty is a witch
> Against whose charms faith melteth the blood.*
> This is an accident of hourly proof,
> Which I mistrusted not. Farewell, therefore, Hero!
>
> (II.i.162–70)

Benedick also believes at this juncture that 'The Prince hath got your Hero' (II.i.179), and considers that Claudio, in allowing the Prince to woo for him, has made 'The flat transgression of a schoolboy, who, being overjoyed with finding a bird's nest, shows it his companion, and he steals it' (II.i.207–9). This remark has something of a latency flavour, carrying a sense of practical possession in the external world; it is also compounded with a cynical sense of values, the examination of which is central to the play. A pull to remain or return to a latency state of mind, with a tendency to emphasize external possessions and achievements – rather than to move forward developmentally, with deeper involvement in seeking to gratify the 'soft and delicate desires' of

---

* i.e. 'before beauty's bewitching spells, integrity melts into desire' (Arden Shakespeare [1984], p. 119).

adolescent love – may be a facet of one's own character, but the world in which one lives may also be relevant. Don Pedro, charged by Benedick with having stolen the 'bird's nest', claims 'I will but teach them to sing, and restore them to the owner' (II.i.216–17). The implication here seems to be that by using his rank, together with his ability to tell an 'amorous tale' (I.i.305) in the wooing, Don Pedro is rendering a service to the novice Claudio – and, furthermore, that such wooing is expected to succeed. Although it takes place at the request of the not very emotionally potent lover it could also, perhaps, be thought of as a kind of strange social variant of *les droits de seigneur*. One may also wonder if Hero, as the 'bird' in question, is meant to know who woos her.

Unlike Benedick, Claudio does not challenge Don Pedro as to whether he has abused his trust. We have been left with some doubts about the strength and depth of Claudio's feelings, and may puzzle over why he originally asks for Benedick's reassurance about Hero's modesty, and why he expresses his love in uncertain terms: 'that I love her, I feel' (I.i.211). To ascertain that Hero is Leonato's only heir (I.i.274) may be a prudent and normal enquiry in his society, but it also underlines a propensity for outward valuation and leaning on the opinion of others. It seems that when he went to the wars he could not sustain incipiently loving feelings for Hero, from whom he was to be absent. As has been pointed out in the Arden Shakespeare (1984) and elsewhere, he is no Romeo. He also has little capacity for self-knowledge, or for experiencing his relationships with others.

Bion adds the dimensions of 'Knowing' to the well-known psychoanalytic concern with Love and Hate, and writes of emotional experiences, or links, of Love (L), Hate (H) and Knowing (K) (Bion, 1962a). The 'K'-link, which is especially relevant here, has to do with seeking to know and be truthfully in touch with intangible, non-sensual aspects of relationships with others and within oneself; as these can never be formally known, the search operates within a context of toleration of doubt. As it does not relate to factual acquisition of knowledge, but is used as a means to discovery, what is learnt is a form of learning from experience. This experiential learning underlies the development of a capacity for deepening responsiveness to the wider emotionality of 'Loving' or

'Hating'. It starts in infancy as part of the relationship between infant and mother, to which we shall return in Chapter 4 (see below, pp. 84–6).

Claudio's eye has perceived Hero's external beauty, but his 'I', he himself, has not been involved in seeking to know her nor in really getting to know his own feelings. His acceptance of Don Pedro's deceptive, immediate and successful second-hand wooing of Hero does not help him to experience the nature of the doubts that accompany his love. Meltzer describes the 'Aesthetic conflict' which originates in the infant's perception of the mother, and 'which can be most precisely stated in terms of the aesthetic impact of the outside of the 'beautiful' mother, available to the senses, and the enigmatic inside which must be construed by creative imagination' (Meltzer and Williams, 1988, p. 22). The central experience of pain in the conflict 'resides in uncertainty, tending towards distrust, verging on suspicion. The lover is naked as Othello to the whisperings of Iago, but is rescued by the quest for knowledge, the 'K'-link, the desire to know rather than to possess the object of desire' (ibid., p. 27). Struggle against cynicism and toleration of uncertainty 'is constantly called upon in the passion of intimate relations and is at the heart of the matter of aesthetic conflict' (ibid., p. 20). Claudio yields to cynicism while protesting that that every eye should negotiate for itself (II.i.165–6). In seeking external reassurance about the nature of his love object from Benedick (I.i.153) he does not tolerate uncertainty, but engages rather in what Keats described as 'irritable reaching after fact and reason' (Keats, 1817a). He cannot construe the 'inside' nature of Hero, the aspect of her which underlies her beauty, and on the basis of his suspicions, beauty for him becomes a witch.

We now turn from some of the consequences of Don Pedro's benignly motivated deceptive wooing on behalf of Claudio to his bastard brother's malicious attempt to wreck Claudio's marriage. Don John 'will endeavour anything' to 'despite' the Prince, Claudio, Hero and Leonato her father (II.ii.30–1). The deceptive plan instigated by Borachio, his confederate, will be to make Claudio and Don Pedro believe that Hero is unchaste immediately before the planned wedding of Claudio and Hero. This is to be done by arranging for Claudio and Don Pedro to see Borachio impersonating Claudio and wooing her attendant Margaret at the window of Hero's chamber (II.ii.50).

The envious, spoiling intent of this 'plain-dealing villain' is not recognized as such in time to prevent the disastrous events:

Leonato   Was not Count John here at supper?
Antonio   I saw him not.
Beatrice   How tartly that gentleman looks! I never can see him but I am heart-burned an hour after.
Hero   He is of a very melancholy disposition.
Beatrice   He were an excellent man that were made just in the mid-way between him and Benedick: the one is too like an image and says nothing, and the other too like my lady's eldest son, evermore tattling.
Leonato   Then half Signior Benedick's tongue in Count John's mouth, and half Count John's melancholy in Signior Benedick's face –
Beatrice   With a good leg and a good foot, uncle, and money enough in his purse, such a man would win any woman in the world – if a [he] could get her good will.

(II.i.1–15)

Humphreys (1984) and other authorities point out that the Elizabethan pronunciation of 'Nothing' could have something in common with 'Noting', and that there could be some punning intent in the title. Perhaps we, the audience, can note how the envious nature of Don John is rightly perceived as 'heart-burning', but that such 'noting' goes on to be treated as 'nothing' by the goodly company, who ignore the effects of his acid, heart-burning, indigestible nature. In this instance the perceptible meaning becomes both masked by and mixed into the shallow, joking discussion of external rather than internal attributes. 'Not noting', hearsay evidence, masked discussions, second-hand experience and apparently well-intentioned deception are part of the social framework. Badness in the Verona of *Romeo and Juliet* was specifically projected into the opposing 'house'. Here in Messina badness may neither be noticed nor differentiated from goodness.

The lack of a trustworthy background of experience in this society must be relevant to all would-be loving relationships within it. Claudio not only has his own problems; the deceptive nature of society itself also bears heavily on him. As well as the prolific deceptions of others within society, there are also what could be called unconscious self-deceptions, which are relevant to much of what passes between Beatrice and Benedick, and which in their case serve to avoid the experience of the pains of love. Their problems are different from those of Claudio. They have each other very actively in mind. Early in the play Beatrice asks a messenger if Benedick has returned from the wars, and clearly minds whether or not he has a close male companion (I.i.73). Benedick also speaks movingly to Claudio of Beatrice's beauty, but also of her 'fury' (I.i.178–9). As soon as they meet they engage in mutual raillery, scorn, self-idealization and brilliant, but often defensive, wit. Thus Benedick: 'What my dear Lady Disdain! Are you yet living?', and Beatrice's response: 'Is it possible disdain should die, while she hath such meet food to feed it as Signior Benedick?' (I.i.109–11). In one of their first exchanges Benedick claims that he is loved by all ladies except Beatrice, but loves none himself, although he laments his hard heart in this respect (I.i.114–18); Beatrice follows by rejoicing at the lack of a declaration of love by a man (I.i.118–22).

Fear of unfaithfulness is an issue for them both. Beatrice implies the existence of some earlier unfaithfulness by Benedick (II.i.261–4). Benedick says to his friends: 'That a woman conceived me, I thank her: that she brought me up, I likewise give her most humble thanks', but goes on to justify his decision to remain a bachelor with a reference to possible unfaithfulness on a woman's part, and claims: 'Because I will not do them the wrong to mistrust any, I will do myself the right to trust none.' Although he acknowledges that he could look pale with anger, sickness or hunger, he insists that he will never 'look pale with love' (I.i.221–31). His reference to his conception and upbringing brings to mind how a baby may feel angry, sick, hungry and unloved on being weaned; a loving and loved infant may experience weaning as an act of unfaithfulness by the 'loved one' who brings him up.

While it is not suggested that an infantile basis to the mistrust is actually described, the language and imagery of the play are evocative of it. The imagery is often oral, sometimes referring to food. Benedick says of Beatrice: 'here's a dish I love not! I cannot endure my Lady Tongue' (II.i.257–8). He sees a lover's words, however, in terms of a 'fantastical banquet' (II.iii.21).

Beatrice says that she could not endure a husband with a beard, but when it is suggested to her that she may 'light on a husband that hath no beard', she replies:

> What should I do with him? Dress him in my apparel and make him my waiting-gentlewoman? He that hath a beard is more than a youth, and he that hath no beard is less than a man; and he that is more than a youth is not for me; and he is that is less than a man I am not for him.
>
> (II.i.26–35)

She follows this with a quip about joining a company of merry bachelors, evoking an image of something like a jolly latency children's party. Here it seems that a beard is too much, too manly, but 'no beard' is too little and perhaps reminiscent of being gently fed and tended as a baby by a waiting-gentlewoman-mother-breast.

Mistrust stands in the way of love, which calls for trust. Anxieties associated with loving are to be avoided by avoiding love itself. Scorn and disdain are used by the pair as a defence against the risk of experiencing unfaithfulness and feeling scorned, disdained or abandoned. Under the cover of their biting tongues, as well as of manic, witty merriment, the pair collude against bearing the risks of loving, and 'lock up all the gates of love' (IV.i.105) before they are completely open.

If imaginative reflection on the subject of marriage in late adolescence gives rise to phantasies which are experienced as leading into areas which feel inappropriate and arouse considerable anxiety, a move forward to giving and receiving love as an adult can be impeded, and in some instances there may be a retreat to latency. Sometimes help for such difficulties is found within the process of adolescence itself. Although the Messina society contributes to the difficulties of Beatrice and Benedick, we shall shortly see that it can also help in their resolution.

Beatrice also conveys that she has longings and standards for love, including a view of what is right for women in regard to the choice of husband, despite any formal expectations of her society:

> Yes, faith, it is my cousin's duty to make curtsy and say, 'Father, as it please you': but yet for all that, cousin, let him be a handsome fellow,

or else make another curtsy and say, 'Father, as it please me' . . . Would it not grieve a woman to be overmastered with a piece of valiant dust, to make an account of her life to a clod of wayward marl?

(II.i.48–58)

She is in touch with her feelings of isolation as Claudio and Hero's marriage is agreed: 'Thus goes everyone to the world but I . . . I may sit in a corner and cry "Heigh-ho for a husband"!' (II.i.300–1). But she immediately rejects a proposal from Don Pedro, telling him he 'is too costly to wear every day', and despite the humorous terms of her response, she gives further evidence of her deep inner well of seriousness.

We now go on to see the response in this society to the possible love of Beatrice and Benedick and the declared love of Hero and Claudio. The wedding of the latter is awaited. With an idea of making time 'not go dully by us' in the interval, Don Pedro leads Claudio, Hero and Leonato, together with Hero's attendants, in a plan to 'bring Signior Benedick and Lady Beatrice into a mountain of affection th'one with th'other' (II.i.340–4). He sees this as a Herculean task: 'If we can do this, Cupid is no longer an archer; his glory shall be ours, for we are the only love-gods' (II.i.362–4). Entertainment and the exercise of omnipotent purpose are the overt motives of Don Pedro and the other 'love-gods'. We are aware, however, that like us, they at least partly recognize the mutually loving aspects of Beatrice and Benedick; Don Pedro has already overtly maintained that Beatrice 'were an excellent wife for Benedick', and designated Benedick as 'not the unhopefullest husband'.

To carry out the plan, Don Pedro, Claudio and Leonato, purporting to be unaware of Benedick's presence in the orchard, maintain and discuss in his hearing how Beatrice is in love with him:

Claudio   Hero thinks surely she will die; for she says she will die if he love her not, and she will die ere she make her love known, and she will die if he woo her, rather than she will bate one breath of her accustomed crossness.

> *Don Pedro*   She doth well: if she should make tender of her love, 'tis
> very possible he'll scorn it, for the man, as you know all, hath a
> contemptible spirit.
>
> (II.iii.169–76)

Benedick is moved, and reflects:

> Love me? Why, it must be requited. I hear how I am censured . . . but
> for loving me – by my troth, it is no great addition to her wit, nor no
> argument of her folly, for I will be horribly in love with her . . . I have
> railed so long against marriage: but doth not the appetite alter?

He finally maintains that 'the world must be peopled' (II.iii.215–34).
Hero and her attendants, Margaret and Ursula, also actively
contrive for Beatrice to overhear their talk. Beatrice is led into an
arbour by the selfsame Margaret who is later used to deceive
Claudio into believing that Hero is unfaithful. From there Beatrice
hears the assertion that Benedick loves her; but because, Hero says,
'Disdain and scorn ride sparkling in her eyes . . . she is so
self-endeared' . . . and turns 'every man the wrong side out'
(III.i.51–68), she would only mock if she were told of Benedick's
love.

Beatrice reflects:

> Stand I condemn'd for pride and scorn so much?
> Contempt, farewell, and maiden pride, adieu!
> No glory lives behind the back of such.
> And, Benedick, love on, I will requite thee,
> Taming my wild heart to thy loving hand.
>
> (III.i.108–12)

It seems that these loving propensities of Beatrice and Benedick
have been 'held' within the group of friends, safely split off for the
time being from their own anxieties and destructive scorn. The two
apparently merry deceptions by the group of friends can be said to
put the couple in touch with their own feelings of love. As we saw
in *Romeo and Juliet*, it is not uncommon for members of an
adolescent group to act as a receptive container for temporarily
unbearable parts of their friends' emotionality. (This aspect of
adolescence will be further discussed in Chapter 4.)

When Beatrice and Benedick, through the activity of the group, believe that they are loved by one another, their mutual distrust disappears. On feeling loved, they become more able to love. They both emphasize the need to requite what is held to be the other's love, and on this account acknowledge their willingness to change their own earlier responses: scorn, crossness and pride are to be withdrawn. Beatrice blossoms into poetry in the process. Actual love of the other is, however, clearly present, although it is acknowledged as a future event. 'Maiden pride' – including, perhaps, some propensity to remain in maidenly latency – can be abandoned once one feels loved. Benedick has thoughts of the next generation, even though they may be expressed in somewhat grandiose terms. Love based in the depressive position, in which the needs of the loved object come first, is appearing.

We soon hear Benedick informing his fellow gallants that he has undergone some change, and that he has toothache – this was associated with love in Shakespeare's time (Arden Shakespeare, 1984). They tease him for shaving off his beard and using scent: 'the sweet youth's in love'. Indications that Benedick may ask Leonato for Beatrice's hand follow (III.ii.63–6). Claudio now believes that 'the two bears will not bite one another when they meet' (III.ii.69–70).

But the sporting, deceptive method employing 'treacherous' and 'false sweet bait' – in which, as Hero says, 'little Cupid's crafty arrow . . . only wounds by hearsay' (III.i.23–34) – again raises questions about this group and the society in which love is to be felt. The initial approach of the 'love-gods' is arrogant and omnipotent. The deceptive quality is also clear, as in Claudio's asides about Benedick – 'Bait the hook well, this fish will bite' (II.iii.109); 'He hath ta'en th'infection' (II.iii.121) – and Beatrice:

> Ursula (*Aside*)   She's limed, I warrant you! We have caught her, madam.
> Hero (*Aside*)   If it prove so, then loving goes by haps:
> Some Cupid kills with arrows, some with traps.
>
> (III.i.104–7)

The aspect of the merry action intended to avoid any dullness in waiting for Caludio's and Hero's wedding appears to predominate here, and the deeper meaning and truthfulness of what is being conveyed become distorted within the group itself. What is love: something catching, an infection, a hook, a chance trap? As part of her contribution to the gulling of Beatrice, Hero describes how she will protect Benedick from suffering unrequited love for her:

> And truly I'll devise some honest slanders
> To stain my cousin with: one doth not know
> How much an ill word may empoison liking.

$$\text{(III.i.83–6)}$$

This light-hearted passage, of course, presages the serious treatment Hero herself later receives in the deception orchestrated by Don John, and leaves an uneasy feeling that we are in a world in which slanders are cheerfully presented as honest, and love can be easily poisoned. This sequence resonates with the earlier construct of a man described in the conversation between Beatrice and Leonato who, furnished with other socially desirable attributes, would have 'Half Signior Benedick's tongue in Count John's mouth and half Count John's melancholy in Signior Benedick's face' (II.i.10–13), with no thought given to the real internal qualities and meaning of what was being put together in an agglomerated form. The group here has an untrustworthy quality which neither sincerely notes nor values what it is conveying – although, paradoxically, the major content in this instance appears to be true and, as such, is effectively received by Beatrice and Benedick, who are helped to recognize their love. One may also question whether Leonato's willingness to participate actively in this somewhat adolescent activity with his daughter Hero concerning Beatrice, his niece and ward, indicates a shallowness relevant to his failure to give fatherly support to Hero later in the play.

Leaving the 'plot' of the 'love-gods' orchestrated by Don Pedro, and turning again to the darker side of the story, we come to the plot orchestrated by his brother Don John, which is designed to lead to the 'death' of the marriage between Claudio and Hero (II.ii.19–20). Don John, ostensibly with Claudio's honour in mind, 'warns' Don Pedro and Claudio how they can witness Hero's alleged disloyalty:

'go but with me tonight, you shall see her chamber-window entered, even the night before her wedding day' (III.ii.101–3). Mistrust comes easily to Claudio. We have seen how easily he was convinced that Don Pedro had stolen Hero from him. Now, even before any evidence of any kind is actually presented, a 'wounding by hearsay' of his love is effected by Don John's 'crafty arrow'. He responds: 'If I see anything tonight why I should not marry her tomorrow, in the congregation, where I should wed, there will I shame her' (III.ii.112–14). What stands out in Claudio's reply is a sense of personal affront, followed by an immediate vengeful plan to shame Hero publicly should the suspicion be confirmed – a plan with which Don Pedro also concurs.

We now meet Dogberry, Verges and the watch. Comic and absurd on the surface, they wrongly describe the nature of their duties and deceive themselves about the level of their own verbal prowess. Despite the deceptive tenor of their talk, they do, however, recognize wrongdoing for what it is. The watch arrest Borachio and Conrade as the former is recounting how he carried out the pretended wooing of Hero, thereby successfully duping Claudio and Don Pedro into believing that she is unchaste (III.iii.139–59). Dogberry and Verges start on a long-winded account of the arrest to Leonato, who, in his haste to get to the wedding, does not stay to note its substance.

At the ceremony, Claudio, supported by Don Pedro, believing the deception instigated by Don John, repudiates Hero as a 'rotten orange' (IV.i.31). Hero swoons. Her father, Leonato, also readily believes the deception, and – concerned for himself rather than for Hero – bemoans that she was ever lovely in his eyes, and that the cause of his shame comes from his own loins. He immediately accepts information that she was absent from her room on the previous night as confirmation: 'Hence from her, let her die!' (IV.i.154).

Beatrice attempts to comfort Hero, proclaiming: 'O on my soul my cousin is belied' (IV.i.146). Don Pedro maintains that he, having wooed for Claudio, is dishonoured too. Claudio, Don Pedro and Don John leave the church, after Claudio's protesting plaint to Hero:

O Hero! What a Hero hadst thou been,
If half thy outward graces had been plac'd
About thy thoughts and counsels of thy heart!
But fare thee well, most foul, most fair! Farewell,
Thou pure impiety and impious purity!
For thee I'll lock up all the gates of love,
And on my eyelids shall conjecture hang,
To turn all beauty into thoughts of harm
And never shall it more be gracious.

(IV.i.100–8)

Auden (1975, p.158) remarks about Claudio:

Had his love for Hero been all he imagined it to be, he would have laughed in Don John's face and believed Hero's assertion of her innocence, despite apparent evidence to the contrary, as immediately as her cousin does. He falls into the trap set for him because as yet he is less a lover than a man in love with love.

We have seen his difficulty in getting to know the quality of his own feelings as well as seeking really to know Hero, to relate to what is inside her mind as well as to her 'outward graces'. Despite his diffidence, his love has a self-centred quality of urgent possessiveness; he was pleased at the quick wooing on his behalf, and wanted the marriage to take place the day after the betrothal: 'time goes on crutches till love have all his rites' (II.i.334–5). One may wonder if there is a double meaning within such 'rites'. Don John's allegations are experienced as a persecutory attack on his idealized manly virtue and honour as well as confounding his fragile picture of external beauty. His mind is easily 'empoisoned' with the belief that it is Hero's thoughts and heart that are at fault, and 'fair' becomes 'foul'.

Critics sometimes see the non-loving aspects of the Claudio and Hero theme as pointless or intrusive, or both, in relation to the rest of the play, and especially so in this denunciation scene. They do, however, appear to be central to thinking about finding and keeping love in the courtly, postwar, meeting-and-courting-ground of the Messina of the play, a place where truth and lies are indiscriminately promulgated by deception and hearsay. Claudio has his own personality traits; he is also a member of the courtly society which lays emphasis on codes of honour and outward appearances.[1] In addition to Claudio, Don Pedro and Leonato also consider themselves dishonoured; male courtly society in particular uses a self-idealizing view of honour as a shield against experiential knowledge of depth in the inner and outer worlds. Don John's lying communication is taken at its outward, face value; he speaks of Claudio's honour, and he is treated as honourable (III.ii.103); the speech purporting to be honest and fair is accepted as such, although it comes from a foul speaker. A clear distinction between a love-god and a robber of love is not so far made in this society.

References to fashion are plentiful, and indicate lack of attention to inner mental states. Hero, as she dresses for her wedding, and the fashion of her wedding apparel is praised in comparison with that of others, says that her 'heart is exceeding heavy' (III.iv.23–4). The mental weight of such inner heaviness receives no more notice than the 'heart-burning' activities of Don John, which Claudio is unable to think about and recognize as real slights on his honour. We, the audience, may ponder the internal consequences for Claudio of a second-hand wooing on his behalf. We may also remember Hero's own joking talk of poisoning Beatrice in Benedick's eyes and the likeness this bears to Don John's attempt to poison Hero in Claudio's eyes, and wonder about these in conjunction with Hero's inner fears. We are aware of an undifferentiated presence within the society of something 'most foul, most fair'. It is Hero who is now the victim of 'wounding by hearsay'. This courtly society, in its preservation of its omnipotent status, 'fair' and 'self-endearing' outward appearances, splits off emotional contact with the knowledge, meaning and possible consequences of its own inner deceptive, hearsay and other second-hand activities. A conflictual perception of what is inside in relation to what is outside is avoided. In depriving itself of trustworthy first-hand experiences, it masks from itself the difference between truth and lies.

Beatrice speaks up for her cousin, and Benedick's stance in relation to the accusation is also noteworthy: he does not walk out with his friends, now the accusers, but seeks space for thought. He bears his initial bewilderment, and pleads with Leonato:

Sir, Sir, be patient.
For my part I am so attir'd in wonder,
I know not what to say.

(IV.i.143–5)

Claudio has claimed that Hero's 'blush is guiltiness, not modesty'
(IV.i.41). But Friar Francis, who has been carefully 'noting of the
lady' (IV.i.158), reads Hero's blushes as 'innocent shames', and
believes her to be guiltless 'Under some biting error' (IV.i.169).
Benedick, although he still believes in his friends' honour, suspects
the villainy of Don John (IV.i.188), and finally persuades Leonato to
adopt the Friar's proposal:

Let her awhile be secretly kept in
And publish it that she is dead indeed;

(IV.i.203–4)

Friar Francis bases his initial conclusions on his observations – his
'notings', as opposed to Leonato's and Claudio's acceptance of
hearsay. Despite some similarity to *Romeo and Juliet* in that there
is a proposal for Hero's 'death', as there is for Juliet's, Friar Francis's
suggestion is very different from that of Friar Lawrence in the earlier
play. Unlike Friar Lawrence, he does not take the law into his own
hands, but obtains the agreement of Hero's father for his proposed
action. There is neither collusion with adolescent actions, nor
recourse to drugs. In fact he provides some paternal functioning,
which Leonato himself is unable to do. The Friar's offer, supported
by Beatrice and Benedick, is of a space in which the slandered Hero
may 'die to live' (IV.i.253), and of an opportunity for a change from
'slander to remorse' (IV.i.211) to take place. The awareness of
Hero's 'death' will, he hopes, lead Claudio to come to value the
Hero he has lost, and regret that he accused her (IV.i.210–54).

In contrast with the initial conversation between Benedick and
Claudio, in which Hero is likened to a jewel which can be bought
and possessed, the Friar introduces a sense of inner valuation,
demonstrated here by loss. He calls for patience and endurance. He
has also introduced a space for thinking, noting and observing, in
the context of his own thoughtful compassion. (This is an
application of the process of 'containment' as described by Bion
[1962a], which is discussed below, pp. 84–6). Benedick con-

tributes to understanding by being able to recognize the possible machinations of Don John. Early in the action Beatrice made a joke about Benedick having lost four of his five wits (I.i.92). In the play itself we see members of society having difficulty in using their wits and senses in conjunction with each other to make sense of what takes place. 'As a criterion for what constitutes a sensible experience', Bion (1963, p. 10) proposes 'common sense, namely some "sense" that is common to more than one sense' [author's quotation marks]. The Friar's intervention, together with the love of Beatrice and Benedick, introduce the concept of a mental space where emotions can come together and love can be thought about in terms of inner mental, emotional depth.

When Benedick is alone with Beatrice he attempts to comfort her, confirms his belief that Hero has been wronged, declares that he wishes to right it, and admits to his love:

> *Benedick*   I do love nothing in the world so well as you – is that not strange?
> *Beatrice*   As strange as the thing I know not. It were as possible for me to say I loved nothing so well as you, but believe me not; and yet I lie not; I confess nothing, nor I deny nothing. I am sorry for my cousin.
> (IV.i.266–72)

The truth that was contained in the orchard scenes has had an effect. The couple are aware of love, accompanied by a sense of mystery. But when Benedick protests that he will do anything for Beatrice, and she demands 'Kill Claudio', he replies: 'Ha, not for the wide world!' Beatrice now believes that there is 'no love' in him if he will not fight with her enemy. Some change has taken place. Not only are the couple aware of the truth about love, but Beatrice recognizes that its enemy, the lie, has to be addressed. Love comes alive – a love which also embraces Hero. For its sake, hate must be recognized and combated in the slandering Claudio. Beatrice laments: 'O God that I were a man! I would eat his heart in the market-place.' Righteously enraged by Claudio's acceptance of the unlikely story of Hero 'talking with a man out at a window', and by his public accusation of her, she decries the male aristocratic courtly society, designates Claudio a mere 'sugar plum' count, and goes on to expose what she sees as the manhood around her:

Princes and counties! Surely a princely testimony, a goodly count, Count Comfect, a sweet gallant surely! O that I were a man for his sake, or that I had any friend who would be a man for my sake! But manhood is melted into curtsies, valour into compliment, and men are only turned into tongues, and trim ones too: he is now as valiant as Hercules that only tells a lie and swears it. I cannot be a man with wishing, therefore I will die a woman with grieving.

(IV.i.287–323)

We are now in touch with feelings of depth. Beatrice, well aware of the superficiality of the 'princes and counties', and the presence of lies, leads the fight for truth and a more profoundly based version of honour than the courtly male one, a version which can embrace and provide justice for Hero, a woman (IV.i.301). She speaks of her desire for a masculine identity – not because of any intrinsic desire to be a man, but because she recognizes a wrong which, in her society, needs to be righted by a male, and feels that Benedick lets her down in refusing to perform 'a man's office'. Symbolically good masculine potency, a sword–penis, is needed to kill the slandering tongue. This stands out in contrast to earlier imagery of masculinity in Messina. Borachio, describing his own villainous attempts to besmirch Hero's honour, speaks of a picture of Hercules where 'his codpiece seems as massy as his club' (III.iii.134), with unclear links between sexuality and force; there is a confused account by Dogberry of a man who would not stand up for the Prince, and so was held to be weak and worthless (III.iii.25–31); and Beatrice herself speaks earlier of the misery of a woman accounting to a 'clod of wayward marl' (II.i.58). Now a strong, honourable man's office is demanded.

Benedick finally asks Beatrice: 'Think you in your soul the Count Claudio hath wronged Hero?', and when she replies: 'Yea, as sure as I have a thought, or a soul' (IV.i.327–9) he becomes willing to challenge Claudio. They both now allow the dominance of 'souls', representatives of an inner world which is believed to provide some truthful guidance.

The shallowness of their 'self-endeared' (III.i.56) defensiveness has fallen away. There is a combined strength and humility in their contact, focused on the necessity of justice for Hero, which takes precedence for Beatrice over any celebration of love with Benedick.

Their mutually biting talk has been transformed into redressing a 'biting error' (IV.i.169) originated by the malice of Don John, who did 'have his mouth', and did bite (I.iii.33). The tongue becomes a vehicle for speaking the truth instead of slander – in contrast to its earlier usage as a means of expression for Benedick's disparagement of Beatrice: 'I cannot endure my Lady Tongue' (II.i.258), or a commodity rated by Beatrice somewhat concretely in similar terms to Don John's leg when she considers features in a male that would win female approbation (II.i.10–15). There is a movement towards a loving, undefended state of mind of the depressive position. The loving, restorative, fighting-for-a-cause, external couple resonates with the desire to fulfil the requirements of their souls; this suggests a feeling of introjective identification with a sense of inner goodness. The 'psychic reality' – the inner reality of the mind, related to this sense of goodness – demands, in such circumstances, that the woman must not be left grieving by the man. The Claudio who is to be killed is the wrongdoing of the 'sugar plum' Count Claudio (IV.i.315), whose self-idealizing tenderness for his own rank and honour (III.ii.105) leads him to dishonour Hero and 'lock up all the gates of love'. Perhaps it is also the shallow, tender self-endearment present in the society of 'princes and counties', with its heart in its own marketplace, which needs to be challenged – a society actively defending itself against the receipt of 'rotten oranges', yet not wanting to know how it deceives itself with its own valuations.

Beatrice and Benedick make contact with their own lovingness through the activities of the adolescent group. They also come into closer contact with their own inner resources, their souls. Outwardly and inwardly enriched, with the help of the thoughtful Friar, they now perform functions of love and concern on behalf of righting the wrong done to Hero. They show a deeper love than we have seen so far – one that arises from their 'first-hand' beliefs; and this love also now makes some impact on their society.

Leonato comes to believe in Hero's innocence: 'My soul doth tell me Hero is belied' (V.i.42), and with his brother Antonio he confronts Claudio and Don Pedro with the villainy that lead to Hero's 'death', only to be pushed aside with epithets such as 'old man' from Don Pedro – very different indeed from the Prince's earlier courteous speech (V.i.62–73). Antonio, now enraged, challenges Don Pedro and Claudio:

> Boys, apes, braggarts, Jacks, milksops! . . .
> Scambling, outfacing, fashion-monging boys,
> That lie, and cog, and flout, deprave, and slander,
> Go anticly, and show outward hideousness,
> And speak off half a dozen dang'rous words,
> How they might hurt their enemies, if they durst,
> And that is all.*

(V.i.91–8)

Antonio provides an older man's jaundiced view of a (male) adolescent society of bragging, swearing, 'fashion-monging' boys. We get a clearer sense here than perhaps we do elsewhere in the play of the youth not only of Claudio but also of Don Pedro. 'Fashion-monging' expresses an older generation's views about the 'outward hideousness' of adolescent clothing, but also reverberates with some sense of inner insufficiency. Insults and polarization pass between the two pairs, now merely categorized by each other as old men or adolescents. Don Pedro recovers his aplomb with a speech of pious self-righteousness:

> Gentlemen both, we will not wake your patience.
> My heart is sorry for your daughter's death;
> But on my honour she was charg'd with nothing
> But what was true, and very full of proof.

(V.i.101–5)

When Benedick appears, Claudio expects him to use his wit to drive melancholy further away (V.i.122–4), quite unsuspecting of Benedick's serious purpose and the challenge he delivers. Don Pedro and Claudio, in their arrogant talk, appear to be totally detached from the emotionality of the recent events; Hero is now even referred to merely as 'the old man's daughter' (V.i.175). Sorrows relating to her 'death' are absent, and individual depressive pain is avoided. John Barton's much-discussed 1976 production of

---

* Jack: rascal; scambling: contentious; cog: cheat; flout: mock; deprave: defame; anticly: grotesquely (Arden Shakespeare, 1984).

the play, set in the India of the British Raj, made it very easy to think of young officers on the move, splitting off and leaving behind any unsatisfactory emotional encounters. The now clearly more manly Benedick addresses Claudio and Don Pedro:

> (*To Claudio*)   Fare you well, boy, you know my mind: I will leave you now to your gossip-like humour . . . (*To Don Pedro*) My lord, for your many courtesies, I thank you: I must discontinue your company. Your brother the bastard is fled from Messina. (*To both*) You have among you killed a sweet and innocent lady. For my Lord Lackbeard there, he and I shall meet; and till then, peace be with him.
>
> (V.i.181–90)

The hard self-protectiveness and defensiveness of Claudio and Don Pedro, who listened to the earlier lies presented by Don John as if they were the truth, is still there, but Benedick – perhaps with his new manly authoritative seriousness – has impressed them: Don Pedro notes Benedick's remark that Don John has fled, and says: 'Pluck up, my heart, and be sad' (V.i.201). Now it seems that, in conjunction with a growing capacity to be aware of Don John's wrongdoing, there may be room for the truth of sorrow and regret to be felt for the killing of Hero's sweetness and innocence. There is some move from a paranoid-schizoid to a depressive state of mind. The healthy acknowledgement of the truth (Bion, 1965, p. 38) does indeed here lead to a 'plucking up' of the heart. The facts become clear as the findings of the comic watch of Dogberry and Verges are finally 'noted', and a deeply repentant Borachio is brought in. Self-righteousness yields to softer feelings. Thus Claudio:

> Sweet Hero! Now thy image doth appear
> In the rare semblance that I loved it first.
>
> (V.i.245–6)

There is no longer cause for Benedick's challenge to Claudio to be carried out in physical terms. But Leonato is sarcastic at first:

> I thank you, Princes, for my daughter's death;
> Record it with your high and worthy deeds;
> 'Twas bravely done, if you bethink you of it.
>
> (V.i.262–5)

Claudio is willing to submit to any penance for his 'sin' that Leonato may impose as his 'revenge', while at the same time he insists that his only 'sin' was 'in mistaking' (V.i.269). He agrees to hang an epitaph to Hero in the family tomb, and to marry the person described as Leonato's 'brother's daughter', without seeing her, and in so doing risks a marriage which his 'eye' has in no way negotiated (II.i.166). In response to Leonato's lack of revenge, he rejoins: 'Your overkindness doth wring tears from me! I do embrace your offer, and dispose for henceforth of poor Claudio!' (V.i.286–9). Claudio goes on to take part in a solemn night-time vigil in which he hangs the epitaph to Hero:

> 'Done to death by slanderous tongues . . .
> So the life that died with shame
> Lives in death with glorious fame.'
>
> (V.iii. 3–8)

The beautifully described dawn which follows is accompanied by a change from mourning to wedding clothes. Claudio's bride is, of course, the veiled and living Hero. Leonato responds to the Friar's question:

> *Friar*   Did I not tell thee she was innocent?
> *Leonato*   So are the Prince and Claudio, who accus'd her . . .
>
> (V.iv.1–2)

Leonato later adds that Hero died 'but whiles her slander lived' (V.iv.66). Can we now confidently believe, then, that the slandered version of Hero is truly dead and buried, that hearts have really 'plucked up' into bearing sadness, and that the dawn issues in a restored, psychically reborn version of Hero into a society that can receive her with love, and say with Don Pedro:

> Good morrow, masters; put your torches out.
> The wolves have prey'd, and look, the gentle day,
> Before the wheels of Phoebus, round about
> Dapples the drowsy east with spots of grey.
>
> (V.iii.24–7)

Certainly in psychic reality, encompassing the 'soul' as described in the play, someone who has been harmed or even felt to have died, such as Hero, may be restored to psychic life if the necessary and inevitably painful emotional experience of regret and mourning takes place. But is Leonato really aware of all that there is to be forgiven, including his own initial response to Hero? Is Claudio's expiatory ritual following on Leonato's forgiveness an accomplishment of true mourning which would call for a thoughtful examination of his relationship with the Hero who had 'died', before she could be put to real rest in his mind? Or could the acquiescence in the ritual in which the slandered and shamed Hero lives with fame in death also have some reference to the disposal of a 'Poor Claudio' from his mind? Both the absence and the biting 'wolfishness' of Don John have now been noted, and Margaret, who took part in the deception, is said to have been 'in some fault . . . although against her will' (V.iv.4–5). Unlike Borachio, Don Pedro, Claudio and Leonato see themselves as exonerated from any share in the actual deception 'but in mistaking'. Some of the causality for the events leading to the repudiation of Hero and her 'death' is still unrecognized in that the mistake of having gone along with the antisocial 'canker' of Don John and not seeking to know – to 'K' – the nature of the inside of society, or themselves, remains unnoticed. Though we are moved by the 'plucking up' of sadness leading to the psychic rebirth of Hero, we, the audience, by whom such differences may be experienced and noted, may be anxious that such 'mistaking' may again be treated as 'nothing' in this society.

But our hearts may 'pluck up' when Benedick and Beatrice discuss their love:

> *Benedick*   And I pray thee now tell me, for which of my bad parts didst thou first fall in love with me?
> *Beatrice*   For them all together, which maintained so politic a state of evil that they will not admit any good part to intermingle with them. But for which of my good parts did you first suffer love for me?
> *Benedick*   'Suffer love' – a good epithet! I do suffer love indeed, for I love thee against my will.
> *Beatrice*   In spite of your heart, I think. Alas, poor heart! If you spite it for my sake, I will spite it for yours, for I will never love that which my friend hates.
> *Benedick*   Thou and I are too wise to woo peaceably.
>
> (V.ii.56–67)

They make serious points with humour. They acknowledge that they possess both good and bad qualities. The 'bad parts' are 'noted' for what they are, and 'the fair' is not spuriously intermingled with 'the foul'. Love is now to be suffered, and carries pain and conflict. The references to Benedick's heart recall his remark at their first meeting: 'I would I could find in my heart that I had not a hard heart' (I.i.116). Such hardness, it seems, is now to be mutually thwarted. Between them they now do have the capacity to sustain a range of deep emotions associated with the inner world of the 'soul'. One may also sense that they have become more adult. The changes we see here do illustrate the development from an adolescent to an adult state of mind, which we shall examine in greater detail in Chapter 4 (see pp. 107–12 below).

When Beatrice and Benedick finally are to join Claudio and Hero in the same marriage ceremony, however, they claim again that they do so only for each other's sake. Claudio and Hero now produce secret sonnets which Beatrice and Benedick have written to each other, expressing their love. The adolescent group is active again! 'A miracle! Here's our own hands against our hearts', exclaims Benedick. From what we know now, we may be unwilling to believe that Beatrice's and Benedick's 'denial' of their mutual love represents a real retreat from the depths of lovingness. Is it an admission of the psychic reality that conflict will continue to exist, or an attempt to mask the truth of their love under the cover of a joking reprise which appears to slander it, in order to keep it safe in the context of the society in which they live? If the latter, what danger is there for the future? Maybe it is still difficult to own deeply felt love with wholehearted openness, and put what Beatrice calls 'good parts' (V.ii.60) at risk of being misapprehended or exposed to unnoted contamination in a society that is unwilling fully to examine the nature of its 'mistaking'. Deception may remain an important part of the currency of a society which, at times, appears to know 'the price of everything and the value of nothing' (Wilde, 1891). But perhaps we can remain hopeful about the laying to rest of the mutually biting tongues which can slander love belonging to this particular couple as Benedick cries 'Peace', seals Beatrice's mouth with a kiss, and calls for a dance. We finally learn that Don

John is captured, and Benedick will devise 'brave punishments' for him.

But how seriously is the effect of deception on the quality of life within society to be taken? There is plenty in the 'ado' worth noting.[2]

3   THE AGITATION OF INEXPERIENCE: A DISCUSSION OF PUSHKIN'S VERSE NOVEL *EUGENE ONEGIN*

An adolescent has to participate in the process of growing up without any first-hand knowledge of the changes that are taking place. The sense of current identity with which to relate to change may also be fluctuating because of the nature of adolescence itself. Exposing oneself to the 'agitation of inexperience' presented by the possibility of change may be feared and avoided. In our discussion of *Much Ado about Nothing* we saw that remaining in a latency frame of mind could be one way of avoiding the impact of anxiety. The verse novel *Eugene Onegin*, written by the Russian poet Pushkin between 1823 and 1831, helps us to appreciate both the potential for change and development which adolescence offers, and also further ways in which such development may become blocked and unblocked.

This discussion is based on the acclaimed translation by Sir Charles Johnston (Pushkin 1979), and I am indebted to this, and also to the introduction to it by John Bayley. I also refer briefly to the music and the presentation of the story portrayed in Tchaikovsky's opera (1879) of the same name. The librettist Konstantin Shilovsky is said to have worked very much in accord with Tchaikovsky, carrying out the latter's wish that he should create lyric scenes which would show something of the characters' inner worlds. Although the opera does not follow the action of the novel very closely, it makes interesting use of some of Pushkin's commentary about the characters and events contained in it. Pushkin's *Eugene Onegin* is an enormously rich work, with a brilliant compound of

widely applicable social, political and psychological insights. It has
its own special position in Russian literature, and the implications
of the particularly Russian nature of its contents have been
discussed by Dostoevsky and many other writers. Matters such as
Onegin's ennui could be thought about both in relation to the Russia
of the time and in a wider social context. The richness of *Eugene
Onegin*, however, like that of Shakespeare's plays, is such that the
work can be thought about from many points of view without
negating those that are not explicitly discussed. Here I again focus
on adolescence and change, but I hope that the references to the
text will enable the reader to maintain contact with the aesthetic
source of the work, or lead him or her back to the multifaceted
wealth of the original.

   Pushkin's verse novel is variously witty, ironic, cynical, racy,
formal and informal in style, and often deeply moving. Pushkin
portrays a fluctuating degree of closeness to his characters: at one
moment he is describing their activities and emotions; at another
he comments on them as his creations ('my Onegin', 'my Tatyana')
or takes part in a discussion with some – but not total – detachment
from his formal subject matter. As readers we feel transported into
a world where we too are involved with the characters and the
varying forms in which the author presents himself, and, as Bayley
(1979) says, led to infer certain perceptions for ourselves within
what Pushkin also called this 'free novel'. Quick changes in mood,
varying between down-to-earth dogmatism and ethereal longing;
between closeness and distance; and between cynicism, idealization and sadness contribute to an artistic texture which is conducive
to a discussion of adolescence in which fluctuating contact with
different aspects of individual emotionality are very apparent.

   The main action of the story can be outlined quite simply. Eugene
Onegin and his friend Vladimir Lensky, a poet, visit the Larins'
country estate. Lensky is already engaged to Olga, the younger
daughter. Her sister, Tatyana, falls in love with Onegin, and writes
him a love letter. Onegin rejects her, but when Lensky, some time
later, presses him to visit again, he is stirred by pity and tenderness
for Tatyana. He attempts to disperse such feelings, and to revenge
himself on Lensky for their presence, by flirting with Olga. Lensky
challenges Onegin to a duel, in which Lensky is killed. Several years

later Onegin re-encounters Tatyana, now married, and now it is he who writes a love letter to her; she finally admits to her love for him, but remains faithful to her husband, Prince Gremin.

Onegin is eighteen at the beginning of the story (1.XXIII), a fashionable dandy in St Petersburg society. He is impatiently awaiting his uncle's death and his own consequent inheritance, reflecting inwardly: 'When will the devil come for you?' (1.I). His falseness of character is portrayed from the start. Participator at innumerable balls and dinners, he is widely flirtatious within a framework of insincere superficiality, and when he is rebuffed he finds instant consolation:

> How early he'd learnt to dissemble,
> to hide a hope, to make a show
> of jealousy, to seem to tremble
> or pine, persuade of yes or no . . .
> how bold or bashful there, and here
> how brilliant with its instant tear!

> (1.X)

In time, however, finding society belles capricious, infidelity cloying, and one day like another, he becomes bored. He is full of spleen. Viewing audience and performers through his glasses in the opera house, he yawns:

>   'Ballet –
> they all have richly earned a pension.'
> he turns away: 'I've had enough – ' . . .

> (1.XXI)

He retreats from society life, and decides to be a writer. He locks himself in his den, but work makes him feel sick. Moreover, 'no word came flowing from his quill' (1.XLIII).

> Idle again by dedication,
> oppressed by emptiness of soul,
> he strove to achieve the appropriation
> of other's thought – a splendid goal . . .

> (1.XLIV)

However, this attempt to take possession of the thoughts of others yields no results. Nothing he reads pleases him, and all the books are critically dismissed:

> he read, and read – no satisfaction:
> here's boredom, madness or pretence . . .
> He'd given up girls – now gave up letters,
> and hid the bookshelf's dusty stack
> in taffeta of mourning black.
>
> (1.XLIV)

Learning of his uncle's imminent death, for which he has been waiting, Onegin rushes to take up his lucrative inheritance of the country estate, but boredom sets in again after two days:

> Yes, spleen was waiting like a sentry,
> and dutifully shared his life
> just like a shadow, or a wife.
>
> (1.LIV)

Onegin's narcissistic, self-idealizing propensities and spleen are apparent. We later hear how he

> without a smile
> burst with cold envy and with bile.
>
> (4.XV)

When he looks disdainfully through his glasses at the ballet and audience, it seems that he 'looks to kill' any potentially enjoyable experience, and to extrude his dissatisfactions into others. Whatever the actual nature of the society may be, his own superciliousness and capriciousness are projected into and identified with it. As we have seen in discussing both *Romeo and Juliet* and *Much Ado about Nothing*, it is common in adolescent life to split off aspects of oneself and locate them in others, making use of the unconscious phantasy of projective identification. If this takes place as part of the 'give-and-take' of adolescent group life, where there is some likelihood of taking back – perhaps changed – projected parts into oneself, some real emotional experience, learning and development may result. There is no indication, however, that this applies to Onegin. His widespread splitting and projective identification has a ruthless, asocial quality in the way it is used to disembarrass him of his discomforts by extruding them outwards. It is accompanied by a concomitant intrusion into the writings and minds of others in an attempt to acquire a ready-made, 'off-the-shelf', identity package, without any need to build an identity up for himself out of his own experience. Any to-and-fro of social interaction is lacking. By such means he bypasses the potential anxieties and painfulness of growing up. Such pseudo-experience can lead to the creation of a pseudo-adult personality, based on infantile emotions (Meltzer, 1973, pp. 51–7) akin to the 'false self' described by Winnicott (1960).

By extruding much of his personality into others, Onegin leaves himself feeling superior, but without anything positive to express; he is also 'empty of soul'. The possession of books, a quill and the phantasy of 'being' a writer clearly does not make him one. Envy lies behind his failure to engage emotionally with new situations and new relationships, and respond to the opportunities adolescence offers. Envy relates to someone else having something that one wishes to possess oneself, and the direct experience of it is painful. An attempt to steal the thoughts of others may avoid the pain of actually feeling envious of what they write. Onegin's unexpressed envy may, however, lead to his finding the books worthless when he reads them. The description of the bookshelf hidden in 'mourning black' suggests that it is failure which is being hidden away from himself. This contrasts with a real experience of mourning, which would require both emotional recognition of the 'death' of himself as a writer and a repudiation of the means by which he sought to achieve his aim. When Onegin takes up his country estate, he expects also to take up the role of a contented country gentleman. It is not difficult to imagine that the indecent haste and greed manifested in his entry into his inheritance – without any mourning for his uncle, whom he has already mentally 'sent to the devil' – is likely to leave him with some devilish emotional legacy affecting his capacity for enjoyment.

Onegin can be contrasted with his fellow landowner and neighbour, the poet Lensky, who can bear 'the uncertainties within his heart' and still find life 'mysterious and enticing' (2.VII). Both Onegin and Pushkin himself poke fun at Lensky, disparaging his youthful, romantic verse with 'roses romantically blowing' within it:

> He sang of grief and parting-time
> of something vague, some misty clime . . .
> he sang of 'lifetime's yellow page' –
> when not quite eighteen years of age.
>
> (2.X)

As Lensky talks romantically, Onegin, biting back his acid comments, succeeds in tolerantly musing that youth must be allowed to 'rave and flare' (2.XV). Onegin and Lensky gradually become friends, and Pushkin, reflecting an aspect of Onegin's cynicism, wryly comments in an aside that such a friendship can bloom 'when there's nothing else to do'. We recall that Onegin was eighteen at the beginning of the verse novel. Lensky, with his ingenuous youthful simplicity and romanticism, appears to serve as a convenient person into whom Onegin can place his own residual youthful longings by means of projective identification, reserving for himself a felt-to-be lofty, manly (although false) perspective.

Lensky has doted since boyhood on their neighbour Olga Larin, and Onegin condescendingly accompanies him on one of his visits to the Larin household. There he and Olga's sister Tatyana meet. Pushkin tells us how Tatyana, as a child, had played neither with dolls nor with other children,

> for she was bored by laughs and noise
> and by the sound of silly joys.
>
> (2.XXVII)

> From early on she loved romances,
> They were her only food . . . and so
> she fell in love with all the fancies
> of Richardson and of Rousseau.
>
> (2.XXIX)

The names of Tatyana and Onegin become linked in local gossip, much to Tatyana's displeasure. However:

> she fell in love – the hour was fated . . .
> so fires of spring will bring to birth
> a seedling fallen in the earth.
>
> (3.VII)

Now the figures from the novels that she avidly reads 'blend into Eugene alone' (3.IX); she sees herself, too, as if created 'By writers of her admiration' (3.X). Tatyana, it appears, 'put herself into' the novels she read by projective identification, and 'lost herself' in the identities of their romantic heroines. To 'lose oneself' temporarily in a book is a common enough experience, from which one can emerge having taken in something of what one has read, with some inner enrichment. The process may provide familiarity with characters whom one might wish to think about and understand – or even wish, particularly in adolescence, to be like; getting 'into them' by projective identification may be a first step towards 'taking in' something about them – in other words, it may result in some form of introjective identification whereby one's inner world may be enhanced. Relentlessly pursued projective identification into the characters of novels, however, seeking to 'be' one of them, avoids having one's own experiences arising out of everyday living, and postpones or evades the ordinary struggles of growing up in the external world. This appears to underlie what we are told about Tatyana up to the time we meet her, with the implication that she seems to have avoided a real experience of childhood and, perhaps, the unwanted, unpalatable fact of being a child as opposed to a romantic heroine. For her there was an absence of the childish play which 'provides an organization for the initiation of emotional relationships, and so enables social contacts to develop' (Winnicott, 1964, p. 145). But it seems that the 'fires of spring', the fires of adolescence, light in her, and she falls in love. Onegin becomes for her the external representative of the heroes of the novels, and she is to be the external heroine, with the pressing desire to be loved by him.

One bedtime, Tatyana, 'hunted by love's anguish' (3.XVI), tries to calm herself by asking her old nurse for tales of the past:

> 'Tell me, nyanya
> your early life, unlock your tongue:
> were you in love when you were young?'

(3.XVII)

But she does not really listen to the nurse's accounts of her hard life. She is now no longer satisfied by some second-hand

experience, that of her nurse, nor by the passivity of 'being' a
romantic character in a novel, and rushes to write an impassioned
letter to Onegin. She makes a headlong attempt to have a
relationship of her own in the external world:

> 'Why did you visit us, but why?
> Lost in our backwoods habitation
> I'd not have known you, therefore I
> would have been spared this laceration.
> In time, who knows, the agitation
> of inexperience would have passed,
> I would have found a friend, another,
> and in the role of virtuous mother
> and faithful wife I'd have been cast.
> Another . . . No, another never
> in all the world could take my heart! . . .
>
> At this midnight of my condition,
> was it not you, dear apparition,
> who in the dark came flashing through
> and, on my bed-head gently leaning,
> with love and comfort in your meaning,
> spoke words of hope? But who are you:
> the guardian angel of tradition,
> or some vile agent of perdition
> sent to seduce? Resolve my doubt.'

(3.XXXI–II)

In any new relationship one must always be inexperienced, and a
first relationship in adolescence has the additional element of an
entry into a new way of being in contact with a member of the
opposite sex. Tatyana's lack of an internal legacy derived from the
to-and-fro of childhood play may handicap her approach to Onegin,
but she does now risk having her own experience. She speaks of
her love, recognizing and acknowledging her 'agitation of
inexperience', although she also reproaches Onegin for making her
suffer in this way. To do this she has to expose herself to her
primitive feelings of persecution and her doubts about her
idealization of him: will he be a guardian angel, perhaps linking with
infantile phantasy of mother or nurse at her bedhead, or is he a
potential seducer, possibly related in her mind to a seducing lover

of fiction, such as Lovelace in Richardson's *Clarissa* (Richardson, 1747)? She does not know. Despite these polarized perceptions, her action portrays her move away from the passivity of living her emotional life within novels; even though she still desires to be a romantic heroine, the romance is to take place in the external world. She also distances herself from a view of accepting herself as conforming to the 'virtuous' experience of her mother, who did not marry the man with whom she was in love. Her crush-like, impetuous, adolescent approach to Eugene indicates that for her the seeking of external relationships has only been postponed, not abandoned; and also, perhaps, suggests that her immersion in novels may have some qualities of 'wanting to know' and 'wanting to be like' as well as of 'being' their heroine. She is able to make use of the new 'fires' of adolescence to test out the reception of her powerfully experienced 'thronging soft and delicate desires' in the outside world, and faces finding out whether she will be a happy heroine or, perhaps, get burnt.

Onegin, in his wasted years of dalliance, has moved from one relationship to the next, evading awareness of rebuffs and of any meaningful content which could have brought pain. The consequent poverty in his internal world is apparent. Any opportunities to experience himself as able or wishing to be in a sincerely loving relationship have been missed: 'he killed eight years in such a style' (4.IX,X). He is nevertheless 'deeply stirred' by Tatyana's letter, and does not wish to betray her innocence. When they meet, he coolly repulses her. He tells her she has 'brought feeling to what had long been heartless' (4.XII), and that he would have chosen her if he was capable of homely life; however, he is not made for happiness, and love would soon fade. He describes himself as unworthy and envious, and ends what Pushkin calls his 'sermon' with considerable condescension:

> 'You'll love again, but you must teach
> Your heart some self-restraint; for each
> and every man won't understand it
> as I have . . . learn from my belief
> that inexperience leads to grief.

(4.XVI)

Pushkin suggests, with some irony, that we will agree that Onegin, in his response, has manifested 'a truly noble disposition', but always finds brickbats hurled at him (4.XVIII). It is only in the final scenes of the verse novel that he can admit how he scorned Tatyana in 'what he deemed the modesty of her condition' (8.XX). Tatyana, too, later refers to this scene:

'But now – oh God! – the thought of you,
your icy look, your stern dissuasion,
freezes my blood . . . Yet all the same,
nothing you did gave cause for blame.'

(8.XLIII)

Onegin attempts to get rid of the stirrings of love which would have to confront his own heartlessness. In a very beautiful Bolshoi production in Moscow in 1983, he was portrayed as momentarily putting his arm around Tatyana and then quickly withdrawing it, graphically conveying a feeling of being moved, but seeking to avoid the risk and possible pain of further experience. Not only are the hurtful implications of his initial admission of heartlessness lost, but as he goes on to speak of his inadequacies in relation to domestic life, he presents them almost as if they constituted a virtue rather than a defect. He acknowledges his envy, but it seems that it is only Tatyana who is to be perturbed by it. He takes refuge in a superior state of mind which claims to 'know about' his own and Tatyana's inadequacies. He lectures Tatyana about restraining her heart, claiming that 'inexperience leads to grief'. But we are aware that he himself is emotionally inexperienced. His own 'self-restraint' rests on a foundation of not knowing himself in any real emotional sense; he does not allow relationships to acquire personal meaning for him, and in consequence the possibility of being called to grieve on their account is avoided. He cannot face the struggle of experiencing his own self-avowed heartlessness, or of examining the envious part of himself. We also saw (see p. 62 above) how he may be out of touch with some less heartless aspects of himself, having located them in Lensky.

Adolescence offers a 'second chance' for growth and development in the context of new relationships, of which Tatyana and Onegin make very different use. Tatyana exposes her sense of identity as a 'grown-up' heroine, stemming from childhood identifications in literature, to her 'agitation of inexperience'; she risks having a real first-hand personal experience, and will have to face any grief that it may bring. This is a further example of the quest for knowledge in an experiential sense, to which Bion's concept of the 'K'-link (Bion, 1962a) is relevant. Onegin, handicapped by his envy, his years of dalliance and consequent 'emptiness of soul' (1.XLIV), is unable to make use of this opportunity for development, in his case occurring later in an as yet unresolved adolescence. Instead he delivers a sermon from a pseudo-adult, second-hand position, in which he claims to 'know about' grief, avoiding any 'agitation of inexperience'. Failure to be emotionally in touch with – to 'K' – one's own experiences stands in the way of the emotional development necessary for growth. The disastrous grief-laden consequences of such non-experience for Onegin become apparent later.

Tatyana languishes. Onegin departs to his estate to lead what Pushkin calls a country 'hermit's life' (4.XXXVII), which includes keeping a good table and the occasional kiss from 'a fair black-eyed maiden' (4.XXXIX). Lensky, full of his love for Olga, succeeds in persuading a reluctant Onegin to accompany him to Tatyana's name-day celebration (4.XLIX). Shortly before this event, Tatyana has a terrifying nightmare in which Onegin appears in the company of a gang of monsters; this portends some of the subsequent events. When she sees him at the festivities she trembles and nearly swoons (5.XXX). Onegin has found such reactions tedious in the past, and when

> He saw the sad girl's trembling state,
> looked down in an access of hate,
> pouted, and swore in furious passion
> to wreak, by stirring Lensky's ire,
> the best revenge one could desire.
>
> (5.XXXI)

But when Tatyana receives the congratulations for her name day he feels differently:

> When Eugene's turn for salutation
> arrives, the girl's exhausted gaze,

her discomposure, her confusion,
expose his soul to an intrusion
of pity: in his silent bow,
and in his look there shows somehow
a wondrous tenderness. And whether
it was that he's been truly stirred,
or half-unwittingly preferred
a joking flirt, or both together,
there was a softness in his glance:
it brought back Tanya from her trance.

(5.XXXIV)

Onegin's revenge against Lensky proceeds, however, and he dances
off with Olga, addressing her tenderly and booking her dance
programme so that she has no space left for Lensky. Olga is smugly
pleased, but apparently oblivious to the emotional import of what
is happening; Lensky, 'crazed with jealousy' (5.XLIV), is provoked
into challeging Onegin to a duel (5.XLV). It is clear that Onegin has
passed his enraged feelings and hatred on to – or, rather, into –
Lensky.

Tatyana's response to her earlier nightmare about Onegin was
an attempt to decipher the 'meanings' of the images it contained
by looking them up in her treasured dreambook under headings
such as 'bear, blackness, blizzard' (5.XXIV), as if the personal
significance of the dream for her could be derived in such an
impersonal and routine fashion. Now she begins to examine her
own experience of Onegin in a first-hand manner, confronting her
contradictory perceptions of him. Sleepless, and perplexed by his
momentary tenderness towards her and his exhibition with Olga,
she feels that her soul has been 'pierced'. She is aware of a doomlike
sense of death, albeit sweet in its association with Onegin, but
acknowledges:

'the truth is this,
it's not in him to bring me bliss.'

(6.III)

Onegin cannot bear Tatyana's trembling emotionality – so clearly
related to him, and serving as a reminder of how she had briefly
brought feeling to his own heartlessness. Nor can he bear his own

fleeting experience of tenderness. Hatred and projection are used as means of dispersing his pain. It is Lensky who is to suffer – not only for having persuaded Onegin to come, but perhaps also for arousing his perception of his envy of a couple who are able to have an effectively loving relationship. The infliction of damage on the relationship between Lensky and Olga suggests a perverse form of compensation for Onegin's reluctance to risk further emotional exploration of potentially loving feelings between Tatyana and himself; the pleasure in such a damaging action replaces any further contact with his own faltering tenderness. Rather than foster an experience of the 'K'-link, seeking to know his own emotions, Onegin appears to prefer an experience of 'minus K', based on a false sense of moral superiority which asserts that 'an ability to misunderstand is superior to an ability to understand', and in which there is a 'hatred of any new development in the personality as if the new development were a rival to be destroyed' (Bion, 1962a, pp. 95–8).

Onegin has successfully distanced himself from his 'wondrous tenderness' and projected his 'hatred' and 'ire' into Lensky, so that it is now the latter who feels vengeful and non-conciliatory. By the next morning Onegin, having received Lensky's challenge,

> found too much that he regretted:
> last night he'd erred in making fun,
> so heartless and so detrimental,
> of love so timorous and gentle.
> In second place the poet might
> have been a fool; yet he'd a right,
> at eighteen years, to some compassion.
> Evgeny loved him from his heart,
> and should have played a different part:
> no softball for the winds of fashion,
> no boy, to fight or take offence –
> the *man* of honour and of sense.
>
> (6.X)

> he should have settled for disarming
> that youthful heart . . .
>
> (6.XI)

From a mentally superior 'manly' position Onegin regrets his action, although this is now described as merely 'making fun', albeit heartless, and shows how he has distanced himself from the experience of his original unbearable emotions, now present in the Lensky whom he claims to love. It seems to him that it is now too late for change, particularly on account of the involvement in the duel of a neighbour, Zaretsky – Lensky's second, and a stickler for protocol. (Here Pushkin slips in a little aside, commenting how the arch-rake and brawler Zaretsky did in fact change later: 'so, if we want to change, we can'! [6.IV].)

When Lensky learns that Olga has been quite unaware of the stir caused in him, he again feels loved by her, and is determined to protect her from Onegin. He departs for the duel with aching heart, leaving some romantic verses behind him. Tatyana does not know about the duel, and pines for Onegin. At the scene of the duel Pushkin, recalling the past relationship between Onegin and Lensky, asks:

> could they not give each other quarter
> and part in kindness? Just the same,
> all modish foes dread worldly shame.

> (6.XXVIII)

In the opera, the sentiments about the duel between old friends parting in kindness are sung by Onegin and Lensky in the form of a canon before the duel. Kobbé (1976) suggests that 'the form of a canon exactly expresses the relationship – the thoughts of the two men are similar but divided by form and come together only as they regret that etiquette precludes a reconciliation at this late hour'. We are also aware that it is also the residual effect of Onegin's own rage and jealousy, as well as his potential lovingness, split off from himself, that he is heartlessly fighting in Lensky. Zaretsky directs the action, and Lensky is killed.

> Onegin, drenched with sudden chill,
> darts to the boy, and looks, and still
> calls out his name . . . All unavailing: . . .

> (6.XXXI)

Eugene looks at Lensky, chilled
at heart by grim remorse's freezing.
'Well, what?' the neighbour says, 'He's killed.'

(6.XXXV)

Pushkin writes mournfully of Lensky's death and loss of his
aspirations, but – 'to be truthful' – also suggests that he might have
got rid of his poetic aspirations and ended up as a stout,
gout-afflicted, middle-aged family man, and died in bed (6.XXXIX).
He leaves the theme of the main narrative, promising to return and
tell us the outcome:

But not today. Although I dearly
value the hero of my tale,
though I'll come back to him, yet clearly
to face him now I feel too frail . . .

(6.XLIII)

Freud (1917) described how death needs to be followed by the
painful work of mourning, calling not only for the recognition of
the death itself but also for a process of detailed relinquishment of
expectations and hopes in the external world in relation to the
deceased before the ego can become 'free and uninhibited'
(p. 245). Klein (1940), following on his work and that of Abraham
(1924), showed the nature of inner disarray following both death
and loss, and how harm suffered by those one loves must be
recognized and regretted before it is possible for harmonious
relationships to be re-established inside oneself. (The inner world
as described by Klein is discussed in Chapter 4, pp. 88–9.)

In *Eugene Onegin*, Pushkin – writing earlier, using himself and
his poetry – brings to life experiences of loss and the need for
mourning, although this may not be satisfactorily achieved. He
helps us to be aware how cynical, manic and persecutory
responses, together with attempts to escape from meaningful
mental life, occur within this process. He also shows us something
of the feelings of lack of goodness and internal poverty which loss
and death can bring, and which some of his characters in the
narrative have difficulty in acknowledging. He writes sorrowfully,
seriously, prosaically and ironically about the 'death' of adolescent
'life' in the form of 'lightheaded youth' (6.XLV), including his own,

and gives thanks for its gifts. (Sadly, one is aware that Pushkin himself died as a consequence of a duel seven years after writing *Eugene Onegin*.) Speaking of himself as poet, he looks back on the past, but calls on 'youthful imagination' to liven his 'drowsing' heart:

> let not the poet's soul of passion
> grow cold, and hard, and stiff as stock,
> and finally be turned to rock
> amid the deadening joys of fashion.
>
> (6.XLVI)

The guilt for the death of Pushkin's fellow poet, Lensky, belongs to Onegin, in whom the capacity for remorse is 'frozen', so that his inner world remains 'cold and hard and stiff', inhabited in the psychic reality of that world by a dead Lensky. Onegin cannot mourn. The love – momentarily seen at Lensky's death, and necessary to subtantiate his remorse – remains 'chilled at heart'. He begins 'a life of pointless roaming', leaving home,

> where every day a bloodstained shade
> had come to him in field and glade . . .
>
> (8.XIII)

Haunted and driven from home by the image of the unmourned Lensky within him and around him, and with his inner world in disarray, Onegin engages in continual roaming in an attempt to move away from and disperse the constantly recurring feelings of persecution within him and render them 'pointless', meaningless.

Olga was too self-absorbed to be aware of Lensky's pain in the events which led to his challenging Onegin, and after his death she is soon consoled by a Lancer. At her wedding 'a light smile plays' on her lips (7.X). An experience of mourning in any depth is avoided; there may even be a little manic triumph in being alive and married.

> Poor Lensky! Set aside for weeping,
> or pining, Olga's hours were brief.
>
> (7.X)

Tatyana feels forlorn when Olga departs – her 'heart is rent in two' (7.XIII). This departure speaks to her of Onegin, although she also feels obliged to detest him as the man who killed Lensky, despite the fact that Lensky himself, and his poems, are soon forgotten. She visits Onegin's house, which he has now left on his wanderings, and sees with trepidation some of his marginal comments on the pages of his few remaining books. From this she gains a greater sense of his 'second-hand' approach to life:

> whether from heaven or from hell,
> this angel, this proud devil, tell,
> what is he? Just an apparition,
> a shadow, null and meaningless . . .
> a modish second-hand edition,
> a glossary of smart argot . . .
>
> (7.XXIV)

Tatyana refuses several suitors, and dreads her mother's plans to take her for a seasonal visit to Moscow, 'the marriage fair' (7.XXVI), where she feels she will be exposed as a provincial ingénue. Weeping, she bids farewell to loved aspects of the local landscape. She is, however, taken up by her young cousins and well received in Moscow society, but she has little use for what she experiences as the pointless gossip of Moscow life, and guards in silence her 'sacred store of bliss and weeping' (7.XLVII) while she longs for the country, her novels, and the place 'where "he" came to her that time' (7.LIII). The chapter ends with her having her attention drawn to the interest of a General of 'majestic bearing': ' "Who? that fat general?" Tanya cries' (7.LIV).

Tatyana's journey to Onegin's house, leading to an examination of his nature and her relationship to him, suggests the testing of reality and an attempt at mourning the loss of her hopes. While she may have largely succeeded in giving up external hopes about Onegin, her sad memories remain held within her in an idealized, romantic form reminiscent of her novel-reading; thus they threaten to stand in the way of complete mourning and the possibility of further emotional development within a new relationship.

Some two years later, Onegin, now twenty-six, bored with his travels,

> was finding leisure's vacuum cruel;
> and with no post, no work, no wife,
> had nothing to employ his life.

(8.XII)

He attends a reception in St Petersburg. Pushkin, in an aside, questions whether he will still be posing in some new role, or whether he will have changed: Is he

> a patriot, a cosmopolite,
> bigot or prude? or has he quite
> a different mask? is he becoming
> someone like you and me, just nice? . . .
> 'You know him, do you?' 'Yes and no'.

(8.VIII)

Pushkin has spoken earlier of his liking for his 'hero' (whom he also, at times, describes by many less attractive epithets), and questions here if we have become overcensorious. He goes on to reflect, in somewhat mixed mood, on the nature of youth, remarking how the fop of twenty, 'in good time, would calmly get fortune, and dignity and glory' (8.X), but he also bemoans:

> Alas *our* youth was what we made it,
> something to fritter and to burn,
> when hourly we ourselves betrayed it,
> and it deceived us in return . . .

(8.XI)

Perhaps what is held for us here is an encompassing view of the many-faceted manifestations of youth, and perhaps some degree of hopefulness in the idea that 'a youthful amateur of caprice and quirk' (7.LV) such as Onegin, may, like other adolescents, be invested with some capacity to change and develop, give up his 'poses', his massive projective identifications into other characters, and grow up to be knowable within his own identity.

Onegin puzzles at the reception whether the young, confident, serene and obviously generally respected guest can really be Tatyana. He asks the General, Prince Gremin, to whom he himself is related, who she is. The General presents him to Tatyana, now his wife. Tatyana engages Onegin briefly in polite conversation. Could this really be the Tatyana to whom he had preached, whose letter he had kept, the girl he'd scorned? Soon it is Onegin who suffers from 'youth's distemper – love' (8.XXI).

While he is awkward in her presence, Tatyana is now transformed from 'the plain, timorous, dejected and lovelorn maiden' into 'the imperturbable princess' (8.XXVII). Onegin, claiming that he can no longer dissemble his love, pursues her in society, to no avail: Tatyana remains polite and equable. It is now he who writes a love letter to her; in it he blames himself for not responding to her earlier approach. He expects it to be received with malicious laughter and wrath. He receives no acknowledge-ment, and when he encounters Tatyana in society he perceives her response to him as 'grim and frozen', with a 'face of stone' (8.XXXIII). He retreats to his room and books for much of the winter:

> What happened? Though his eyes were reading,
> his thoughts were on a distant goal:
> desires and dreams and griefs were breeding
> and swarming in his inmost soul.
>
> (8.XXXVI)

Onegin is now clearly preoccupied with his inner world. Thoughts of 'a dim, warm-hearted past' (8.XXXVI) emerge in his reverie, followed by recollections which include those of Lensky's death and memories of the earlier, spurned Tatyana. Pushkin comments:

> He got so used to this immersion,
> he almost lost his mind, expired,
> or joined us poets.
>
> (8.XXXVIII)

Onegin is now mourning, and facing some of the frozen contents of 'his inmost soul'. With genuine grief and regret, internal images can change: a mourned Lensky ceases to be an implacably persecuting inner 'bloodstained shade', and a rejected Tatyana can become less internally frozen. An internal spring in Onegin accompanies the external one in St Petersburg. He suddenly races

to Tatyana. He finds her softly crying, reading what is by implication
his letter, and evoking the 'hapless Tanya' of the past:

> An emotion
> of wild repentance and devotion
> threw Eugene at her feet – . . .
>
> (8.XLI)

Tatyana responds by asking him if he remembers how long ago:

> 'humbly I heard your lesson out?
> Today it's turn and turn about.'
>
> (8.XLII)

Although she expresses gratitude for his straightforward response
then, she suspects that he may now seek to shame her when her
fortunes have changed and she moves in high society. She would,
however, exchange the 'modish whirl', which she hates, for her
old home with her bookshelf, and where her nurse is now buried.
She married when she was sad, to please her mother. Now she relies
on Onegin to leave honourably:

> I love you (what's the use to hide
> behind deceit or double-dealing?)
> but I've become another's wife –
> and I'll be true to him, for life.
>
> (8.XLVII)

She goes out, and Onegin hears the sound of her husband in the
distance. Pushkin abruptly closes the story, but says goodbye to us,
and to the creation of the 'free romance' of the poem, speaking
sadly of those related to its making who are now distant or dead
(8.LI).

Tatyana suspects that Onegin may be maliciously seeking to shame
her now that she moves in high society, and Pushkin suggests that
the presence of envy is not unusual:

> We all resemble more or less
> our Mother Eve: we're never falling
> for what's been given us to take;
> to his mysterious tree the snake

is calling us, for ever calling –
and once forbidden fruit is seen,
no paradise can stay serene.

(8.XXVII)

While we may agree with Bayley (1979) that Onegin cannot bear the idea of domesticity until he sees Tatyana married, his envy does not predominate as it did at the beginning of the verse novel. Earlier – as at Tatyana's fateful name-day celebration, which led to the duel and Lensky's death – the envious part dominated to the extent that he preferred to treat his own potential lovingness with misunderstanding and hatred. Now he does allow himself to be 'deep in love, just like a boy' (8.XXX). After what one can call his winter of reverie, Onegin makes contact with depressive, sorrowful feelings, and his love deepens. The account of his wintry immersion suggests that painful mourning calls for such a degree of change in the inner world that it feels mad and deathlike to him. Pushkin also allows us to see the situation from the point of view of what could be an ongoing – but lessening – cynical part of Onegin, represented here by Pushkin himself, expressing some mockery of the immersion in this painful process and its integrative drive. It is with this part of himself that Onegin has to struggle.

The oppression 'by emptiness of soul' which we heard about early in the novel, and which led to the 'appropriation of other's thought' (1.XLIV), has lifted; he is experiencing rather than dissembling his own emotions, and no longer taking up roles. He is becoming more of a whole, 'together' person, no longer heartless, but aware of his feelings in a heartfelt manner. His new capacity to regret and repent of his mistakes indicates a growing ability to learn from experience. He is also becoming more adult. Tatyana's final speech leaves him with the 'agitation of inexperience' of a heart plunged in a 'wild round of tempests' and a 'raging ocean' (8.XLVIII). How will this deeper emotional awareness respond to an ongoing internal presence of the Gremin couple, of which Tatyana remains a faithful member? We are left wondering about the future.

The Tatyana of St Petersburg is represented as a serene woman, much changed from when we met her last. We may puzzle over how this change has come about, and also over the nature of her marriage and her decision to be faithful to her husband. Are we to take the latter as a manifestation of formal moral expectations, linked with the fear of what the modish world would say if she left Gremin for Onegin? We are not told about the marriage in detail. It is clearly not one of passionate love on Tatyana's part, but some sense of a committed couple is conveyed. Something of the relationship is portrayed in the opera: Tatyana's husband, Prince Gremin, tells Onegin of the love and beauty that she has brought into his life, and in Kobbé's opinion (1976), 'the single aria, in fact, creates the impression of a truly noble figure'. In response to Onegin's declaration of love, Tatyana recalls the past in a tune derived from Prince Gremin's aria, which supports a notion of some inner enrichment evoked by the poem. Tatyana's husband is certainly no longer the 'fat general' of their original Moscow encounter as perceived by her adolescent self, however much her feelings for him differ from her feelings for Onegin. Tatyana is described as being without vain artifice or affectation (8.XIV), and it seems clear that it is not the Prince's rank nor 'the favour of the Court' (8.XLIV) that she values, however 'well she's studied her new role' (8.XXVIII).

This lack of falseness about her position, in contrast to Onegin's earlier usurpation of identities, stands out. Tatyana may have emulated her mother's acceptance of marriage while loving another, so that in this respect her position may resonate with a heroine of a romantic novel, such as Goethe's *Werther* (1774), which she so often read, but it does seem – as Bayley (1979) also comments – to be her own 'self' that speaks. Her reference to her fondness for her nurse, and her wish to please her mother by her marriage, suggest that it is with inner representations of these loved figures that she now identifies. This introjective identification with these inner objects appears to have contributed to the development of a firmer sense of being herself, and to have largely replaced the predominant earlier process of projective identification, associated with being – or becoming – a romantic heroine. 'Imperturbable and free' in her early encounters with Onegin in St Petersburg, Tatyana can also contain her love for him within herself. This is very different from the approach and sentiments of her original letter, and from her earlier pining for him in 'girlish grief', supported by a dream that they 'would jointly tread life's humble way' (8.XXVIII). She now tells him:

> 'Bliss was so near, so altogether
> attainable! . . . But now my lot
> is firmly cast . . .'
>
> (8.XLVII)

Her soft crying on rereading Onegin's letter may nevertheless represent some re-emergence of her 'sacred store of love and weeping' for him as her romantic hero – perhaps revived by his expression of love for her, but now on a longer-term basis held within a deeper framework of relinquishment. It may also represent a world of youth, where something as ideal as bliss was felt to be achievable. Clearly, Tatyana now has no thoughts of an external outcome for her love for Onegin. Her new serenity when we meet her again in St Petersburg appears to stem from a cumulative process of attempting to 'know' and learn from her experiences, and from being a loved member of a mutually respecting couple. The griefs occasioned by the series of events that began with her 'agitation of inexperience' in response to the 'fires of spring' have, it seems, been internalized and used as first-hand emotional experiences, allowed to 'pierce her soul' and thus contribute to her serenity, maturity and growing up, even though she has not achieved the actual relationship and marriage for which she longed.

Pushkin has shown us how both Tatyana and Onegin have changed and developed, know more of themselves, and have a deeper capacity to love. They are also more adult. We shall think more about this when we discuss the nature of the move from adolescence to adulthood in Chapter 4 (see below pp. 107–112). Although they have both learnt to know themselves better, they do not, however, perhaps really know each other, as Bayley also indicates. Tatyana's original feelings about Onegin were founded on her need for him to be 'the hero', while his were not open to being emotionally experienced. We, the readers, are left to experience some of the sadness at the fact that they could not share an exploration of their potential lovingness in the context of a youthful 'agitation of inexperience'.

Pushkin helps us to recognize that the pains and pleasures of adolescent love need to be borne with a truthful recognition of their emotional impact, and that this experience may form the basis of more mature development to come:

> Love tyrannizes all the ages:
> but youthful, virgin hearts derive
> a blessing from its blasts and rages,
> like fields in spring when storms arrive.
> In passion's sluicing rain they freshen,
> ripen, and find a new expression –
> the vital force gives them the shoot
> of sumptuous flowers and luscious fruit.

(8.XXIX)[1]

PART TWO:

ADOLESCENT DEVELOPMENT AND THE SOCIAL FRAMEWORK

4   ADOLESCENCE:
A PROCESS OF CHANGE

THE PROCESS OF CHANGE

I turn now to the experience of change in becoming, being and no longer being adolescent. The adolescent process covers the period of movement from the mentality of a dependent child to that of an adult. A dependent relationship with external parents will gradually diminish and end. Although an individual adolescent state of mind can recur at different ages, one can think in terms of broad chronological norms encompassing a psychosocial process which may often extend, in both directions, somewhat outside the actual teenage years. Early adolescence starts with the emotional responses to the bodily changes of puberty. It brings psychic energy to the surface in a sexual context, and ushers in the mental tasks and changes of the whole process. Major preoccupations at this time are likely to be around these bodily changes and concomitant confusions as to who one is in relation to this child-into-adult body. Soon there may be awareness of beginning to feel 'out' of the family, but not yet 'into' the heterosexual group life of adolescence, although groups of one's own sex may be prevalent. In the central years of this process life in the mixed peer group becomes predominant, and forms a background to the development of a personal and sexual identity. A working identity, in practice or in thought, also begins to take shape. Later stages see the lessening of the predominance of group life, frequently alongside the develop- ment of more established sexual coupling and the beginning of adult life. A sense of adulthood which carries deep personal conviction also calls for a relationship in the inner world of one's mind with a figure, or figures, which could be thought of as a helpful inner couple.

The revival in puberty of the forceful emotionality originating in infancy, although it is soon to be directed towards new relationships in adolescence, indicates that we should begin by thinking about the emotions and sexuality of childhood. These are relevant to understanding the development of adolescents, and to therapy with them. We also need to think about the development of an inner world that can help, or hinder, the process of change. I propose to do so against a background of established psychoanalytic theory, but making particular use of Kleinian and post-Kleinian contributions, some of which expand earlier work, while – as in any subject of study – some differ from it.[1,2]

A CONTAINING SPACE

In the Verona of *Romeo and Juliet* there was no containing space for the new idea of turning the opposing 'households' rancour to pure love' to be held and thought about attentively; catastrophe ensued. Bion's theory of containment (Bion, 1962a,b) is based on the need for infantile anxieties to find a containing space if they are to become manageable by the infant; in this respect it has much in common with the primary maternal preoccupation or holding of the ordinary 'good-enough' mother described by Winnicott (1956a). Bion describes how a mother relates to her infant's feelings in what he calls her maternal 'reverie' – a form of thoughtful and emotional attentiveness by means of which the fears which are initially devastating to the infant may become contained, so that they may support, rather than hinder, growth. The infant can arouse in the mother feelings of which it wishes to be rid, by communicating them to – or, perhaps more accurately, 'into' – her by means of projective identification: 'A well-balanced mother can accept these and respond therapeutically: that is to say, in a manner that makes the infant feel it is receiving its frightened personality back again but in a form that it can tolerate – the fears are manageable by the infant personality' (Bion, 1962b, pp. 114–15). Pain which is thought about may be modified and borne, instead of being evaded and becoming subject to some form of enaction. Interwoven in the mother's containing ability is her attention to her infant's embryonic thoughts and wish to be understood, thereby increasing meaningful contact.

All this is a form of 'learning from experience' (Bion, 1962a,b; Harris, 1978). As an outcome of feeling psychically 'known' – 'K'd' – by the mother, a capacity to know oneself and relate to one's own experiences can develop. In conjunction with the multiple experiences of actual containment, the infant also takes into him- or herself a helpful, containing and thinking maternal presence, which can further the development of containment from within.

Containment of infantile anxieties is primarily described in terms of the mother and infant, but as the process relates to the capacity of being in touch with, bearing and thinking about emotional experiences, it can be carried out by others: a father may look after a baby and, in particular, may frequently contain a mother's anxieties. We have already seen, in our discussion of *Romeo and Juliet*, that the concept also has wider social applications, to which we shall frequently return.

The potential for containment in family life can go awry owing to problems within child or mother (or other caretaker), or within the interaction between them, although I will comment on these separately. Such problems may be re-experienced and readdressed in a therapeutic encounter in adolescence. A mother may, because of her own difficulties, be unable to take in or tolerate what her child is seeking to convey to her, so that the child may feel that its anxieties fall through her in a sieve-like manner, rather than being held in mind. A 'brick wall' type of response to anxiety can also occur, experienced as harshly throwing it back, as opposed to receptively taking it in. We may recall Juliet's experience of finding no place for her grief within her parents or Nurse (*Romeo and Juliet* III.v.196–8). It is also possible to be too willing to spare a child pain: a mother can mentally wipe or soak away anxiety, acting more like a sponge or a toilet than a thoughtful container, so that the child has no chance of learning from its own experience and getting to know itself and its own feelings. But a child – or, in our context, an adolescent patient – may envy the mother's or the therapist's capacity to contain and seek to spoil it, or even prefer to demonstrate that some kind of misunderstanding is superior to being understood (Bion, 1962a, p.95). This is an example of '–K', ('minus K'), which we saw in *Eugene Onegin* (see above, p. 69). Therapists and others working with adolescents within the wider society discussed in the next chapter, by opening themselves to the painful impact of what is conveyed to them, may be experienced as having space in the mind for a young person to feel 'known', in the sense described here; this may, as in the process between mother and infant, lead to further development.

EMOTIONAL DEVELOPMENT AND THE INNER WORLD

Klein believed that the ego – that is, the organized part of the self – exists in a rudimentary form from birth. She describes how we can:

> observe that at an age of only a few weeks the baby already looks up to his mother's face, recognizes her footsteps, the touch of her hands, the smell and feel of her breast or of the bottle that she gives him, all of which suggest that some relation, however primitive, to the mother has been established. He not only expects food from her but also desires love and understanding. (Klein, 1963a, p. 3)

This simple description of the infant's relatedness to the mother may also help – for those who are unfamiliar with it – to clarify and soften the nature of the rather harsh-sounding 'object' in object-relations theory. This can – and usually does – refer to a person, or something felt to represent a person; similarly, the term 'part-object' refers to part of a person. A small baby can relate to different parts of his mother and the functions she performs for him at different times – her feeding breasts, the sound of her voice, her eyes, hands or holding function; when unaware of her total 'oneness' – his contact may be with part of her, a 'part-object', but nevertheless an aspect of a human relationship. Primitive, deathly anxieties of falling to pieces into nowhere (Bick, 1968) and other 'nameless dreads' (Bion, 1962a) accompanying unintegrated states need maternal containment.

Klein thought that early infantile perceptions of the self and objects (including part-objects) tend to be 'split' into good or 'ideal' and desired ones on the one hand, and bad or persecutory and unwanted ones on the other, and kept at a distance from each other. Thus an infant, seeking to hold on to loving experiences of care, safe from unmanageable anxiety and rage, may, by splitting, project bad and frightening ones outwards. This state of mind belongs to what Klein (1946) called the paranoid-schizoid position. Its presence in the frequently somewhat unintegrated emotionality of adolescence comes to life in the pages of *Romeo and Juliet*, where both the Capulets and the Montagues can see themselves as good and aggrieved, and the others as persecuting and bad. Although actions and relationships based on such polarized states of mind are likely to be primitive, and the projections carry social dangers, the clarity of the splitting does convey a necessary differentiation between good and bad. Plays such as *Much Ado about Nothing* – and, in grimmer form, *Macbeth* – illustrate how the confusion between 'fair' and 'foul' is inimical to positive development.

When a baby becomes aware that the varying functions to which he or she relates, such as being fed, cleaned and emotionally attended to, are all part of a whole mother, and that the mother who tends lovingly is the same as the one who at times is experienced as depriving, feelings of love and hate are directed to the same person. Such perceptions support a capacity to feel concern founded on an awareness that one can harm the person one loves. This state of mind belongs to the depressive position. Such love is also more tolerant: 'In the depressive position the object is loved in spite of its bad parts, whereas in the paranoid-schizoid position awareness of the bad parts changes the good object abruptly into a persecutor' (Hinshelwood, 1991, p. 141). The word 'depressive' in this context does not have a connotation linked to illness or morbid feelings; it refers, rather, to the capacity to bear the pain of loving another despite one's own and their shortcomings. Winnicott (1955) suggested that an alternative title, 'the age of concern', would make its meaning clearer. Where such object-related concern is felt, the greatest anxiety is now that one's loved ones

could be harmed, could die; while in the paranoid-schizoid position
the drive for narcissistic self-preservation is paramount, and the
greatest fear is of being made to die oneself.

Klein saw the paranoid-schizoid and depressive positions as
successive developmental stages of infancy. Infant observation,[3]
psychoanalytically based therapy and theoretical development
support the presence of such early developments, but raise some
questions about specific order and clear stages (Meltzer and
Williams, 1988). A state of mind related to the depressive position
is not now thought of as a once-and-for-all achievement for any of
us; reversible movement between the paranoid-schizoid and
depressive positions, depicted by Bion in the form of 'Ps↔D',
remain throughout life as a constantly recurring phenomenon
(Bion, 1963). A move from a paranoid-schizoid to a depressive state
of mind is graphically conveyed in *Much Ado about Nothing*, when
Don Pedro – shortly after his polarized harangue with Antonio and
Leonato, and helped by the intervention of Benedick – is able to say:
'Pluck up my heart, and be sad' (V.i.200–1).

Containment of anxieties in an actual infant, or the infant part of
an adolescent in therapy, can make them more bearable and
available for integration into a more depressive state of mind. It also
supports the growth of a capacity for reinternalization of projected
parts of the self, and again underpins struggles towards integration
and development. The fluctuating states of mind of Ps↔D are also
relevant to therapists' work with patients. Therapists who are
seeking to gain understanding of what is brought to them have to
be prepared to put aside any tendency to cling to what is known
and, when they are in a state of not knowing, and not
understanding, patiently to contain their own unintegrated state of
mind analogous to the paranoid-schizoid position, until some
pattern emerges akin to the depressive position. They also need to
be able to bear a feeling of depression when an interpretation has
been given (Bion, 1970).

Klein describes how in phantasy (that is, our unconscious
expression of mental life, as opposed to conscious daydreams) we
build an inner (or internal) world within us from infancy. This world
has its own inner, or psychic, reality, and its contents feel real to
us. It contains versions of objects, starting with parents, internalized

in various situations, and is influenced by both our external experiences and our own emotional response to them, and can therefore change (Klein, 1955, pp. 309–10).[4]

We see the enactment of a painful disparity between inner and outer worlds when Romeo, once he has fallen in love with Juliet, inwardly holds the name of Capulet as dearly as his own; in the external world, however, this is seen as dishonourable, and is dangerous. In *Eugene Onegin* we can glimpse something of the concreteness of the reality of the inner world, and the interaction between internal and external worlds. Onegin's external love for Tatyana leads to his withdrawal into inner grief and mourning, in the course of which we are aware of the presence in his mind of an inner version of a dead Lensky, 'stiff and chilled', and a spurned Tatyana, who:

> still
> sits there beside the window-sill
>
> (8.XXXVII)

His winter of mourning culminates in internal change. This is followed by a renewed external approach to Tatyana, the outcome of which, in turn, leaves him to face an inner 'wild round of tempests' (8.XLVIII).

The quality of internalization in early life, and the extent to which the adolescent can remain in contact with – or return to – good internal objects with the concern of the depressive position, will affect the use that can be made of the new relationships of adolescence.

INFANTILE SEXUALITY

Freud (1905a) made us aware of the existence and nature of sexuality in infancy – associated with the primacy of specific bodily zones, moving through oral and anal stages to the infantile genital phase. These findings were further developed by Abraham (1924). Klein's conceptions of the paranoid-schizoid and depressive positions do not supersede these phases but contribute to the understanding of the emotionality within them. On the basis of her actual psychoanalysis of small children, however, Klein came to believe that some development occurred earlier than Freud had thought, and saw some of it differently.

Freud considered the Oedipus complex, the 'group of largely unconscious ideas and feelings centring round the wish to possess the parent of the opposite sex and eliminate that of the same sex' (Rycroft, 1968), together with its 'negative' version, in which the wish to possess is centred on the parent of the same sex, to be 'the central phenomenon of the sexual period of early childhood' (Freud, 1924b, p. 173). He thought it emerged from around the age of three, in the phase of genital primacy. He described its dissolution at the end of infancy at around five years of age, followed by internal identifications in the ego related to both parents, in some way united with each other, in the form of an 'ego ideal or super-ego' (Freud, 1923, p. 34) as heir to it. Klein (1932), on the other hand, saw the Oedipus complex as rooted in the baby's first pre-genital suspicions of the father taking the mother's love and attention from him or her.[5] She also thought that the figures internalized – taken, in early infantile life, into the inner world in an idealized or persecuted state of mind – already carried super-ego functions, and contributed to what was perceived as the severity of the super-ego, although this was subject to later modification as aspects of objects which were loved with deeper 'depressive' concern were taken into the inner world (Klein, 1963b).[6]

It is well known that Freud saw the infantile genital phase as phallic in nature, maintaining that 'the little girl is a little man', with the clitoris as her leading erotogenic zone, and that 'the truly feminine vagina is still undiscovered by both sexes' (Freud, 1933, p. 118). He was aware, however, that what he could say about femininity was incomplete, acknowledged that what he said did not always sound friendly to women, and thought that some of the complex nature of female sexuality might become more comprehensible through patients' work with female analysts (Freud, 1931). He also suggested: 'If you want to know more about femininity, enquire from your own experiences of life, or turn to the poets, or wait until science can give you deeper and more coherent information' (Freud, 1933, p. 135). According to Klein, a little girl had an unconscious – and sometimes conscious – knowledge of the vagina. She also considered that the penis is turned to orally in phantasy on weaning by the boy as well as the girl (Klein, 1932); thus she saw development for boy and girl as more parallel.

First-hand analytic experience with small children has revealed an infantile preoccupation with the wider sexuality of both parents. This includes an understanding of how the very young child in phantasy sees the mother's body as a kind of world in which life goes on: a world in which babies, for example, may live and be gratified (Meltzer, 1967). The infant, in its phantasy, can enter this world. This can be for the purpose of wanting to know and understand, and thus an expression of an embryonic epistemophilic instinct. It can also be to avoid feelings of exclusion, or – when predominantly motivated by emotions such as envy, jealousy, hatred and greed – to spoil the gratification of others. Drawing on Klein's work, it is possible to follow such phantasies from an infantile point of view in psychoanalytic psychotherapy with an actual small child, or an infantile part of an adolescent. Here Freud's (1933) description of a child's reproaches against its mother, such as that of being given too little milk, can come graphically alive. Parents can, for example, be perceived as feeding and gratifying each other with some form of oral or combined oral and genital 'milk', or in some way gratifying babies inside the mother, instead of feeding the infant. This may be followed in phantasy by an attack, based in envy or jealousy and carried out by the infant's bodily parts or substances, such as teeth, urine or faeces. Such phantasies may, understandably, be followed by fears of vengeful retaliation. Klein considered that the fear of her insides being attacked and becoming irrevocably damaged are the leading anxiety for the little girl, while for the little boy the major anxiety remains the fear of castration as propounded by Freud (Klein, 1932). These developments are particularly relevant to the phantasies that arise in puberty about the nature and contents of adolescents' own bodies and the parental figures in their inner worlds, as we shall shortly see in an extract from psychotherapy with a pubertal girl.

THE CHANGES AND CONFUSIONS OF PUBERTY

The pre-school years are followed by latency, with a focus on the external world, frequently accompanied by some rigidity of emotional life which normally disappears with the advent of puberty. A child may have phantasies about his or her parents' sexual togetherness and numerous sensations within his or her own body, but cannot take part in the creation of children. It is in the process of puberty that the body changes, and the physical characteristics and capacities of adult sexuality and reproduction are gradually acquired. The male becomes able to produce semen, and the female to ovulate. Physical strength increases, making the commission of acts of violence towards others and oneself possible in external reality as well as in phantasy.

A preoccupation with bodily changes, some of which are not initially visible, tends to occur. Phantasies may abound, based largely on the experience of infantile sexuality, often in conjunction with an increase in masturbation. There may be confusions affecting a sense of identity with no clear answers to inner puzzlements such as: Who am I? Does this adult-like body actually belong to me? What is inside? What can it produce? It seems more powerful; how powerful? Powerful enough to create? Or to destroy? Until now its only physical products, apart from saliva, have been urine and faeces. Menstruation may arouse anxieties. What kind of blood is this, and what is its meaning? Is it related to some kind of internal destruction, or to the making of life? Is the equipment for making babies really present? A pubertal girl may feel confused, on a fleeting or longer-term basis, between the nature of her anus and her vagina. She may also harbour unconscious anxieties that menstrual blood may represent vengeful damage inflicted by an internal mother whose own fertility has been attacked in the phantasies of infantile sexuality. A wet dream may also be problematic. Can semen and urine be clearly differentiated? A boy whose penis has been massively used in masturbation in the expression of hostility to parental intercourse, with phantasies of urine being used as a burning, dangerous substance, may find it difficult to trust its use in the service of new 'thronging soft and delicate desires'. A fourteen-year-old patient told his therapist, with dismay, that he did not know whether his wet dream produced 'piss or pus' (Woods, 1988). There is no existing personal model of adult sexuality to which to refer; this has to be created.

Adolescence is the emotional response to puberty, although physical and emotional development do not run along smooth parallel lines. A baby part of the self within the adolescent may still be longing for renewed infantile care, while another part wants to move forward. Infantile sexuality remains relevant. A positive relationship between a baby's mouth and the nipple, proffered and taken in with love, provides a prototype for a later good relationship between the vagina and the penis. In contrast to this, some degree of perverse valuation may be set up which places the infant's anal functioning and its faecal bodily products above that of the mother's breast and her milk, and may also extend to denigration of parental intercourse and baby-making. The part of the self that has begrudged parents their sexual life may remain envious of reproductive pairing. Also, if members of the opposite sex have been treated with contempt in latency and used as receptacles for scorned parts of the self, turning to them now, hoping for love, may be difficult. Nevertheless, adolescence provides opportunities to grapple with anti-developmental aspects of infantile sexuality, as well as for new development.

One method of refuge from potential confusions and conflict is to stay in the relative safety of latency. Some young people may feel unconsciously so closely linked with the authoritarian aspects of their internal objects that they may, as Hoxter (1964) points out, remain in a mental state of protracted latency, afraid that so-called 'growing up' really means a regression to unbridled expression of their infantile sexuality.

We saw in our discussion of *Much Ado about Nothing* how the presence of infantile anxieties in late adolescent life could endanger the move into a loving adult relationship. Beatrice, following on her protestations about a husband with or without a beard, jokingly conveys, albeit with an underlying wry note, the idea of remaining a maid, evocative of latency (II.i.30–45). A feeling of some movement between a latency state of mind and one which can risk actively embracing loving feelings is also graphically conveyed in the same play by Claudio (I.i.278–85) and Benedick (II.iii.6–36). The outcome of the processes of change cannot be known in advance; ways in which the anxieties of inexperience may be faced or evaded are vividly portrayed in *Eugene Onegin*.

A PUBERTAL GIRL

Material from the intensive psychoanalytic psychotherapy of a twelve-year-old girl, Ruth, illustrates the diversity and fluctuating nature of her emotionality at this time. On one occasion, after doodling a monogram which included the entwined initials of the therapist and herself, Ruth drew a little two-seater car, adding that it was not like the one that had been made by 'that silly man', naming a male inventor: this was a communication in psychic reality from the baby-girl part of herself to an idealized 'mummy', here associated with the therapist, in which she unconsciously claimed that their intertwined, 'two-seater' set-up surpassed anything provided by a silly, excluded 'daddy' inventor. Some time later, just before a weekend, Ruth represented what seemed to be a little-boy part of herself by what she called 'the long letter with a tail' in her surname, curled up inside a representation of a maternal figure, passively partaking in what, from the context, appeared to be an idealized version of parental weekend intercourse, thus avoiding the pain of exclusion. A few weeks later Ruth told the therapist that she would rather be a man who could plant seeds than a mother, and that she didn't want the pain of childbirth; after a further few weeks, she spoke of waiting impatiently for her first menstruation.

Some time before a seasonal break, Ruth, a gifted drawer, sketched parts of a wall frieze based on a school project intended to represent human development from prehistory to the present time. She joined the two ends of her sketch by merging one side of a cavewoman in a leopard skin into one side of a modern girl in a spotted leotard, saying that 'everything must be joined together without any jagged edges, so you can't see any beginning or end, or any difference between the people'. Deep infantile anxieties concerning separation, and the defences against them, were apparent. Ruth sought to block awareness of the coming separation to escape from an experience of an absent therapist, representing a mother of infancy, 'jaggedly' piercing into her from as far away as prehistory: instead they were to be joined 'as one'. In a later session, a caveman was drawn in and quickly rubbed out: the therapist must not open her 'cave-genitals' to a husband. In more general terms, the experience of time, and the absence or presence of another, must be obliterated to avoid pain.

As awareness of a potentially 'jagged break' in therapy increased, an even more primitive aspect of Ruth's anxiety became apparent. One of her doodles showed a wall, out of which the bricks were falling one by one into space. Spread over the bricks were letters taken from the names of the therapist and herself, together with letters from the words 'break up', conveying a catastrophic anxiety of breaking up from the therapist and falling apart, uncontained, into nowhere.

Some time later – probably fuelled by 'the fires of spring' of her own pubertal sexual development, and helped by therapeutic recognition of the psychic reality of her response to separation – Ruth brought dreams which showed violent infantile resentment about exclusion. These were understood in terms of phantasies about the therapist's weekend activities with a husband and family. In one dream the therapist was represented as drinking with adults and children at a bar when Ruth had wanted a session; in another Ruth's experience of swinging with the therapist in a 'tree tops' house in a lush setting was spoilt by the branches being pulled downwards and away from her. In the latter part of the dream nuts were being thrown down violently near the bottom of the trees, followed by a bomb which 'exploded everything' with a bang and smoke. Ruth, who had awoken in terror, said that although the scene was confused, the worst thing was that she herself was down below, directing operations. It was possible to understand with her how these dreams related to her jealousy and envy of others felt to be drinking at the 'breast bar' of the therapist; how the 'tree tops' breasts and maternal supporting arms were experienced as having become 'untwined' and drawn away from her by the pull of the parental genitality. In response, under the directions of her excluded baby self, the potentially fertilizing, seed-giving testicles, the 'nuts', were thrown down, and 'everything', including her own world, was exploded with an anal bomb of faeces and flatus.

A few days later Ruth told her therapist, with great excitement, that she had started to menstruate. Both pleasure and anxieties tumbled forth. She was, however, worried that her periods would be messy and smelly, and leak out all over the place, and that it would be embarrassing if other children at school found out that she was menstruating. But she also said that her mother had reassured her about her periods, and that she hoped she would now become prettier.

The complex interactions between infantile and pubertal components in Ruth's inner world are apparent alongside her hopes and anxieties for the future. We see aspects of her infantile sexuality in quick succession: feminine, masculine, active, passive, hetero-sexual and homosexual (the active, homosexual baby girl, little car, and mummy; the passive, heterosexual little boy and mummy). We learn of her wish to be the seed-planting daddy, but also of her wish to start her menstruation. This material provides a glimpse into early difficulties in adolescent striving towards adult sexual identity when parental sexuality is still under attack by a child part of the self, and the problems for development when the internal world is inhabited by damaged objects. The attack with anal weapons on parental coupling came from an infantile part of Ruth which was smarting at exclusion from the breast in favour of the daddy. This also linked her to the world of internal parents whose intercourse has been spoilt: a mother who has had to undergo a shameful, messy explosion, and a father whose fertility has disappeared in anal bombing, leading to the psychic presence of vengeful, unborn children. Ruth's response to her menstruation with anxieties about making a smelly mess and having difficulties about managing it at school if other children knew about it is understandable in the context of her inner world. She did, however, hope that she would become prettier, perhaps with therapeutic help, and also felt helped by her mother in the outer world. (We discuss an adolescent boy in Chapter 6.)

A SENSE OF IDENTITY

'You know him, do you?' 'Yes and no.'
(*Eugene Onegin*, 8.VIII)

Young people, beset by the emotional complications of early
adolescence in particular, may sometimes retreat from a depressive
to a more paranoid-schizoid state of mind, with their aggressive
propensities split off from any more loving feelings. We saw
examples of this in the rivalries between the houses in *Romeo and
Juliet*, and in Leonato's and Antonio's abusive altercation with Don
Pedro and Claudio in *Much Ado about Nothing* (V.i.93–175).
Adolescents can also lose contact with parts of themselves, giving
rise to a fluctuating sense of identity. We may recall Romeo's
complaint:

Tut, I have lost myself, I am not here.
This is not Romeo, he's some other where.
(*Romeo and Juliet*, I.i.195–6)

An awareness of having lost part of oneself in an adolescent is
unusual, but adults can be bewildered by the sudden disappearance
of what appeared to be a responsible young person. When a
dependent child part is largely to the fore, an adolescent can
experience expectations of more adult behaviour from him or her
as persecuting and uncaring, but when he or she feels grown-up,
he or she can feel any attribution of childishness to be unfair. Parts
of the self with which an adolescent has lost touch may be felt to
be located in someone else. The process of projective identification
is relevant here. This concept was named and introduced into
psychoanalytic theory by Klein (1946).[7] It relates to an omnipotent
phantasy that some part of the self is placed in another object. This
can be an actual external object, such as an external mother, or an
internal object in the mind, separate from a sense of self, such as an
internal mother. It extends the simpler process of projection, in that
a part of the self as well as an emotion is located elsewhere, although
the difference may not always be clear. Klein (1955) was aware that
aspects of the process, such as the way one can put oneself
temporarily into someone else's mind when empathizing with

them, had been taken for granted before being incorporated into psychoanalytic theory. We have already seen emotionality to which this concept can relate portrayed in *Romeo and Juliet, Much Ado about Nothing* and *Eugene Onegin*.

Bion's work, which followed that of Klein, clearly shows how projective identification, when it is used by an infant to convey his distress to his mother (see pp. 84–6 above), forms part of a vital process of communication within a two-party relationship further-ing development (Bion, 1962a,b), and has wide therapeutic application.

Klein's original work, however, related largely to the intrusive use of an object (which Meltzer [1982] considers could usefully be differentiated under the name 'intrusive identification'). The purposes can be various: to avoid separation from the object (as in Ruth's attempt to merge with the 'cavewoman' mother); to keep good parts of the self safe in the object, or get rid of unwanted parts of the self into it, sometimes intending to hurt in the process (some of which is conveyed in Onegin's varying extrusions into others of his contempt, his tenderness and his jealousy). The object can also be entered in phantasy from a variety of other motives: in order to find out something about it, to 'be' it, get something out of it, or avoid envy of it. Motives may overlap; in *Eugene Onegin*, one can think of Tatyana's reading including an element of finding out, avoiding being a child and somewhat passively having the identity of a novel heroine (2.XXIX; 3.X). Onegin, more intrusively, attempts to 'achieve the appropriation of other's thought' and acquire the identity of a writer for himself (1.XLIV). What is largely avoided in these instances is the mental pain of being oneself and having one's own feelings. As we saw with Onegin, the extended use of the phantasy of entering into others to avoid one's own experiences stultifies development, with a danger that one might become a 'second-hand edition' (7.XXIV) of a person, a 'false self' (Winnicott, 1960).

A sense of identity is deeply related to unconscious processes of identification with others in the internal or external world. The use of projective identification, by means of which parts of one's self are felt to be elsewhere, may provide an immediate feeling of success or grandiosity, but may frequently be followed by feelings of confusion, and claustrophobic or persecutory anxiety. A sense of identity of a very different kind arises out of a relationship with objects which have been introjected. It is with identification linked with introjection that Freud himself appears to have been mainly concerned (Freud, 1921; Klein, 1955). The term 'introjective identification' as used here describes a relationship with objects taken into and existing in the inner world; good introjective identification implies a positive relationship with loved inner parental objects whom one aspires to please, while at the same time having a separate sense of self, and actually being oneself (Meltzer, 1973). Although the actual state of identification with objects fluctuates in all of us from time to time, the wish to maintain positive introjective identification with good inner figures on a longer-term basis may arise largely as a benign outcome of developments in both infancy and adolescence itself, and we shall return to this subject at the end of this chapter (Meltzer, 1973).[8]

While much projective identification may take place in phantasy, being in receipt of the impact of a projective identification of any kind is liable to evoke some response in the recipient. We shall see later, when we discuss work in community and clinical settings, that it may be possible, and therapeutically beneficial, to extract some communicative understanding, just as a mother may with her baby, from a projective identification, even if it has a largely hostile intent.[9]

Projective identification is used widely, in a manner particularly associated with adolescence, within what can be thought of as an identity workshop aspect of adolescent group life, to which we now turn. I also discuss adhesive identification in this context.

THE INDIVIDUAL AND THE GROUP

Deutsch (1968, pp. 70–4) described the presence of groups of adolescents of both sexes in the streets of big American cities, attired alike in jeans and barely distinguishable from each other in what she saw as their mutual imitation: 'One may call this uniformed masquerade "identity card: *we*"' [original emphasis]. Deutsch thought of this as a somewhat rebellious and immature way of marking a sense of difference from the older generation, but also as providing group cover for anxiety about infantile and adolescent gratifications. According to Bick (1968, 1986), infants with an experience of satisfactory maternal containment feel that uninte-grated parts of the self are being held together within the boundary of a containing skin, and those who lack this experience can suffer catastrophic fears of 'spilling out', 'falling-into-space' or coming to a 'dead-end'. To avoid such a disaster, a psychic latching or sticking on to others, as if joined on to their skins, can take place, or some form of continuous movement can be used to provide an actual experience of something like 'keeping going', and act as what Bick describes as a 'second-skin'. This primitive, shallow way of being – sometimes seen in early infancy, and also in autism – has become known as 'adhesive identification' (Meltzer, 1975; Meltzer et al., 1975). Anxieties leading to this kind of identification, such as catastrophic fears of falling apart, can also be suffered by normally more 'together' people such as Ruth (see p. 95 above). In her teaching Bick said that the idea of adhesive stickiness and the continuous movement of the 'second-skin' was applicable to the wider culture of adolescent group life.

The work of Bick and Deutsch, taken together, allows one to think of an adolescent community holding itself together in an adhesive, sticky manner, constantly 'on the go', making – and adhering to – its own changing culture of clothes, music and speech, and thus forming its own 'identity card: *we*' skin container. This can be used for what Meltzer (1973, p. 88) calls an infantile greed for pleasure in the flaunting of new aspects of sexuality, as well as a psychosocial space in which to experience the anxieties of being adolescent in an 'age between' (*The Winter's Tale*; see below), the emotional containment of family life and becoming adult. The container also marks a boundary, perhaps providing some sense of safety from intergenerational hostility. Such antagonism is not new. In *Much Ado about Nothing*, an incensed Antonio globally condemns (male) adolescents as a group of 'fashion-monging boys' who 'Go anticly, and show outward hideousness' (V.i.94–6). In *The Winter's Tale*, a father complains: 'I would there were no age between ten and three-and-twenty, or that youth would sleep out the rest; for there is nothing in the between but getting wenches with child, wronging the ancientry, stealing, fighting' (*The Winter's Tale*, III.iii.59–63). (The editor [Pafford, 1963] of the Arden edition maintains that 'ten' is not an error, and points out that no claim is made that all the offences are committed at every age!) Adults, then as now, could be seen by adolescents as belonging to a different category of social beings, as if they had never known youth: in the eyes of Juliet, her Nurse not only lacks 'warm youthful blood', which would make her 'swift in motion as a ball', but is seen as one of the 'old folks', many of whom 'feign as they were dead' (*Romeo and Juliet*, II.v.12–17).

Within this skin of adhesive identification, smaller adolescent groups and groupings emerge. Small, discrete groups or gangs form from puberty onwards and are likely to be composed at first of members of one's own sex in some continuation of latency life. (Although the terms are not exclusive, and are sometimes used by some writers on an interchangeable basis, 'gang' here implies a state of ganging up within the membership, fuelled and held together by some form of shared destructive intent. The ganglike quality of pubertal groups may be variable, and other groups can become ganglike.) Although single-sex groups, sometimes of a delinquent nature, may continue, smaller heterosexual groups gradually spring to life as adolescence develops, providing a central forum for adolescent social life.

These groups provide conjoint playground-cum-workshops concerned with identity where young people can find out, in conjunction with others, what it is like to be this changing version of themselves: what interests them; whom they get on with, and why; how they experience their new sexuality. This may be too much to manage within one personality at any one time. Parts of the self may be attributed to others by projective identification. Such projective activity can arise and change with great rapidity, but it can also exist on a longer-term basis. A projective identification may be passed with safety into the group 'skin' and circulate within the membership, contributing to the 'identity card: *we*' aspects of adolescence. Parts of the self may frequently be split off and attributed specifically to a particular member or members, who may seem able to carry them, so that one member becomes 'the' representative of a particular propensity within the group, accompanied by some group awareness that this is happening (Winnicott, 1961).

The general purpose of the projective identification taking place in these adolescent groups need not be seen as predominantly intrusive, although this must vary from individual to individual. Nor does there appear to be a communication with an expectation of being met with direct, containing one-to-one receptivity. It seems, rather, to function as a means of divesting adolescents of currently conflictual or painful elements in their own personality with some degree of safety, but also allowing some contact with them to be retained. The projected part of the self may be followed in others, and taken back later, possibly in altered form. The group process provides containment for what is unmanageable by any one adolescent at any one time, and allows aspects of the personality which are not projected some expression and chance of development, unhindered by what may currently be experienced as antithetical parts of the self. Members may be in particular need of group contact in order to feel 'themselves' if they have some vestigial awareness of the loss of parts they have projected into the group. (An individual's sense of identity may change as a consequence of the projective activities within the group, but it is not suggested that the group is made up of anything more than a collection of individuals.) Winnicott (1961) sees such group life as part of containing what he calls the 'doldrums area' for adolescents: 'a phase, in which they feel futile and in which they have not yet found themselves', but which they have actually to experience (p. 84). Meltzer (1973) considers that while antisocial aspects of such group activities must be monitored, the groups should not be intruded upon by adult guidance. To remain outside group life may leave the individual isolated, without a testing ground for his or her own feelings, but possibly subject to projections from it. (This may occur to some extent with John – see Chapter 6 below.)

Examples of such projective activity appear in Chapter 10, on group therapy, but may have already come alive for us in *Romeo and Juliet*, and particularly so in *Much Ado about Nothing*. The lovingness of Beatrice and Benedick may be thought of as being held in safety within the group and later relayed back to them in such a form, and at such a time, that it may be assimilated, as in the orchard scenes.

The view of group life described here overlaps with some descriptions from other psychoanalytic perspectives. Blos (1979) proposes the concept of an adolescent-initiated 'autoplastic milieu', within which the peer group can be seen to facilitate certain kinds of internal change. There is also accord with Erikson's concept of a psychosocial moratorium which allows a limited delay before a commitment to adulthood, and with his call for some tolerance of necessary adolescent play in a peer 'clique', however 'irrelevant, unnecessary or irrational' it may appear (Erikson, 1968, pp. 163–5).

Although necessary containment is provided, the splitting and projective identification so common in adolescent group life imply an at least temporary move away from any integrative achievements of the depressive position, and are thus not without cost. The progression towards adulthood implies a further process of change.

Relatively benign aspects of adolescent groups have been referred to here. More problematic ones will be discussed in the next chapter.

INDIVIDUAL ADOLESCENT SEXUAL AND EMOTIONAL DEVELOPMENT

The movement towards adult sexuality is liable to be complex and uneven. Sexual desires towards the actual parents may resurface briefly with puberty, but in normal development they are quickly redirected towards peers. There can, however, be difficulties. With Ruth we saw how residual infantile emotionality towards parental sexuality in the internal world may hamper new development. With John, in Chapter 6, we shall see how the presence of omnipotent infantile phantasies combines with a degree of passivity to hinder his wish to achieve an active male sexual identity. An adolescent may discover something about his or her growing sexual capacity and desire in the course of masturbation, but it is in the peer relationships that these come to life.

Oral and anal phantasies, based on the experience of infancy, are likely to precede and perhaps accompany early genital strivings in the adolescent world. Experience of being a loving adult is clearly lacking, and initial approaches may express a degree of idealization or aggression towards the object of desire. The imagery of *Romeo and Juliet* and *Much Ado about Nothing* brings us into imaginative touch with progressive emotional responses in adolescence. At the beginning of *Romeo and Juliet*, in the context of offensive oral and anal sallies, a Capulet servant aggressively asserts that he will cut off 'the heads of the maids, or their maidenheads' (I.i.24). In contrast, Romeo's first idealistic approach to Juliet is akin to that of a pilgrim to a shrine (I.v.92–108) (with Mercutio's coarser phantasies split off in the background: I.i. 37–8). Juliet soon speaks of their deepening mutual 'bud of love' (II.ii.121). But the quality of a Claudio-like assertion 'that I love her, I feel' (*Much Ado about Nothing*, I.i.211) which may play havoc with 'thronging soft and delicate desires' (I.i.284) of blossoming adolescent love, needs to tested out. The difference between 'loving' and mere 'doting' (*Romeo and Juliet*, II.iii.78) may also need to be learnt by experience before a deeper love can develop.

The 'falling in love' of adolescence is to a considerable extent 'an attempt to arrive at a definition of one's identity by projecting one's diffused self-image on another and by seeing it thus reflected and gradually clarified' (Erikson, 1968, p. 132). With an increasing sense of knowing oneself, fostered by experiences within the adolescent group, relationships can increase in depth and gradually become based on a true intimacy, a relationship between two 'selves'. Only then can a love that 'Doth grace for grace and love for love allow' (*Romeo and Juliet*, II.iii.82) develop. Such a relationship involves a sense of self in which strength has become joined with love in a move from a self-based, narcissistic position to one of concern for someone who is loved for themselves in the depressive position. In utter contrast to the raping potency of the Capulet servant, Juliet, waiting for Romeo to leap into her arms on her wedding night, voices her deep and impassioned sexual love, eager:

> to lose a winning match
> Play'd for a pair of stainless maidenhoods.
>
> (III.ii.12–13)

Freud (1905, p. 229) wrote: 'One of the tasks implicit in object-choice is that it should find its way to the opposite sex. This, as we know, is not accomplished without a certain amount of fumbling. Often enough the first impulses after puberty go astray, though without any permanent harm resulting.' He (1923) considered bisexuality to be a constitutional element in basic human endowment; the term is used here to denote 'masculine and feminine psychological attributes and attitudes in a single person' (Rycroft, 1968), not actual sexual practice. While the giving up of any enacted bisexuality is a normal outcome of adolescence, a mature person has the capacity for identification with internal parents in both masculine and feminine roles; such bisexual qualities are meaningful in enhancing understanding of a partner's sexuality in adult life (Meltzer, 1973).

Ruth's oral, possessive love of the breasts, although it was not experienced in the form of physical homosexual desire, represented a kind of female coupling in competition with the 'silly male inventor' daddy, and exemplifies some adolescent 'fumbling' in the mind about sexual identity, as did her wish to *be* a planter of seeds. Her anally based attacks, fuelled by infantile sexuality against parental togetherness from which she was excluded – as occurred in the tree tops bombing dream – faded as they became the subject of concern from a part of herself that was becoming tolerant of parental sexuality. Ruth went on to develop a feminine sense of identity, supported by positive bisexuality.

Relationships of a homosexual nature may occur in early adolescence. Boys, particularly in all-male schools, may use each other to experience their burgeoning sexuality, and to test out their prowess for heterosexual encounters. Girls may use each other to share and explore their phantasies about the nature of their changing minds and bodies: what it is like to change from being fed at the breast to feeding babies and having sexual intercourse. For a minority of young people, sexual relationships with the same sex may develop into a lasting pattern. Relationships between members of the same sex of a transient and to some extent exploratory and predominantly loving nature, whether or not they are actually physically enacted, may, sometimes somewhat mysteriously, help to link infantile lovingness for a parent of one's own sex with further heterosexual development. Anne Frank (1947), at the age of fourteen, writes movingly in her diary one day of her need for a mother whose example she can follow, of her love of the beauty of the female body, and of a wish she has had to feel a girlfriend's breasts; the next day her longing for closeness with a boy emerges. Such loving, exploratory desire contrasts with perversely motivated relationships with a member of the same sex founded on infantile rivalry with the feeding breast or reproductive parental intercourse (Harris, 1976, p. 31). Experiences within adolescence may be sufficient to clarify confusions around sexual identity for some young people. Others, such as Ruth and John, need help.

Freud described the final sexual organization as involving a convergence of the affectionate current with the sensual current of genital, reproductive sexuality, and thus focusing all desires on a single object: 'The sexual instinct is now subordinated to the reproductive function; it becomes, so to say, altruistic' (Freud, 1905a, p. 207). Although he had an opinion about sexual 'normality', Freud pointed out that where homosexuality 'is not considered a crime it will be found that it answers fully to the sexual inclinations of no small number of people' (ibid., p. 229), gave recognition to an organic factor, and considered that its origins were incompletely understood (Freud, 1922).

The term 'perverse' has sometimes been applied to homosexuality as an entity. Sexual relationships between adults of the same sex are now in general politically and socially recognized. Generalized terminology with a pejorative tone is not acceptable. It is important, however, to understand and recognize perversity in any relationship. Meltzer proposes that 'perversion', with the meaning 'characterized by perversity of purpose', is an apt term for states of mind engendered by the leadership of the destructive part of a personality from which love has been split off, which enviously seek either to destroy the qualities of goodness, or to achieve an even greater perverse satisfaction by setting up a world which is essentially anti-nature, with Satan's 'Evil, be thou my good' as its motto. In such a world the differentiation of good from bad is undone, so that, as in Orwell's *Nineteen Eighty-Four* (Orwell, 1949), 'hate is love' (Meltzer, 1973, pp. 90–8). Chasseguet-Smirgel (1985) has, with some similarity, described perversity in terms of the erosion of differences, including those between the sexes and the generations. The perversity of confounding differences between the generations is, of course, descriptively true in child sexual abuse. In *Much Ado about Nothing* a perverse state of mind is conveyed by Don John, who nurtures his malevolent discontent and attempts to spoil any goodness in the impending marriage and sexual love of Claudio and Hero. Successful struggles with perversity as described here can be seen in the description of psychoanalytic psychotherapy with John in Chapter 6.

FROM ADOLESCENCE TO ADULTHOOD

The process of change between latency and adulthood is likely to be uneven both within an individual and among individuals, including the degree of personal turmoil that may be experienced during it.[10] In some adolescents a gradual process of maturation may be apparent. In others more problematic areas – such as that of feeling and being 'REAL', to which Winnicott (1963b) draws attention – may be very visible and need to be overcome; these are discussed in the next chapter, along with family and social difficulties accompanying and influencing change. Winnicott (1961, p.79) nevertheless maintains that 'The cure for adolescence belongs to the passage of time and to the gradual maturation processes', and that an adult person will emerge if the process is not broken into or destroyed. He also cautions us (1963a, p. 92) that 'Adults must be expected to be continuing the process of growing and of growing up, since they do but seldom reach to full maturity.' These statements help us to think about the ending of adolescence in two ways: descriptively, and in relation to the meaning of mature adulthood.

Somewhere around the age of twenty is often seen as a marked psychic boundary between adolescence and adulthood (Laufer, 1975; Miller, 1969). Major bodily changes are probably completed by this time, and have probably been accompanied by a degree of social and mental change. When one reaches what may be thought of as adulthood, relations with external parents are different. The concepts of obedience and conformity which existed at the

beginning of adolescence are clearly no longer relevant, and actual
dependence ceases. Infantile sexual desires experienced directly in
connection with the actual parents will have been replaced by those
with peers. In benign circumstances, external dependent parental
ties may be in the process of replacement by friendly relationships
between adults, but with a link to, and a recognition of, the past,
and perhaps with thoughts towards future generations. The
relationship with internal parents, which I shall discuss shortly,
will, however, be important. The centrality of what may have
become a variety of involvements in the mêlée of the peer group
will probably be replaced by that of a couple, accompanied by some
sense of an established personal, sexual identity, and very probably
some form of working or student identity. The fall in first criminal
convictions towards the end of the teenage years, discussed in the
next chapter (see below, p. 130), indicates an increased capacity
for social conformity around this time. Social, family and working
issues of adulthood now become important; couples may seek
housing and services in a social and perhaps even parental context.
One can thus think of a process of change as having come to an end
with its culmination in adulthood.

The degree of change at the threshold of adult life may, however,
indicate, at least in part, a fitting-in and conformity with social
requirements rather than the presence of a deeper sense of
personal, adult motivation. Despite the presence of sexuality as one
of a partnership, something in common with a return to a latency
frame of mind may be apparent, in which a sense of an externally
ordered and settled way of life may inhibit a degree of emotional
liveliness in which meaningful conflicts occur. Sometimes an
adhesive quality seen in adolescent group life may remain, but it is
now experienced very differently, with routine sexuality and
specific working experiences providing some form of glue to a
domestic and social way of life. States of mind indicating this kind
of adjustment to society may recur in individuals at intervals in
between a sense of deeper concern. In a counselling service such
as that described in Chapter 7, one may meet young adults in their
mid twenties who conform externally to an adult lifestyle, with
potentially long-term partners and settled housing, sometimes even
with children, but feel that something is lacking, indicating some

awareness of not having reached a degree of 'growing up' and maturity to which they may aspire, and of which Winnicott (1963a) speaks. On exploration, what appears to be absent is a sense of a firmly established relationship with inner objects, validating a deeper experience of identity.

In contrast, there are those in whom no firm engagement with an ongoing adult existence is apparent. A sense of settling down, accompanied by some commitment to a partner or lifestyle, may be absent. Adolescent states of mind may – and often do – recur in all of us from time to time as a fluctuating phenomenon, but for some the passage of ongoing time is denied, and the idea of the future is felt to remain open, indicating an ongoing, unresolved, adolescent state of mind.

In very broad terms, it seems that in these instances it has not been possible to reach, or maintain with any degree of stability, the love, and particular kind of pain, of the depressive position, which in itself provides and seeks to sustain a sense of value in life, and can be thought of as supporting a move towards a more mature adulthood.

The first strand in development supporting a move of any kind from adolescence to adulthood probably follows decreasing splitting and projective identification of parts of the self into others, followed by an increasing perception of being a whole person with an inherent sense of a personal, working and sexual identity. It is, however, perhaps the combination of this first strand with the second and third strands – which I am about to mention – which contributes to fostering internal and external relationships that may underpin an attempt to maintain, or return to, an ongoing 'process of growing' supported by depressive concern.

The second strand is concerned with the attainment in late adolescence of a state of mind which can sustain an intimate and truly loving relationship with a partner who 'Doth grace for grace and love for love allow'. This is likely to lead to the emergence from the microcosm of adolescent life as one of a couple with the necessary degree of sexual intimacy which, according to Meltzer (1973), can allow an atmosphere of potential parenthood to be present in the coupling. (This does not imply a specific intention to have children immediately; I explore the question of 'children' later in this chapter.)

The third strand is the establishment, or re-establishment, of internal relationships as a central force in emotional life. Introjective identification, carrying the concern of the depressive position, with loved internal parental objects, in both their masculine and feminine roles, is intrinsic to the formation and maintenance of a mature adult state of mind. This inner, benign couple can be thought of as the enhanced ego-ideal or super-ego described by Freud (1923), based originally on the figures of both parents, but it will have been changed and enriched by absorbing qualities distilled from others who have been admired in life (Freud, 1924a). These parents of the inner world need to be allowed to lead their own life, freed from intrusive attacks arising out of envy and the jealousy of the infantile part of the personality, and identification must be made with them in their mutual love for each other and the children in their minds. This does not mean 'following in the footsteps' of actual parents and trying to be what they are, or do what they do, or did, in any concrete terms. There is, rather, a sense of needing to fulfil an aspirational task in relation to the loved inner objects, appreciated in their creative functioning, while at the same time accepting an adult responsibility for one's own life (Meltzer, 1973).

These three strands may link and overlap somewhat mysteriously. A sense of self enables loving intimacy to take place. Being loved as one of a couple in the external world supports the withdrawal of infantile intrusion into internal parental sexuality. Closer introjective identification with internal parents helps ego development and the capacity for deeper, external love, and lessens the need to project. Such an introjective relationship – in particular, perhaps, with the parent of one's own sex – enables a sense of sexual and gender identity as a loving adult person to develop and to become deeply meaningful. It is to this sense of relatively mature adulthood that I shall now turn.

It comes alive in *Much Ado about Nothing*. A feeling of being able to love is no longer deposited in the group but recognized directly, by both Beatrice and Benedick, as each comes to believe that they are loved by the other. Benedick's claim to hard-heartedness and determination to avoid marriage have already given way to being in love and to a dawning sense of himself as a begetter of children (II.iii.226–34). Beatrice's loving concern for Hero, suggestive of an identification in psychic reality of the mother's depressive concern for her children, is recognized as needing attention before their love for each other. Under the aegis of Beatrice's 'soul', akin here to her inner parents, they form a couple who seek to right the wrong to Hero; the now manly Benedick, fighting for the truth, challenges the 'boy' Claudio. Inner objects appear to have gained strength and accessibility: a representative of inner masculine potency can be called upon in the outside world to fight in the restorative process, first by Beatrice and then by Benedick. Conflicts involving the heart are to be faced; love is to be 'suffered'. The inner meaning of their masculine and feminine genders has changed and developed; they are now an adult, mutually loving couple in introjective identification with their 'souls'.

The acceptance of being adult and being oneself, motivated by depressive concern, will probably be very different from a child's view of what it is like to be grown up: childish phantasies such as those of projecting oneself with grandiosity into the identity of a mother or father, or of a powerful self-indulgent adult, or of being able to 'do what what one likes', no longer make sense. Pushkin's *Eugene Onegin* helps us to understand that becoming an adult in psychic reality does not promise happiness related to external circumstances, immediately or at any time, but relies rather on a developing sense of self with a firmer, more coherent identity, in conjunction with a concerned reliance on good internal objects. There is no conventional 'happy ending' here, but we can nevertheless sense in Tatyana the presence of an identity linked to an aspirational relationship to internal objects represented by her mother and nurse, as well as to sincerely held external bonds with inner meaning: 'But now my lot is firmly cast' (8.XLVII).

Can we expand and apply Freud's statement about the sexual instinct becoming 'altruistic' when it is subordinated to the reproductive function (see p. 106 above) in a wider social context? Erikson (1968, pp. 138–9) spoke of 'Generativity' as the 'concern for establishing and guiding the next generation'. He recognized that this does not necessarily mean actually having children, and that parental drives may apply to other forms of altruistic concern. In an adult sexual state of mind, motivated by depressive concern, the internal parents must be allowed freedom to care for the needs of each other, and their internal children. Meltzer (1973) suggests that depressive concern can lead to the 'combined object' of loved internal parents becoming externalized and felt to relate to 'all the mother's babies', worldwide. Something of this state of mind (as opposed to actual physical genital sexuality), which relates to the next generation as a whole, is conveyed in Arthur Miller's *All My Sons* (1947).

5 THE ADOLESCENT AND SOCIETY[1]

In this chapter I discuss various interfaces between the adolescent and society: leaving home, but also having no home to leave; aspects of school, work and sexuality; the area of drugs, drink and delinquency, and problematic aspects of adolescent groups. I then think about suicide in adolescence. This is followed by thoughts about the needs of troubled adolescents and those who help them, together with some wider issues affecting the relationship between adolescents and adults within society.

SAYING GOODBYE TO FAMILY LIFE

Family life inevitably diminishes as sexual and emotional development within the adolescent lead to deeper involvement in group life. This does not mean that parental functioning is completed, rather that home life may be complicated by the fluctuating nature of an adolescent's sense of identity (which we discussed in Chapter 4). What Winnicott calls the 'need to defy in a setting in which dependence is met and can be relied on to be met' (Winnicott, 1961, p. 85) remains. Parents have to respond to new problems in the light of their ongoing experience. This may be a time when children and parents are frequently viewed by each other as unreasonable. Parents, by acknowledging the child's changing status and bearing the altercations as best they can, may, despite external difficulties, contribute to the development of helpful *internal* parents within the adolescent.

Relinquishment of family life may be particularly hard for either or both generations where some special degree of closeness exists, such as the involvement of the adolescent in the care of a disabled parent. Quite apart from actual sexual abuse, which we discuss later, a regressive pull may exist between parent and child, resulting in mutual idealization and hindering a constructive approach to development. In some such instances, a lack of interest in school work may alert a sensitive teacher to the need for help. Preparing to leave the family may also be accompanied by an upsurge of strife about what has, or has not, taken place within it. Even though family life is ending, adolescence does provide a 'second chance' to relate constructively to family difficulties. There are examples of therapeutic work with family conflict relating to the end of adolescence in Chapter 8.

PHYSICAL AND EMOTIONAL HOMELESSNESS WITHIN SOCIETY

Some adolescents leave home with good internal objects, based on a 'good-enough' response to 'good-enough' parenting. Such a 'home in the mind' provides emotional containment for the relinquishment of external family life. But it is also possible to suffer from a kind of inner homelessness. Lucy, who will be discussed in Chapter 7, clearly experienced her external and internal family as 'broken'; an external 'second chance' within the family was not available, and when she was about to leave her mother and cross the world to stay with her father – to which she also looked forward – she felt like a homeless child. Lucy had a sense of inner, emotional homelessness; family conflict lay behind the possibility of Doreen and Tony, who are discussed in Chapter 8, being sent away from home. All three came from financially secure, physically well-housed backgrounds.

For many young people, unemployment, actual homelessness and other economic and social factors magnify and contribute to emotional problems. Some adolescents find it impossible to remain at home. There may be actual sexual or physical abuse, as well as a lack of containment or a capacity to feel contained. Whether they are, or feel, thrown out may be an open question. A vulnerable young person, having left home under adverse circumstances, may lack external help, but feel touchy and uncooperative in relation to what may be available. It has been estimated that more than 98,000 young people run away from home or care each year (Children's Society, 1990a). Some manage to find helpful support in hostels orientated to their needs. Others do not. Groups of young people can be found sleeping in doorways or cardboard boxes on the streets, residents of the so-called 'cardboard cities'. Adolescents in such situations clearly risk exploitation, prostitution and involvement in drug abuse. They also lack developmental opportunities.

Two well-groomed teenagers, sleeping in doorways with other young people, maintained in a press interview that if they could be at home they would not be on the streets, and that they could not get work in their present circumstances. They said that they preferred the company of their own age group to being moved on from short-term hostels for young people or staying in others they described as being full of 'winos and fleas', adding that new, better hostels would need to be central, as they could not afford to travel to beg! (Bunting, 1990). A great emotional distance from any meaningful home life, with little expectation of change, is conveyed here. This pair appear to be passively dependent on the crumbs from the table of society, perhaps sticking together in some form of adhesive identification with others in a similar plight. Henry (1974) describes an emotionally disturbed adolescent as 'doubly deprived': suffering not only from the cumulative effects of earlier adverse external circumstances but also from the operation of rigid internal defences against pain; the instance reported here suggests that the social plight of some young people may add a triple element.

IN AND OUT OF CARE

An estimated 40 per cent of all homeless people sleeping rough in London have been in care (Doyle, 1991). Some failure of external or emotional containment of family life – through death, physical or mental parental illness, sexual abuse, neglect, or breakdown in relationships – underlies admission to care. We read, shocked, of failures within the care system: instances of sexual abuse by staff; of unruly teenagers who have been kept 'pinned down' in solitary confinement in night clothing in sparsely furnished accommodation; of homes having to be closed. We also read about severe financial problems. Report after report refers to a high proportion of poorly paid, often unqualified residential staff, dealing with an extremely difficult task. Although perverse and abusive events have occurred all too often in care, and must, of course, be dealt with as such, some of the criticisms may arise at least in part out of the interface between unhappy young people and staff with insufficient skills and support.

Young people need help with their responses to the unhappy events which lead to their admission. Their feelings about being taken into care can be complex, even though they are not immediately apparent. Residents may think of care as a 'non-home' – either because it is not in fact their home, or because it is experienced as a further, persecuting version their own non-containing home, and also fails to provide a longed-for state of idealized 'care'. Staff who are trying to do their best are likely to be perceived by residents at one time or another as unhelpful or persecuting. Distress, withdrawal, mistrust and even some violence can be expected. Some of the running away from care may be founded in earlier external and current inner experiences, with little reference to the detailed nature of the place from which the absconders are running. Some very primitive solace may also be found in joining together with others in a similar predicament. The pain of an adolescent running away, under the pressure of inner, largely unconscious feelings, from schools that might perhaps ordinarily be 'good enough' in themselves is movingly conveyed in *The Catcher in the Rye* (Salinger, 1951).

In the course of professional consultation to the staff of one adolescent home, the consultant became aware of an atmosphere that was often desultory, with some of the longer-term residents sleeping late, passively watching television or playing pool. An apparently small incident, such as a disagreement with a staff member about the time of a meal, could spark off violence and sometimes led to a staff request for police assistance. A number of residents made little emotional contact with the staff; alongside this, some of the staff represented their job as being the provision of a clean and correct physical environment, and so not calling for deeper contact with the residents. Here residents' own varied, unclear and unworked-through responses to admission to care, including their own feelings of being rejected, complicated their attitude to non-involvement with the staff. Lack of emotional contact in the home formed an unconscious, collusive process which evaded the actual experience of the residents' mental pain, and thus excluded the possibility of any constructive containment. Conflict was also largely evaded, but when persecution and violence did emerge there was little experience of a containing presence to work with it.

The Wagner Report (1988) rightly maintained that staff must not feel blamed (except, of course, in cases of actual wrongdoing) or abandoned by society. Adolescents coming into care may themselves feel blamed by, and/or blaming towards, their parents, and the caring institution may thus be housing a variety of feelings of blame and abandonment, some of which may be projected on to the staff. For staff, themselves subject to possible violence, to work effectively with the pain of being made to feel rejecting, while struggling to provide a good and caring service, requires not only stamina but professional skills and possibly some additional form of help, of which external consultation, as in this instance, might be one. The work can be more stressful if the staff are largely part-time, so that it is more difficult both to start and to sustain meaningful relationships with the young people.

In contrast to the particular experience described here, some pioneering institutions have formed communities in which the relationship between residents and staff, and the meaning of the emotionality between them, is seen as central to the work (Menzies Lyth, 1979, 1985). Such approaches, although they make heavy demands on the staff, can help the adolescent to feel contained, and provide some space for inner development.

An experience of physical and emotional homelessness can arise on leaving care, as well as entering it. In contrast to a more rigid demarcation at eighteen, some duty to advise and befriend those up to the age of twenty-one is now in the process of being implemented by the statutorily responsible local authorities in the United Kingdom (Children Act 1989). Young people leaving care at eighteen have sometimes found themselves homeless, or have felt too lonely, inwardly and outwardly, to be able to maintain themselves emotionally in the accommodation found for them. Some young women, on leaving, have quickly become pregnant, partly looking for comfort *from* the baby, and are clearly in need of further help. Authorities may attempt to place those who are due to leave in 'bed-sit' accommodation or flats, and supervise their progress. Although this is well intentioned, it can feel persecuting and abandoning to those leaving care, and experienced as a preparation for psychic homelessness. One sixteen-year-old girl described the offer of a flat, together with some supervisory support, as a preparation for 'cardboard city'. This led to some painful but necessary emotional work surrounding leaving care – in this instance with a skilled worker with the ability to bear being experienced as part of a rejecting establishment. The provision of ongoing accommodation must be related to the ability to use it, supported by workers skilled in understanding the needs and manifestations of psychic reality. Leaving care contrasts bleakly with leaving a family of one's own, with whom contact will be maintained, at a time that may feel right. Paradoxically, in such circumstances the offer of a flat might be welcome, but unlikely. Many young people whose capacity for relinquishment has been severely strained by their life experiences may be leaving what has become for them a needed, although not necessarily a loved, base to their existence. The Children's Society describe units which help to prepare young people for independent living, but – somewhat unusually – also have an open door through which those wanting 'to share their joys or sorrows' can come 'home'. Some young mothers, who left care some years before, return with their children for reunions (Children's Society, 1990b, p. 6). Vulnerable young people need positive ongoing experiences if they are to sustain belief in an internal carer. This calls for contact with some known aspect of the care system to be available on an informal basis unrelated to age. Such contact may make some contribution to the avoidance of a repetitive cycle of deprivation affecting future generations.[2]

LEARNING, EDUCATION AND CONTAINMENT

Relationships with teaching staff provide a major contact with working adults in the everyday life of young people. Schools function in a society which puts varying degrees of emphasis on what it expects of them, ranging between producing evidence of having taught children certain specific skills, and helping children to learn and to want to continue learning 'for life'. The way in which the staff view themselves and respond to these expectations, and the degree to which their professionalism and status are accepted by society, must convey itself to the adolescents with whom they relate.

Traditional methods of teaching have an appeal for a latency child keen to gather information, but after puberty new factors influence the adolescent's response to education. Intellectual capacities and interests should increase, and can go hand in hand with emotional development, bringing further meaning to new experiences. A love of literature may serve as a conveyor and container of discovery of a new world, as Keats describes in 'On first looking into Chapman's Homer':

> Then felt I like some watcher of the skies
> When a new planet swims into his ken . . .

(Keats, 1817b)

As adolescence proceeds, the firing of imagination and of opportunities to pursue interests beyond excessively rigid boundaries furthers development. Such a climate is conducive to learning from experience (see above, p. 85), which in itself stimulates a capacity for further learning. The ability to learn in this or any other way is an outcome of personal development and family background, but one which can be fostered by a teaching institution. Other ways of learning – by projective identification, in which there may be a feeling of getting something out of an object, or by an obsessional collection of facts – provide a less rich relationship within the process itself, and hence make less contribution to an internal valuation of what is learnt. Children and adolescents do need to acquire factual knowledge and skills; but also, ideally, an interest and pleasure in learning itself. Meltzer and Harris have suggested that learning by a method commonly referred to as 'the stick and carrot' may stimulate anti-learning from somewhat rebellious adolescents; knowledge may be jettisoned on removal of the 'stick', or, in identification with it, used in an aggressive manner (Meltzer, 1973, pp. 164–5; Meltzer and Harris, 1986, pp. 155–7).

Going to secondary school may be a step towards independence, although this in itself can also arouse anxiety in the child part of the self. Actually being at school may provide some containment for adolescents with unstable backgrounds; in such circumstances the 'breaking up' at the ends of term and the final leaving may also carry some degree of anxiety of the kind experienced by Ruth (see above p. 95). Many children and adolescents who are in distress, or cause distress, may need special help. The referral to psychotherapy of several young people discussed in this book was initiated by their school. Such therapy may, however, be unavailable, or the ability or motivation to use it may be lacking in child or parent, so that the staff may have to find a way of responding themselves to special needs that arise within the school.

Kit, aged fourteen, a girl with asthma which had been described as life-threatening, attended a support unit led by Mr G. Kit's parents had separated; Kit was distressed, but had been unable to sustain psychotherapy. She had, however, become very attached to Mr G – to the extent that she tended to drop into the support unit at non-scheduled times, and had once asked Mr G personally to take her to hospital when she was anxious about her asthma. Mr G had become for Kit 'the' person able to sustain her life, and he felt that he had to respond to what she asked of him on the basis of 'a matter of life and death'. He was, however, concerned about Kit's reliance on him, her somewhat denigratory attitude to other children in the support unit and, at times, also to himself, and her use of the unit without prior consultation with her form teacher or himself. He clearly needed to talk to Kit about this, both for her sake and for that of others, but to do so he had to understand the feelings evoked in him, the countertransference, in relation to what was happening between Kit and himself. He painfully came to realize that he had to bear feeling rejecting and even non-life-preserving if he was to help Kit to think about the way she used him as a constantly available 'life-safer' in relation to her anxieties.[3,4] (Countertransference and transference are discussed at the end of this chapter, and in the following clinical chapters.)

WORK AND UNEMPLOYMENT

Young people seek employment for more reasons than that of financial necessity. Occasionally personal difficulties may lie behind a reluctance to take up a working attitude to life; we have seen how regressive family involvements could impede a move forward. A deep sense of inadequacy may also sometimes lead to what Erikson (1968, p. 184) calls 'work paralysis': one eighteen-year-old in therapy felt that to leave the support of home and go to work would be like having the walls of a maternal house collapsing around him. But for the majority of adolescents, becoming a working individual is intrinsic to development. For some – especially those with less trust in inner objects, as we saw earlier (see above, pp. 108–9) – actually having a job may provide an essential basis for belief in personal adulthood. For others, to work and be able to support a family may deepen such a belief.

Employment will probably be relevant to companionship, and can highlight recreation as leisure from work, enriching the texture of life. To work with others and function as a co-operative 'work group' member (see p. 11 above) can also enhance the sense of being adult, and can apply at all levels where some form of genuine teamwork is required. Some employment can involve being, or feeling, used very much as a 'part-object'. For such work not to be deleterious to a sense of identity, some form of 'work group' membership could be useful, such as an opportunity to participate in some of the ordinary day-to-day arrangements, however matter-of-fact, surrounding the working experience. Some young people may have an inner motivation leading to the acceptance of apparently unrewarding work; future students may extend their horizons by finding all sorts of occupations, often in the process of travel, and even learn something from them. On the other hand, the offer of work experience under the guise of training, which is not clearly appropriate to it, can lead to a persecuted response in vulnerable young people who need a positive experience to enhance their sense of worth.

Unfortunately, in our society, we have not found a way of avoiding cyclical mass unemployment, or of helping those who are unemployed to feel and be useful, without either feeling or being exploited. Reactions to unemployment can range widely: young people can feel deprived by society and vengeful against it because of the non-receipt of adult working status, or acquiesce in the passivity of 'signing on', also thereby losing an active sense of adulthood. It can lead to feeling, or feeling made to feel, a member of an underclass, in terms that are wider than purely economic. It can not only lead to external poverty but also contribute to a sense of inner poverty. Reaction can take the form of accentuation of personal anxieties, and stimulate feelings of depression. The inability to provide an independent income can be experienced as socially shameful. Long-term unemployment on leaving school can feel like being put on the scrapheap before one starts, 'pensioned off' with benefits. Such an atmosphere forms the breeding ground for dangerous boredom, and an escalating grudge against society. Coleman and Hendry (1990, p. 185) report findings that the young unemployed worried more about their appearance and money, died earlier, especially by suicide, and had greater physical and mental ill-health than those in work.

ADOLESCENT SEXUALITY IN SOCIETY

Winnicott (1961) wrote of adult society's need to tolerate the modern adolescent's ability to explore 'the whole area of sensuous living' (p. 83), in order to avoid what he called 'a false solution' to adolescence. Deutsch (1968), writing soon after, appeared to be more doubtful about sexual trends, and thought that girls involved in 'free love' showed both very little inner participation and a lack of any real relationship with their partner. The freedom for sexual exploration within a variety of relationships may provide an opportunity for bringing together what Winnicott (1961, p. 81) called the instincts and 'the personal pattern'. This does not by itself, however, necessarily lead to the formation of 'adult' relationships, the basis of which we discussed in Chapter 4 (see above, pp. 107–12). It is sad that, as the increasing divorce rate indicates, numerous 'false solutions' to would-be long-term loving sexual relationships do appear to be found. One may wonder if there is some perpetual adolescent manifestation within society itself which seeks a 'better' partner as an ongoing aim.

Adolescent sexual activity is increasingly recognized as a social reality. According to a MORI survey, prepared for the Health Education Authority (1992), 52 per cent of the sixteen-to-nineteen-year-old age group have had full sexual intercourse. The majority of them described their most recent partner as their 'regular' boy- or girlfriend, or long-term partner. In contrast, however, 17 per cent of men said that they had had intercourse with four or more partners in the past twelve months (p. iii).

Although it is frequently denied, a risk of AIDS can now accompany sexual experience. The Health Education Authority, on the basis of the same survey, describes 23 per cent of young people aged sixteen to nineteen as willing to have unprotected sex with a new partner (p. v), and 44 per cent as feeling that they had been given insufficient information about AIDS (p. vi). The report concludes that 'there is a general recognition, held by around three in ten young people, that the risk of AIDS may require lifestyle adjustments. This recognition, however, is not linked to young people's actual sexual behaviour' (p. 69), and stresses the need for educational efforts to enforce this linkage.

Katz (1991) describes an educational approach which makes use of highly explicit, colourful, adolescent sexual vocabulary in the encouragement of pupil participation in discussing the risks of specifically named sexual practices. After one lesson all the seventeen-year-old participants said that they would use a condom if sleeping with a new partner, some adding, on leaving, that they were going 'to do their homework'! Is such an approach to be criticized for making sexual activity seem technical and casual, rather than helping to further the development of a genuine loving relationship? Or is it to be recognized as a way of reaching the adolescent on matters of safety in a realistic manner, forming a component part of wider education and experience?

How are we to think about the largely denied fears of AIDS? Do we prefer to live in a world of deception? Although the Association of British Insurers (1991) state that an HIV test with a negative result and no risk factors present will not of itself prevent someone from obtaining life insurance, questionnaires may still enquire about tests: this may discourage an openness towards finding out facts and relieving, or facing, deathly anxieties. Splitting and projective identification are common in adolescence, and may be used to maintain a belief that it is someone else who will be at risk, and also possibly subject to pejorative social attitudes. Heterosexuals may seek to comfort themselves by regarding such anxiety as belonging solely to homosexuals. Young people embarking on their own sexual life with some degree of hopefulness may find it particularly difficult to allow themselves to be aware that they could be either the recipients or the donors of some hidden, 'bad' sexuality; this could make unwelcome links with earlier infantile masturbatory attacks on parental sexuality and the creation of life. Adolescents sometimes consider that sexual intercourse with 'protection' refers to contraceptive measures only – again with an implication that it may be difficult to think about an activity associated with love in conjunction with the possibility of death.

A BACKGROUND OF SEXUAL ABUSE

Sadly, an earlier or current experience of abuse inevitably influences adolescents' perceptions of themselves and their view of sexuality. Although abuse can take a heterosexual or homosexual form, there is evidence of greater abuse of girls than of boys, and perpetrators are predominantly male (Bentovim and Boston, 1988). Abuse may take place in childhood – some may continue into adolescence; some may start in adolescence. Kenward (1987) quotes a twelve-year-old boy who had been abused by a male friend of the family: 'When people look at me, will they know? Will I be homosexual? When I have a girlfriend will I know what to do? Will I be able to be a parent?' His sense of present and future identity, including his masculinity, had been invaded and undermined, and he was left with an anxiety that there was now something undesirable inside him, and that it might be visible. Although many young people are not able to be so explicit, his experience speaks for that of others: a feeling of being sullied, of containing bad sexuality – the residue of a bad penis, threatening to undermine strivings towards adult sexuality and parenthood.

Of course the adult is the abuser, and is responsible for the abuse. However inappropriate and unfair it may feel to one's sense of justice on behalf of the abused person, it is possible that sexuality in a young child or adolescent can be stimulated by such attention from an adult, and that an abused person may be, or feel, involved in some contributory seduction. Confusion, bewilderment and even pleasure, as well as revulsion, can arise from the closeness involved. (Freud considered that 'under the influence of seduction children can become polymorphously perverse, and can be led into all possible kinds of sexual irregularities' [1905a, p. 191].) Without departing in any way from the view that the adult is the abuser, it is important that therapists should recognize and work with any feelings the abused person may have of being sullied or worthless, and acknowledge any sense of complicity on his or her part, however externally unwarranted. Without this acknowledgement, the abused person may be left with an experience of something bad inside him- or herself that no one can bear to recognize. Victims may fear to disclose abuse through fear of what they feel is their own sense of shame, which may sometimes be linked with having been made into a conspirator with the guilty perpetrator: 'Don't tell Mummy'. Also – unfortunately, sometimes correctly, as was initially the case with the twelve-year-old referred to above – they may feel that they will not be believed.

The report of the inquiry into child abuse in Cleveland (Butler-Sloss, 1987) found that attempts to grapple with the problems were affected by the main agencies' failure to understand each other's functions, and their lack of communication. A polarized position – in some instances between supporters of the professionals and supporters of parents, or in others between sets of professionals, such as doctors, social workers or police – has frequently been reported in the context of child abuse over such issues as the removal of a child from home. An underlying difficulty here may be that it is painfully hard to recognize the appalling fact that some abuse is perpetrated by a parent who is also loved, so that in such instances a sudden removal from home and lack of parental contact constitute in themselves an additional emotional trauma for the child or adolescent who has been abused. Forryan and I have attempted elsewhere to illustrate the way in which the painful nature of such a problem can 'get into' the professionals involved, and become split between them, to the extent that one worker can even suggest removal of an abused child from contact with the other worker (Copley and Forryan, 1987, pp. 65–76). Such countertransference responses, if they are understood, can help to illuminate the problem at a professional level, as opposed to being seen simply as examples of professional rivalry. Psychodynamic consultancy may be useful in such instances.

It is not uncommon in clinical work to meet older adolescent girls, or even young adults still living at home, who have been sporadically abused over very many years by their father, or by their mother's current partner. Complex feelings may be present; the adolescent may have to engage with emotionality that she should not have to bear. Several adolescents girls have said that they submitted so that their mother should not know, and that their father should not be sent to prison. Sometimes their mother is aware of the situation, covertly or openly, and there may be some collusion over the family's 'guilty secrets'. One adolescent felt that she held the family together and protected the younger children, accepting a role of suffering tinged with pride; in another instance one could glimpse some triumph over a mother, left with more menial chores.

As well as being physically abused, the abused child or adolescent is emotionally deprived of thoughtful and comforting parental help. Lack of containment increases the possibility that the abuse will be experienced as an event that has taken place in the body, but cannot be thought about. The inner world of the adolescent bears the scars, which may be re-enacted: an adolescent can leave home in order to to get away from the abuse, but find that she carries the expectation of it with her. Such uncontained abuse may come to feel part of life, with little strength in inner objects to support a move away from its ongoing presence. A residual physical response based on an experience that has had no mental containment may seek repetition. Tragically, an abused adolescent may thus feel some ongoing residual, basically inappropriate, sexual impetus. One older adolescent, until she was helped by intensive psychotherapy, engaged compulsively in brief sexual encounters stimulated by her abusive sexual experiences, but could not commit herself to any long-term tender relationship; tender feelings had to remain idealized and apart from any possible contamination.

Abusers who have themselves been abused may also suffer from physical experiences that they have not been able to think about. Some organizations that help abused children and adolescents are now seeking to understand and treat perpetrators of sexual abuse, hoping that this will contribute to helping young sufferers and their families (Children's Society, 1990b).

THE ANTISOCIAL TENDENCY AND THE CONTAINMENT OF MENTAL PAIN

The question of whether mental pain can be borne, thought about and modified by some form of containment, or whether it is evaded, often with deleterious consequences, arises throughout life (Bion, 1962a). The adolescent – as a result of diminishing family containment, together with a propensity to split and project – is particularly liable to evade pain at the cost of development. This tendency is relevant to the use of what A.H. Williams (1975a, p. 38) has called 'the false gods of drugs, drink and delinquency', and extends to some problematic aspects of adolescent groups and adolescent suicide, a discussion of which follows.

DRUG, ALCOHOL AND SOLVENT ABUSE

Groups of young people may be seen in a pub enjoying themselves in a relaxed manner: there is oral pleasure, linked perhaps with the imbibing of infancy, but in the context of an adult or incipient adult status of being a provider, standing a round in turn. A little –

sometimes manic – indulgence may provide some escape from what Winnicott (1961) calls 'the doldrums'. Adolescents are clearly not alone in such indulgence, and there is an obvious wider link with adult use of substances such as alcohol, tobacco and medicinal drugs. There may even be some family link with the more social aspects of drinking: Coleman and Hendry (1990, p. 81) report from a review of research findings that while a high proportion of drinking starts within the home setting, those who start in peer groups in parks and other public places tend to be the heaviest drinkers, with more hostile attitudes towards authority and the older generation.

Much adolescent drinking, however, does not fit this relatively benign description. At times adolescents speak with pleasure of an intention of getting drunk, often, but not necessarily, as a group activity: 'pissed out of their mind'. This escape from the mind takes place not as an unfortunate consequence of a relaxing experience of taking alcohol, but for the purpose of uncoupling the self from thought and emotion, for which some hatred is felt (Bion, 1959). Sometimes a drinking group of adolescents occupy space, such as a town centre, in a manner that is intrusive to other citizens. This is suggestive of basic assumption group mentality, which includes both pleasurable flight from individual mental life and some degree of forceful 'fighting' entry into the space of more settled groups within society.

Drug abuse in adolescence includes solvent-sniffing, largely by the younger adolescent; the use of stimulants that give a 'high', taken individually or in groups; drugs such as LSD, which produce so-called inner 'experiences'; cannabis, which relaxes and may lead to feeling 'stoned', and the use of addictive narcotic drugs. Some usage, such as that of sedatives and tranquillizers, overlaps or has parallels with that of an older population, in dulling the experience of personal pain. Other substances can be used in similar way: a food binge can drug the body into feeling full and camouflage an inner mental sense of emptiness. The use of drugs can create a false feeling of being grown-up, while simultaneously masking the pain of knowing that this is not real. Usage may sometimes conform with an established family pattern, but is often overtly anti-parental; it may form part of a particular adolescent group culture and even be a requirement for membership.

> Sasha, aged twenty, lived in a commune; she had a job and an active social life. Disappointed at her failure to embark on her desired career or to have a long-term relationship, she sought therapy. When she was alone, she stuffed herself with food. She did not think that her use of cannabis, which formed part of her group culture, had any particular significance. As her therapy became more meaningful to her as mental nourishment, her stuffing of food lessened, and she became aware of the degree to which she also tried to 'stuff her mind' with cannabis, in order to camouflage what was emerging as an inner sense of worthlessness and loneliness. As she gave up her reliance on the drug, she became more able to allow her problems to acquire meaning, and to think about them. An increasing sense of inner resourcefulness followed, leading to both a career change and an enhanced sense of adulthood.

A somewhat blurred, continuing argument about the use of drugs takes place in society; it has something in common with their function of blurring, or temporarily changing, the emotionality of their users. The condoning of substantial drinking by adults, except when driving, may convey mixed messages about the desirability of its use, and young people may distrust advice not to start smoking given by adults who continue to smoke. Arguments occur as to whether cannabis, probably most widely used by young people, is 'worse' than the drinking and smoking of many adults. The majority of drug offences relate to the personal possession of cannabis, and there are frequent discussions of how the penalties for its use and possession should be classified (Goodsir, 1991). The fact that HIV can be passed on by dirty needles can lead to the adult world being cynically held to condone serious drug usage by the issue of clean needles, actually undertaken for reasons of safety. Pushers combine with those who are 'hooked' in an alliance between falsely induced 'need' and greed. On the other hand, some of the real needs of the unemployed and homeless may be insufficiently attended to by society, leaving a degree of pain beyond the capacity of many to contain, and leading to attempts to evade it through the use of drugs.

While alcohol and the use of drugs at one end of the scale may be accompaniments to social relaxation, they are also used to evade the mental pain which is of necessity involved in living as a whole person. Their offer of false alternatives seductively bypasses the truth of mental life, and can lead to varying degrees of physical and mental risk and suffering by the self and others. Apart from physical dangers, there is a grave psychological danger: the use of and possible mental or physical addiction to a substance as if it were a good or ideal object, as opposed to a false god. 'Foul' becomes confused with 'fair'.

THE QUESTION OF CRIME

There are well-established links between sex, age and crime, irrespective of the total quantity of crime committed. Females have a considerably lower rate of offending (NACRO Briefing, 1990). The long-term Cambridge Study in Delinquent Development (male) found, in general accord with other studies, that the 'behaviour of delinquents genuinely and spontaneously changes in the direction of increasing social conformity with increasing age' (West, 1982, p. 143). The number of recorded first convictions in the teenage decade decreased towards its end. Most young delinquents, especially those who had not been arrested more than once or twice, were not reconvicted after the age of nineteen or twenty. Although a backcloth of variables depicting multifarious forms of family, economic and intellectual disadvantage and a history of 'troublesomeness' in school was seen to be relevant to much juvenile delinquency, the Cambridge Study found that the actual commission of crime arose from an accumulation of pressures as opposed to any particular cause (p. 3). The most common motives admitted to by the young people concerned were a desire for quick material gain, followed by excitement, 'kicks' and relief from boredom (p. 24); group solidarity was also a factor.

Aggressive drives may become intensified under the stimulus of puberty, and with an increase in splitting and projective identification they may be split off from a more potentially socially responsive self. The rising and then declining curve of delinquency during adolescence accords with a view that most adolescents' antisocial tendencies may diminish, along with an adolescent state of mind, when they are brought into relationship with more positive – or at least law-abiding – feelings within the self, and some inner authority is found to help to govern them. A disadvantaged background, with possible deprivation and/or a belief that one has been deprived (Winnicott, 1956b), together with a degree of 'troublesomeness', may make it more difficult for the adolescent to be in touch with a positive part of the self, to further integration. The presence of what A.H. Williams (1975b, p. 15) calls 'criminal corrupt authorities' within the adolescent's conscience also makes it more difficult to find benign inner figures with whom to identify. Some adolescents need help in the process of integration; society also needs protection.

Adolescence is also 'an age between' and an age-in-waiting whose members often do not want to wait. An aggrieved response, based in the paranoid-schizoid position, to feeling excluded by an adult world which may be perceived as flaunting its riches may now be enacted with the power of an adult body, against both parental imagery and a wider society, frequently in the form of theft for immediate gain. Problematic for adolescents, especially boys, in this 'age between', and troublesome for society, is what Winnicott calls 'a sense of REAL': 'Especially in boys, violence feels real, while a life of ease brings a threat of depersonalization' (1963b, p. 243) [original capitals]. This can be linked with the drive for 'kicks' and the relief from boredom. Offences affecting cars and their contents are prominent in crime statistics, and as news items. A car is widely experienced as representing potency; Menzies Lyth (1989b) likens its power to paternal potency and its interior to the maternal body. In this context, theft and 'joy-riding' may provide an adolescent with a 'sense of REAL'. Pubertal girls may attempt to fill up a feeling of inner emptiness by shoplifting from a well-stocked store, representing a fully furnished maternal inside.

Evidence indicates that the formal processes of justice, and in particular detention in a penal establishment, are liable to worsen rather than improve antisocial behaviour (West, 1982). Although we live in a society in which crime as a whole has increased, the crime rate has fallen among 'juveniles' – that is, those under seventeen. In recent years some juveniles have been cautioned rather than prosecuted, and Intermediate Treatment schemes of community-based supervised activities and discussions have been introduced as alternatives to custodial sentences and care orders. Evidence suggests that reconviction rates for those who have taken part in such schemes are substantially lower than those for offenders given custodial sentences, among whom the reoffending rate is high (NACRO Briefings 1990, 1991).

Blom-Cooper maintains that 'There is no such thing as "crime", only crimes' – each event must be approached with a different preventive policy: 'The essential point about a policy for persuading people not to behave badly towards one another is that it does not belong primarily in the department of criminal justice' (Blom-Cooper, 1987). Such a thoughtful approach, however, is not widely accepted. Custody of dangerous and some other offenders is necessary for public protection or their own care and can hardly be a matter for argument. Although the evidence indicates that imprisonment does not tend to lead people to behave better towards each other, 'Crime produces public revenge feelings' (Winnicott, 1946, p. 114), and there are frequent demands for it for other reasons than necessary custodial ones. This is suggestive of a wish to treat offenders as bad people, as opposed to people who have done bad things. Depressive concern is not absent only in the commission of most crime, but also frequently in society's reaction to it.

Some form of reparation – if this is in fact possible – to those who have suffered from the crime may be appropriate. But we must be aware, as Money-Kyrle (1953) has said, that it is doubtful how far making people do what they ought to want to do helps them to want to do it.

Enactment of delinquent tendencies in general diminishes as the process of adolescence ends, but young people with families who do not notice or cannot respond to their difficulties need particular attention. A number of troublesome young people may need considerable trouble to be taken if they are to be helped. This may also be of long-term benefit to society. (Help may also, of course, be needed by those who suffer from their actions.) Winnicott (1946) thought positively of institutions that are able to exercise some protective paternal authority, which is often missing in the young person's background, but can also recognize the often violent demands that deprived adolescents make on society. Intermediate Treatment schemes which succeed in combining a personal interest with a firm setting of compulsory, but not specifically punitive, attendance may be able to help young people to get closer to their more positive aspirations and use these in the recognition and combating of their antisocial selves. Probation or psychotherapy may be appropriate.

Alan, aged sixteen, and his parents had accepted it as axiomatic that he would prefer to take a responsible part in his youth group's camp, rather than go abroad on a family holiday with his parents and younger sisters. One evening, however, when a group of French girls were enjoying themselves in a sporting event, a camp fire near their tent got dangerously out of hand. This was finally traced to Alan having secretly attempted to burn some of their possessions. Fortunately, no one was hurt. What stood out was the strength of feeling that was consciously unknown to both Alan and his family. Alan's projective identification with his father, and the family's acceptance of what they thought was his tolerant 'grown-up' attitude to his sisters, had hidden the existence of his burning jealousy and feelings of exclusion, which were brought to light only in the context of the family holiday abroad. The crime was serious and frightening for society, and a psychiatric assessment was needed to determine whether a custodial order would be necessary for public protection. It was thought, however, that the magnitude of the event and the discovery of his involvement had in themselves made their impact on Alan. Therapy provided an opportunity for him to experience – albeit with some resistance – what he felt were totally unacceptable emotions, such as virulent childish jealousy. A 'false self' representing itself as a 'grown-up' personality needed to be recognized, both for communal safety and for personal development.

It took a near-tragedy for the rivalrous little boy who felt excluded from parental attention to be found within the 'good' adolescent. Social and educational disruption understandably followed the event for Alan, with some inevitable 'punishing' publicity. But a custodial sentence based on 'making the punishment fit the crime' according to some external tariff, would probably have stood in the way of his being willing to get to know himself, and try to take some responsibility for his malicious jealousy, and to identify, at least to some extent, with some benign authority – first external and then internal – who would help him to do so.

Dirk, a fifteen-year-old boy with a very different background, was convicted and fined for a burglary with a friend, in which a small quantity of food was taken. Born outside his parents' marriage, he had violent rows with his father, and was possessive of his mother, who herself had a history of mental hospitalization and found him so difficult to manage that he was often sent to his grandparents. He was educationally backward, with a history of truancy. Here was an unstable adolescent in an unstable family. There was tangled oedipal emotionality between mother and son, but despite this his mother sought help in a family consultation where attention was given not only to Dirk's rivalry with his father and possessive jealousy of his mother, but also to his pleasure that he was now starting to go out with girls, the fact that he would leave home, and his increasing ability to relate positively to the support of the special educational unit he was now attending.

The consultation provided space for thinking about the motivations and relationships which impeded development, but also recognized his less easily discernible positive strivings. Help was need if these were to be brought together with the delinquent and socially inadequate elements. This called for attention in a wider framework than that of punishment. Dirk would neither have accepted, nor have had sufficient attentive stamina to use, longer-term therapy, but he did need further help. In his particular case, it was possible that this might be provided by the special educational unit he was attending, although the authority of an Intermediate Treatment scheme could have been helpful.[5]

The company of delinquent associates, and the disengagement from them, can be relevant to the commission and giving up of criminal activity (Rutter and Giller, 1983; West, 1982); Dirk's burglary, like many other delinquent juvenile activities, had been committed with a friend.

PROBLEMATIC ASPECTS OF ADOLESCENT GROUP DYNAMICS

Here we continue to be aware, now in a group context, of aggressive activities linked with 'a sense of REAL' (Winnicott, 1963b). As we saw in Chapter 4, adolescent group activity can have a containing function, but it can also be used for antisocial and anti-developmental purposes.

Groups may have a specific subculture of their own, while they also highlight particular aspects of the wider culture. In an exploration of adolescent subcultures, Sinason (1985) discusses a punk group, whose members had flamboyantly coloured hairstyles and wore a standard attire of leather trousers, safety pins and chains. One of the group described how members vigorously fought not only others outside the group, but also each other when they were bored; they nevertheless still liked each other and felt very isolated when they were not with the group. Sinason thought that this group was held together by a 'second-skin' of adhesive identification, and that the resort to violence as a means of feeling some sense of identity within subculture groups was evidence of the extremity of their deprivation. Aggression in such a group appears to be central to its survival, and is both interwoven into the group itself and projected into society at large. There is no evidence of any clear splitting, which could provide a base for positive development; any idealization here is of the aggressive capacity of the group itself, within which members enjoy fighting each other. Boredom – including, it seems, boring, penetrating anxieties of disintegration – are kept at bay by aggressive movement. Members of such subculture groups seem to present an extreme version of adolescents who need to be held together in some form of group skin, but probably lack the ability, found in the ordinary mainstream culture, to use each other to change and develop; this suggests the presence of the kind of emotional poverty conveyed by some severely deprived children (Boston and Szur, 1983).

There can also be an element of pleasure in a group membership which avoids conflict. Sinason quotes a punk girl: 'I like being punk because you know who you are and who you can go out with and what music you like' (pp. 88–9). But if this is compared with the plaintive comment of a fifteen-year-old football supporter, who felt that she would like to be 'a person all on their own' (p. 82), instead of needing to move in an amorphous mass with the group, we can sense some pain in feeling almost literally stuck into a group. Such a group, although it provides a sense of identity to its membership, is, on account of its violent aggressive 'glue', largely antisocial in its operations, and probably should be described as a gang for much of the time. Members of such subgroups, however, may feel that it is society that gangs up against them. Sinason quotes a skinhead: 'If you want trouble you get it. But if you don't you still have to watch because some people will hate you when you're a skin. Even if you were seeing an old lady across the street' (p. 89).

Group dynamics of the kind portrayed in *Romeo and Juliet* illuminate ganglike confrontations between the kind of adolescent groups in our society which have clearly defined opponents, whether these are based on racism, extreme political or other allegiances. Demonstrations may be intended to provoke and justify aggression: 'let them begin' (I.i.37). Emotions which feel incompatible with an image of the self may be projected and fought in others; thus a group membership with anxieties about any kind of homosexual feeling in the context of a sought-after powerful heterosexual identity may indulge in denigrating imputed homosexuality in others in the form of 'queer-bashing'. The contribution that such fight/flight ganglike destructiveness makes to their 'sense of REAL' may give pleasure to its protagonists while plaguing a more modern version of a potentially peaceable 'Verona' mother country. As we saw in *Romeo and Juliet*, groups in such a state of mind ignore suggestions of more thoughtful members. Benvolio's attempt to 'scape a brawl' when the 'Capels are abroad' and there is 'mad blood stirring' (III.i.4) was ignored, together with his more 'work group' based counsel that grievances might be discussed (III.i.51). Although there may be individual friendship within the membership, individual thoughtfulness is likely to diminish as enemies are found, and the drive to mindless basic assumption fight/flight mentality increases. What might at one moment be called a group becomes a destructive gang. Basic assumption activity allows the overriding involvement in the fight to avoid attending to cautionary, thoughtful 'Benvolio' voices or other individual misgivings.

Winnicott (1963b, p. 243), in thinking about the drive of the male adolescent in particular to feel REAL, asked: 'Can adolescence in general gather all its aggression into the competitive or dangerous sport? Will not society clamp down on dangerous sport and make even this unrespectable or antisocial?' In recent years, however, it has not been first-hand sporting risks, but aspects involving spectators that have been particularly prominent in discussions

about what may be antisocial. Sinason (1985, p. 89) quotes one
football supporter who is a member of a subculture group: 'I like it
because you can see straightaway whose side you are on . . . If we
feel like being rough we can all gang up against the other side. If
we stay together we are usually safe.' Although football violence
may in fact be rare, as Canter *et al.* (1989) demonstrate, the
magnitude of a particular event can be horrendous. Although
disaster may occur in all large crowds if something goes wrong,
events where the atmosphere is already vibrant with fight/flight
basic assumption activity may be particularly dangerous.[6] It is
unfortunately rare for society to use positive driving energy for
major life-saving activities, drawing on work group as opposed to
basic assumption activity, although this was undertaken under the
leadership of young people in 'Band-Aid' on behalf of famine-
stricken nations.

Boredom can increase the feeling of unREALity to which
adolescents are prone, and form the tinder for the growth of
fight/flight basic assumption states of mind, violent disruption and
wider activation of gang activity that thrives on the use of violence
as a protection against inner emptiness. A social background which
incorporates ingredients of psychological and social disadvantage
makes it easier to draw support from those who are motivated by
envy and perversity. Vandalism can occur on its own or as an
extension of other gang activity, sometimes with an appearance of
non-confrontative mindlessness, but suggestive of envious spoiling
and denigration of something that may be valued by others and not
available to oneself. Such perversity may be further supported by
the passive acquiescence of others with some feelings of grievance.

Recent so-called 'copycat' violence in United Kingdom towns is
an example of violent and dangerous group action, some of which
has taken place in locations subject to youth unemployment. Some
instances may have been examples of flight/fight basic assumption
activity sparked off by such events elsewhere. Provocation, perhaps
experienced as being of the kind present at the beginning of *Romeo
and Juliet*, is frequently present. Where there is confrontation, the
police, in their official role, are obvious candidates for polarization,
and the 'fight' of basic assumption mentality itself, as opposed to
the restoration of order, is in danger of taking over as the actual

purpose of the intervention. Taunting and mockery of failed adult potency to provide work may be triumphantly present in a series of adolescent driving stunts in stolen cars. These, both dangerous and providing a sense of REAL, may be intended to force a sense of impotence into the adult world, and reverse what is held to be provocative adult withholding of opportunities to grow up. Wider destructiveness may follow.

With considerable unemployment, there is a failure of opportunity for developing a sense of identity through work, giving rise, among other things, to an income that could make buying and legitimately driving some kind of legally owned transport in an adult manner more achievable by some young people. Grievances based on lack of realization of normal opportunities may get caught up in wider forms of protest.

> One of the greatest disservices which can be done to adolescents is to give them a legitimate grievance. Being wronged helps them to abdicate from ownership of responsibility into a feeling of being wronged and being persecuted. In other words there is a sliding down the scale from a state dominated by depressive anxiety to one which is pervaded by persecutory anxiety. It is in this aggrieved state that a lot of adolescent delinquency takes place. (A.H. Williams, 1975a, p. 38)

SOCIAL SPACE WITHIN SOCIETY

Some intrusive use of space by drinking adolescent groups was referred to above (see p. 128). Comedia (1991) describe a number of town centres which are dominated by cars and commercial developments in the daytime. After the shops close, pub drinking and other facilities for young people, particularly male drinkers, take over the life of these centres. They point out the presence of dual carriageways obstructing pleasant pedestrian access, together with the absence of safe public transport which might make an intergenerational social mix more likely. The material and commercial use of space by society may contribute to divisiveness which supports unconstructive group life within it.

SUICIDE IN ADOLESCENCE

Shakespeare helps us to be in touch with a state of mind that envisages death, but also conveys a subtle aura of somehow not dying. Romeo expresses a clear intention to kill himself, but intertwined with this we may sense a suggestion of something like a belief in some form of continuing life (with mortal as opposed to religious connotations). In his dream, which takes place just before he hears of Juliet's 'death', she revives him from death with kisses (V.i.8). When he hears of her 'death', his determination to lie with her that night (V.i.34) is clearly linked with suicide, but also with something different: the violent, quick poison becomes cordial (V.i.85); he will 'remain with worms' to protect Juliet from 'Death' making her his paramour (V.iii.103–9). (This sequence is, of course, related to the fact that Juliet is not really dead at the time, but even so, it illuminates emotionality accompanying suicide.)

Suicides or suicidal attempts are rare before adolescence, and those of adolescents may cause a particular sorrow. One can think of an attempted suicide as the outcome of a particular phantasy of getting rid of unbearable, frequently mental, pain, and believing that this is what is being killed off, without the necessary realization that the death of the whole self is involved. This view clearly draws on the concept of severe splitting of mental capacity within the self.

Part of the mentality accompanying thoughts of suicide may be an intention to redistribute suffering; someone else is to feel bad or guilty. The Samaritans have drawn attention to the fact that a number of teenagers have to be rushed to hospital every year on the fourteenth of February because they have not received a Valentine; some of them die (Samaritans, 1991). We do not know the details, but we may wonder whether it is the feeling of being unloved oneself that has to be killed, and it will be the one who did not send the Valentine who will have to suffer the death of the teenager. If so, the fact that one's own death is involved may not seem real. This account underlines the emotional vulnerability of some adolescents at a time when the love objects of childhood are being or have been relinquished, internal objects may be in a state of flux, and some external guarantee of being loved may be desperately wanted. The need to take seriously what might be thought of as only dramatic gestures is also clear; adolescents are often dramatic.

Actions with minimal danger to life do also take place; Ahmed (discussed below, pp. 203–4), made a gesture as a means of conveying what he felt but could not say, and this also needed attention. A suicidal attempt carries meaning, even if it is unlikely to succeed in medical terms, and it is important to try to understand the nature of the pain that was to be disposed of in any suicidal attempt, whether it was intended to succeed or not. Such pain might be associated with part of the self, as in the case of one adolescent patient who spoke of wanting to kill what was felt to be a dirty baby part of herself impeding recovery. Alternatively, it might be felt to be inflicted by someone alien: a young man wanted to silence the intrusive thoughts about his sexuality which, he felt, were being voiced by an inner critic; he experienced his attempted suicide as an attempt to kill off a persecutor, rather than himself.

Therapists and other workers with adolescents have to be aware of suicidal possibilities, arising in particular around times when there is no external contact with the worker. Exploration with the patient about the possibility of an attempted suicide may enable the pain to be thought about rather than enacted, possibly leading to contact being be made with a more life-preserving aspect of him- or herself. Therapists also have to make clear to their patients, and also to themselves, that they do not possess omnipotent powers to protect life. Protective measures may be desirable, although sometimes they are far from easy to arrange with young people who may not have supportive contact with their families or feel that they do not actually need such help, and, by splitting, make such flights into health that they appear convincingly well, even to specialist carers.

There have been a number of recent suicides in the United Kingdom of young people in solitary confinement in prison. Bleak, lonely conditions which leave vulnerable young people feeling 'imprisoned' in a particular frame of mind, without access to any good external objects, can form the immediate background to a suicidal attempt. The perception of something 'bad' or 'mad' within a part of themselves, or of a bad, unloving experience, may be what some of these young people in mental distress plan to kill off. Such conditions have been criticized, and the contrasting need for staff support and family access has been stressed (Howard League for Penal Reform, 1990). Some reform is proposed, but it sometimes seems to be easier for society to isolate those who are suspected or known to have harmed it, responding at the paranoid-schizoid end of the Ps↔D spectrum, rather than to help them to be in touch with some form of positive support which might provide some alleviation or change.

THE NEEDS OF TROUBLED ADOLESCENTS AND THOSE WHO HELP THEM

How does society respond to its troubled adolescents – or, one could say, to the adolescents who trouble it? Some pain and disturbance are experienced within the adolescent; much is experienced by society. Two points stand out from the discussion in this chapter.

One is that adolescents with developmental difficulties do rely on the professional workers with whom they come into contact for help, although such help may not be openly sought. Such workers can fulfil a therapeutic function by containing and thinking about what is 'put into' them by the adolescents. A care worker needs to be able to relate to a young person's fear of being prepared for 'cardboard city'; residential workers in an adolescent home need to be able to respond actively to the adolescents' silence, and not collude with it; a support unit teacher needs to be able to recognize that he may be experienced by an adolescent as someone relied upon to maintain life, but that this can have a prejudicial impact on his work unless it is understood and responded to actively. Feelings engendered in the professionals provide some understanding of how they are being seen and used by the young people with whom they work, and thus form part of the raw material for responding to the adolescents' needs. These are matters of countertransference and transference, discussed further in the clinical chapters of this book.[7] Workers carrying burdens of a therapeutic nature need training and support to help them to be open to the pain of the adolescent and to respond to what at times may seem unclear and unsocially expressed demands, as well as to separate out emotionality related to the adolescent's needs from what is personal to each worker. There is an urgent need for society to respond to what is fundamentally its own suffering by making appropriate training available.

This leads on to, and links with, the second point. Many adolescents who need help are caught in the paranoid-schizoid position. Those who seek to help them may, in consequence, be seen to some extent as persecuting, and this may be difficult for workers to bear individually without professional training or support. Society in a more general sense has difficulties in containing the pain inflicted upon it, and in responding with depressive concern to the needs of some young people, as we have seen from some of its responses to offenders. This does not mean – to quote Winnicott (1961, p. 87) – that adults have to say 'Look at these dear little adolescents having their adolescence; we must put up with everything and let our windows get broken'. Society does need to notice the 'ado' and try to respond constructively, but without vengeance, thus acting protectively both to itself and to its developing adolescents. The adolescents do need containment in the sense used here. This in itself may provide a positive experience for internalization, and may in turn contribute to an increased capacity for some young people to be able to experience and relate more constructively to their own pain.

ADOLESCENTS AND ADULTS AND THE WORLD THEY LIVE IN

One may question whether there are impediments which affect adults' ability to relate to the next generation with the altruistic concern we discussed at the end of Chapter 4, and in turn hinder adolescent development towards concerned adulthood. The possibility of an adolescent element in the increasing divorce rate in society has already been raised (see above, p. 123). One may also wonder, in the context of decreasing church attendance within the established Church, and diminishing demands for a 'God-slot' on television, how far matters of the 'soul' are being attended to more inwardly, or how far material interests are becoming more predominant. Vast, impersonal advertising, some of which receives attention in the process of normal television viewing, certainly invites massive and speedy intergenerational consumption of all kind of new things which 'show well outward', a number of which are known not to be good for our environment. Lasch (1990, p. 239) refers to prevailing social conditions in America having brought out what he describes as narcissistic personality traits, present in varying degrees in everyone: 'a certain protective shallowness, a fear of binding commitments, a willingness to pull up roots whenever the need arose, a desire to keep one's options open, a dislike of depending on anyone, an incapacity for loyalty or gratitude'. This also has an adolescent ring.

Here I can raise for reflection only the presence within the adult world of possible preoccupations and difficulties which do not encourage emotional growth because they do not sufficiently delineate the 'fair' from the 'foul'. Nuclear weapons, believed by some to be preservative of peace, but with massive power for annihilation, exist. Even 'good' civil nuclear energy can suddenly be devastatingly destructive. Something treated as life-enhancing can suddenly portend death on a massive scale, and may exist as an uncontained dread, confounding issues of life and death. Influenced by these things, one may wonder if there is a lack of hopefulness within current society, which cannot be thought about but is drugged by an alliance between speed and greed for current satisfactions. It may be increasingly difficult to believe in the restoration of a good, minimally uncontaminated Mother Earth. This may lead to increasing failure to seek or maintain a state of introjective identification with an actual and symbolic maternal world which is not to be plundered or abused, but used with care, with children, born or unborn, in mind. It may be easier to seek to gratify a more adolescent mentality, with an emphasis on speedy, external satisfaction. This, in turn, may add to the difficulty, for adolescents, in finding and maintaining an adult quality of life.

PART THREE:
STUDIES IN THERAPY

6 PSYCHOANALYTIC PSYCHOTHERAPY WITH INDIVIDUAL PATIENTS: A STRUGGLE TO GROW UP

In this chapter I follow a three-year period of therapy with John, a fifteen-year-old boy. Experience of individual psychoanalytic psychotherapy forms the background to all the work with adolescents discussed in the following chapters. The case is discussed in detail in the hope that it will bring to life the psychoanalytic approach underlying the rest of the book, and that as a result we shall be in a better position to share what can appropriately be applied from this intensive form of relationship to other forms of intervention. I include a number of dreams that portray the actual unconscious thinking that is taking place within the patient (Meltzer, 1983) and also illustrate and substantiate some of the changes that occur during the course of his therapy. The work with John amplifies aspects of adolescence discussed elsewhere in the book – the establishment of sexual identity, struggles with perversity, the presence, and the lessening, of splitting and projective identification, and the move towards adulthood.

The core of such work at any age lies in the extensive use of the transference relationship between therapist and patient and the interpretative process based upon this as the means to change and development. In the Kleinian approach followed here, considerable attention is given in the transference to infantile feelings which influence the adolescent in his drive towards adulthood. The method of work and techniques employed normally remain the same, irrespective of the frequency of attendance, ranging between five times and only once a week. One would normally hope to be able to relate to the same range of feelings in all these instances, but with a very general expectation, qualified by issues such as the degree of illness and the drive for health, that more frequent attendance is likely to facilitate deeper understanding. Many patients, such as John, do, however, have the capacity to work in considerable depth in once- or twice-weekly therapy.

BACKGROUND

John was an only child. His father was a businessman who travelled a good deal; his mother taught part-time. During much of John's childhood the family were based in France, because of his father's work, and they still had a holiday house there. Their social life in the United Kingdom was centred around a club frequented by French visitors, and they had a series of French *au pair* girls, who appeared to be treated as visiting members of the family. John came to the clinic on his headmaster's advice, saying that he did not know how to get along with other boys at school, and had no friends. The headmaster, consulted with John's consent, said that John was recognized as being bright but also inordinately competitive; his pushing to the fore could stir up others, and his occasional attempts to placate his rivals were so heavy-handed that they often led to further disruption.

John had a consultation and some brief psychotherapy with Dr P before the latter's return to Australia. On asking for further help he was referred to Mrs E for psychoanalytic psychotherapy, for which he had a short wait. His parents were not directly involved in John's referral; they had met a member of the clinic staff and accepted that John should attend, but did not want any help for themselves. Mrs E usually preferred to meet parents of younger or 'middle' adolescents personally before starting psychotherapy, but John's parents had felt that this was not necessary. An interview with the person who is actually going to treat their child can be useful in helping parents to understand what is being offered and to feel in some alliance with it, whether or not they also seek help for themselves. Possible difficulties that might arise, perhaps around a seasonal break in therapy, can be thought about. Consideration can also be given to whether further occasional meetings between parents and therapist would be useful, or too intrusive to someone of John's age – in this case, some other contact for the parents might appropriately be discussed. The lack of an initial interview can lead to awkwardness if parents want to see a therapist at a later date because a problem arises, and at that point have to be asked to see someone else. Mrs E would also have found it useful to hear directly from the parents about John's early history and their feelings about him.

INTRODUCTION TO THERAPY

John's first session with Mrs E gives some indication of the contact. I shall use the present tense in an attempt to portray John's lively, direct, 'adolescent' manner of speaking, even though this some-times leads to sacrificing some consistency of tenses in the discussion. Questions, comments and information pour forth from him. 'Are you Australian?' Mrs E takes up Dr P's departure and John's anxiety that she is poised to leave from the start, and says that she has no such plans. She outlines the way she works (which is different from that of the brief work with Dr P and includes the use of the couch), and how John can co-operate by relating to what is currently in his mind, and by bringing dreams. In further clarification of the setting she confirms the times and length of sessions and the approximate timings of her holiday intervals. She says that she is sorry that she can start only once a week, but expects to be able to increase to twice a week shortly.

John looks around and says Dr P's room was bigger; Mrs E suggests that he feels he is coming down in the world by seeing her, and that he may be judging what she might have to offer by the size of her room. John responds: 'What am I doing here? What's wrong with me? Am I not normal? Am I a queer? What does that mean anyhow – homosexual?' Mrs E recognizes John's anxiety about something being wrong with him and his sexuality, and also some bewilderment about his contact with her. She makes it clear that understanding can arise only out of shared work. In response to some exploration by Mrs E, John demands forcefully: 'Haven't you got notes? Its all written up.' Mrs E refers to her earlier remark about how she works, comments that John seems to know what was recorded and had expected her to have done some advance homework regarding it. She takes up his possible disappointment that she does not work in exactly the same way as Dr P, and is also perhaps frightened by what she has said. She explains that although Dr P has left some indications about what is troubling John, it would be better for their work for her to hear about it directly from him.

John responds: 'Oh, all right then, I'll tell you from the beginning. It started at eleven. I was lonely. My parents did nothing; I even asked to see a psychiatrist, perhaps I should have said a sex therapist.' He laughs ruefully. 'Oh, I hate the idea of that. I used to play around with these girls in this garden, I used to make them jealous, I used to get an erection.' 'At eleven?' 'No, last year. Then Yvonne, a daughter of family friends, came to stay when we were in France, and was quite nice to me.' 'Nice?' 'Oh, just friendly, worse luck! I danced at a party last summer. Michèle, a girl like Yvonne, came, but wouldn't look at me, but I met a nice girl one night and thought she was marvellous, but I paid no attention to her next morning. I don't like asking girls to do things. The girls [referring to the consecutive *au pairs* in the family's London flat] are not at home much. I'm very worried, because I look at dirty pictures and get no response. I feel people say "filthy little boy" when I go to buy them.' 'Them?' 'Oh, just pornography, people in intercourse, naked girls; it's all quite normal.' Mrs E wonders aloud if he feels that he 'knows' her reaction to the pictures: she is saying 'filthy little boy'. She adds that although he might be differentiating between particular kinds of pornography, he is also making a statement about it being perfectly normal. She makes it clear that when he speaks of getting no response, she assumes that he is talking about his masturbation.

'Oh, I can't sleep without it. I don't really think about people.' John goes on to describe his accompanying fantasy of being Sir Jasper, an imaginary character, immensely rich and powerful, who makes great inventions, can fly off and rescue people, 'gets' girls, and has others hold down women for him to rape. 'I can't work.' 'Can't work?' 'Oh yes I can, very rarely not, I come top, but I heard that a fifteen-year-old boy committed suicide because of masturbation.' Mrs E voices what she takes to be his fears that his masturbation, linked with the superman-boy Sir Jasper part of himself, could be the death of a potentially working self, and that parts of himself could be held down by this great raper, Sir Jasper. 'Oh well, I get an "A" all the time and I came first in the exams.' Mrs E notes inwardly that any worry about suicide is left with her. John goes on to outline his A-level subjects and intentions of getting a prestigious degree. 'My parents have degrees, so why shouldn't I?' 'Perhaps a higher one,' ponders Mrs E, and John laughs. 'But I'm anxious about being a queer; I once wanted to put my head on a boy's lap and be stroked, although I didn't do it. I can't go into a urinal and see all the others; it's terrible. Oh [glancing at his watch], you're going to say it's time soon. We'll have to talk about it next week [said in quite managing tones]. I hate this place, you could do a test and let me know.' Mrs E speaks of John's hatred of the clinic and of her for not giving him the immediate answers that a Sir Jasper part of him demands, his resentment at having had to wait for her to see him, and now at having to wait again till next week, with the feeling that others take her time. She says it is time to stop. 'Oh yes, Friday, marvellous, I'll have to come.'

Thinking about the session, Mrs E was aware of being expected to go along with the Sir Jasper 'superman' little-boy part of John, who sought to dominate her management of the session. She sometimes consulted with colleagues in thinking about new pieces of work, and did so here. When she reflected further on some of the material of the session, the loneliness, referred to by John in the context of sex and the two little girls, seemed to be something to think about in association with John's being an only child, and his feelings about little girls as missing from the perhaps not very fruitful 'garden' of his parents' sexuality. Projective propensities were apparent in his stimulation of jealousy in the little girls. Many of his difficulties, possibly including those associated with the penises in the urinal, were probably linked with the daydreams and phantasies associated with his 'Sir Jasper' self. It would be important to draw his attention to the ways in which his masturbation, with its underlying projective identification of flying up into a powerful 'superman' daddy or penis, and possessing its powers, was clearly indulging the omnipotent little-boy part of him at the expense of engagement with his developmental struggles.

John's complaints and demands for answers continue. In the second session he grumbles that Mrs E leaves him to look up bad sex books from the corner shop, which doesn't do him any good, while she has a library: 'You've got the answers down there, you've got thousands of cases, you must know.' Mrs E says that he feels that by withholding information with which he believes she is powerfully endowed she drives him to his 'dirty picture' activities, and adds that he may well have seen a notice downstairs about a 'Records Department' in the clinic as he came in. John smiles. Mrs E suggests that to a little-boy part of him this arouses a feeling that she represents a mother in his mind, fully endowed with knowledge, somewhere 'down there' inside her; this part of him believes that she is withholding the answers to which he feels entitled, and does not accept the way she says she works. She recognizes his worry about his sexuality and personal relationships, and reclarifies her method of work. John says complainingly that Dr P sat back while he, John, talked, and only then asked questions. Mrs E – who does in fact listen to John speaking first, and tries to follow what he says – comments that she thinks he objects to the way she is talking at this moment in comparison with a nicer Dr P, who, he implies, treated him as if he, John, were in possession of some kind of library, while he feels that she is taking away such an attribute.

John pours out his problems: 'Am I homosexual? I can't go out. Look at my face! [The implication was that it was childish.] People will laugh. I used to get bullied. Is it wrong to like girls? I used to, but then perhaps I never did really. Boys hate and ignore you if you don't have a sixteen-year-old girl to bring to a dance. I have to take two tickets. I have to show old love letters from a twelve-year-old girl.' John implies that the only girl he could have asked to the dance was a French girl whom he had met at the club his family go to, but that she wouldn't do: 'Sir Jasper got her!' 'Sir Jasper got her?' 'Oh well, that's actually me in my daydreams: Sir Jasper is intelligent, successful, commanding.' Mrs E comments that in this instance he seems to be describing a need to 'have' a girl in the same way as he believes other boys do – not only not to be ignored, suspected of being homosexual or hated by them, but to be like them in having a girl who would like to go to the dance with him. The activities of Sir Jasper in his daydreams, representing an instantly successful little-boy part of himself who, in his masturbation, can fly off, get and sexually possess a girl, appear to avoid finding out in practice whether he does like girls, and if they like him. He also seems to be puzzled about the idea of 'liking': will he like coming here, for example, or come solely to get answers?

By the third session John has chosen to lie on the couch, but he begins to feel uncomfortable with Mrs E 'sitting and staring behind him'. He proclaims firmly: 'You are a computer, not human; you are not allowed to be involved with patients.' Then he looks round and, speaking softly, exclaims: 'Miracle, miracle, you're not writing!' He talks about his parents, and how badly he feels about the fact that they have to stay in this country just for him and his education. His father might get promotion if they went back to France now, and his mother cannot practise her profession here in the way she liked doing when they lived there, and has to do housework, which she hates, but then (said dismissively) she *has* to be there to nurse his colds. Mrs E talks about John's fear that she will penetrate into the back of his mind, or alternatively make him feel bad when he decrees that she must be only a kind of uninvolved houseworker-computer, programmed to solving his problems and loneliness, and not allowed to practise her profession in the way she would like. On the other hand, he is also relieved that she is not behaving as depicted in the popular press, and seems able to listen to him in a human manner.

John asks if he is a queer because he wanted a master to see his new flashy outfit? It makes him feel sick. This master brandishes his essay all over the place, saying it is very good. He, the master, is not bright, and takes a quarter of an hour to do what takes only two minutes. Boys tell him that he, John, is bright to be chosen as a representative for an external school competition. He also recounts how he undid his coat in the tube, hoping that a girl he knew would notice and admire this new outfit. Mrs E wonders if he feels that it is queer of him to want to brandish his developing intellectual and sexual potency, with the emphasis on others of either sex seeing and admiring it, but to feel able to present only a brief showing-off 'flash'. She points out that he presents himself as intellectually ahead of the master, so he may doubt the latter's judgement. He may also imagine that he surpasses him in the speed of his sexual potency, thus doubly triumphing over him in his mind, but then leaving himself anxious about the meaning of showing him his new outfit, with a fear that it includes a sickening, placatory aspect. He may, in addition, have some fears about the degree of friendliness of the boys who have not been chosen for the competition.

John now recounts what he calls a terrible daydream, in which Jasper (he often omits the 'Sir'), watched by the master he has spoken of and some boys from school, is with a girl, but does nothing – that is, he just pets, and isn't in love. Mrs E comments about his fear of what he describes as the potency of his Jasper part being seen by the master, the boys, and also herself – and even himself – to be just a 'flash', nothing to do with being powerful or in love. Somewhere here John talks about the size of his penis, with an implicitly favourable comparison to that of other boys, but conveying some uncertainty. Mrs E recalls his difficulty in seeing others in the urinal and suggests that some fear of failure associated with rival penises may be relevant there too, whatever other significance this may have for him. In his mind, the Jasper part of him may consider himself to be a better performer than the husband he believes her to have, or than her other patients, and he wants them to know it, but also has a terrible feeling that he may just be something like a pet patient.

John comes twenty minutes late for his fourth session, tossing off an apology. As he lies on the couch, he remarks: 'Back to bed again, I suppose I'd better take my boots off.' Mrs E says he is showing her a 'back to bed' little John, apparently conforming to what he seems to see as her wish that he should be a compliant child, but accompanied by some defiance. 'Perhaps you're hurt because I was twenty minutes late,' John replies. Mrs E says that she thinks he feels hurt that she could not provide the second weekly session immediately. John maintains that Dr P had said that he could come five times a week. (It is unlikely that such an offer was actually made, but Mrs E recognizes that there may have been a misunderstanding.) She comments that John has told her that he does not like asking 'girls', here representing herself, to do things.

He would like her to offer more, and wants her to feel how painful it is not to have the amount of sessions he wants, and may suspect others of having. Through his lateness it is she who is to feel the hurtful impact of his absence, and perhaps also to be jealous about the little-boy him feeling that 'Daddy Dr P would be much more forthcoming than the Mummy her'. John says that he has sometimes come between his parents, stressing that this is a past event; Mrs E speaks of his current response to Dr P and herself as representatives of parents of the 'little' John.

Mrs E can currently only offer one session, but she would want to have some further understanding before increasing sessions to more than two. One a week provides little time in which to relate to such pressure of material, but much more might be an unnecessary gratification of greed in John, who is able to make good use of limited time.

SOME DISCUSSION OF THE METHOD

I should now like to pause and look at the method of work, and in particular the understanding provided by following the trans-ference and countertransference relationship.

> In Kleinian thought there is a particular emphasis on the totality of transference. The concept is not restricted to the expression in the session towards the analyst of attitudes towards specific persons and/or incidents of the historical past. Rather the term is used to mean the expression in the analytic situation of the forces and relationships of the internal world. (Spillius, 1988b, pp. 5–6)

Significant features in John's inner world can become alive and meaningful between Mrs E and John by means of the first-hand experiential life of the session, and thus available for change and development. From the beginning Mrs E draws whatever she can in the material into the transference relationship with herself. This includes negative reactions, such as John's hatred of her for not giving him the immediate responses he demands, or his early comparison of her approach with that of Dr P. It also includes John's perceptions of the building, such as the size of the room and the location of the Records Department. She also listens, clarifies and thinks about external issues, and draws his attention to ways in which he might be contributing to some of the difficulties he experiences.

She tries, however, to avoid getting entangled in any detailed commentary about the external world of her patient's adolescent activities, in regard to which he might – quite probably correctly – feel her to be out of contact, and also to be talking down. This is not a great problem with John, owing to his limited adolescent involvement, but to do so would be to stray into a more hearsay, second-hand world away from the immediacy of their contact. Material related to school may receive some exploration and understanding in its own context, but, as in the instance of the daydream of Jasper's failure to perform, she gathers what she can into the transference for understanding 'live' in the session. Similarly, while she may attempt to clarify and think with her patient about some of the events at home, she avoids making active comments about what are felt to be the rights and wrongs of adolescent/parental conflict which could only serve to stir up issues about which she has no first-hand experience, and could encourage acting out. She seeks, rather, to draw infantile aspects of relationships with parents into the transference experience of the session. We shall, however, see and discuss some changes which do take place in John's relationship with his parents later in the therapy.

Throughout her work Mrs E is informed by her own counter-transference. The earlier view of countertransference in psycho-analytic work was solely that of inappropriate responses arising from the therapist's own problems, and therapists such as Mrs E naturally hope that their own psychoanalytic experience has helped them to be able to be aware of these and put them aside. Work by Heimann (1950), Bion (1959) and others has, however, led to the recognition that the therapist's inner rejoinder to what is conveyed to her by the patient by any means, including projective identification, may serve as a route to potential understanding. At the end of the first session Mrs E was aware of a developing working relationship with a troubled adolescent, but she also felt under the impact of a demand that she provide immediate answers which helped her to be in touch with dominating aspects of the little-boy John. In the fourth session she was aware of being made to feel envious of Dr P's apparently more generous provisions, and jealous of John's preferring him to her. These countertransference responses helped to formulate her understanding of what John was conveying, and its implications for the transference.

Adolescents need to be helped not only to differentiate emotionality with an infantile basis from that coming from a more adult part of the self, but also to explore the meaning and status of what may feel like separate parts of themselves. There can be some overlap in this: Sir Jasper has a basis in John's omnipotent infantile sexuality, and can also be felt to function separately from other aspects of him, as in getting the girl John wanted for the dance. Change may not be welcome if it threatens the loss of omnipotent powers, such as those ascribed to Jasper, which John may feel to be adult, but are in fact infantile.

In the light of adolescents' fluctuating contact with different parts of themselves, it becomes important to try to find some adult structure that is interested in the overall therapeutic task. Mrs E, without herself taking any moral view, can point out to the more adult aspect of John, which is interested in development, that his indulgence in Jasper-dominated masturbation could hold him back from facing his inexperience of real girls, and that he himself has some anxiety, although he wants to brush it off, about its murderous qualities for his working self. She can also hear and acknowledge Jasper's complaints that she spoils his masturbation. In this context Mrs E and her colleagues try to find a way of speaking that maintains the session as a living experience for all aspects of the participant self as well as addressing a therapeutic ally (Hoxter, 1964). Such an approach can, in fact, help the growing-up part of the adolescent not to feel infantilized.

Mrs E tries to use language that may help John to differentiate more infantile structures from more adult ones (Meltzer, 1973, p. ix). Thus when the little-boy John seems to be showing her his preference for his previous male therapist, she speaks of his finding 'Daddy' nicer than 'Mummy', in contrast to talking about John's actual parents as 'Father' and 'Mother' when references to them occur in the session. We shall soon see clearly how John, with his infantile self, relates to what can be understood as 'part-object' aspects of Mrs E in the transference, especially her breasts. For many patients it seems appropriate to talk about their relationship with the functioning aspects of these part-objects without talking about them as anatomical structures (Spillius, 1988a, p. 5). This holds for John at times, and Mrs E talks of his relationship to a feeding aspect of her, but when his drive to possess and control what represents the actual feeding objects themselves, or to become involved in other parts of a maternal, or paternal, body dominates, Mrs E finds it more meaningful to talk of both function and anatomy. In puberty and early adolescence, when mixed infantile sexual phantasies re-emerge in adolescent clothing, anatomical references may also help in understanding and clarifying feelings related to the functioning of part-objects and sexual identity. As the work proceeds, we shall see that John appears to make use of such language for this purpose, and also draws on the visual imagery of the breasts to convey his dream thoughts.

ONGOING PSYCHOTHERAPY

One of John's night dreams, as opposed to frequently recounted daydreams, was brought to the session in the fifth week of therapy. It is the first in a series of 'jungle' dreams which in themselves show some of the change that takes place in his therapy. Mrs E's comments about all his dreams took place as part of the to-and-fro of the life of the session, but are presented here in a more orderly form to aid clarity, with some sacrifice of the spontaneous interchange.

The dream is preceded by an account of how awful everything is at school and at home: 'I can't face people; I can't even masturbate regularly since you told me it was bad for me; my parents tell me I swallow every second word; I feel sick; no one can understand what I say.'

It is at school, which is also a jungle. There is an open window. I am there and give a warning about a tiger. No one pays any attention. A boy called Andrew changes into a tiger, pounces, and eats other boys. I have moved to the front, and sit on the desk and say I was right. The tiger comes to eat me and I wake up.

No overt anxiety is apparent in the telling of the dream. John refers to his fear of wolves when he was little, and how this fear gradually changed into one of tigers; he had been afraid when his father was away, both in childhood and also recently, and once thought his father was a wolf. (He says he does not recall the *Red Riding Hood* story, but does know of the powerful tiger in the petrol advertisement.) The school in the dream is his, and he speaks contemptuously of the master he imagines to be taking the lesson, on whose desk he sits at the end of the dream. He used to like this master, but now yawns throughout his lessons. He went around with Andrew five years ago, when there was no one else available. Andrew was ahead then, but he, John, is far ahead now. He and Andrew, as part of some school community project, visited a terminal case (John's words), an old man of fifty or so (his father's age approximately), in hospital to get out of some even worse school activity. 'Oh no, the man wasn't dying, he just would never get out of hospital. He used to say I was afraid of Andrew, but it wasn't true, and in any case I am strong! I am the tiger!' John goes on to describe how young he is for his class, how he frequently comes first, how he hates mixing things in chemistry, and how this and other subjects that he hates make him feel empty and full of hot air. He implies that some of his subjects are irrelevant to his ambition: he wants to be a managing director or a president. 'A president of what?' 'A country, of course!'

Mrs E talks to John about his world being presented as a jungle-school of ruthless ambition in which there is no safety. Companionship is on the basis of no better choice being available, and if you get ahead of your previous mate, as he does with Andrew, your mate can be hunting you, and there's no use in thinking you are liked on a friendly basis. An Andrew-tiger part of himself may pounce on rivals as part of his presidential coup in which he moves to the front desk and becomes the presiding master, the President of the Jungle-School, but as he is about to be eaten, he is made aware of the danger of ignoring his own warning about the tiger in this competitive jungle. This inner jungle life may link with his feeling of being unable to face school when he is successful.

Mrs E also talks about the fears of the little-John self who is frightened when the daddy is away and in whose mind a daddy can return as a wolf or tiger, and also about his frequent feelings of sickness. When John, as the strong tiger, pounces to become President of the Jungle, he does not want to know about matters he feels are irrelevant to his presidential ambition. These include the consequences of his own wolf-tiger competitiveness, wolfing and swallowing up or contemptuously disposing of – 'yawning away' – any ideas of competent, presiding Daddy or master, and leaving him with indigestible explosive internal hot air inside which makes him feel sick, and also empty of any internal protective fatherly presence against fear. The jungle of his mind may then be inhabited by a vengeful, predatory tiger-wolf-Daddy threatening to devour him and a displaced old-man-Daddy whom he has swallowed up, stuck and decaying in the undergrowth of his inside, like the old man who won't come out of hospital, and makes him feel ill.

Mrs E links these two aspects of a father in John's internal world with feelings about herself: in pointing out some of the implications of his masturbation she may represent a father trying to get his own back by stopping him from feeling that he is a Sir Jasper President; he may also be afraid that she will just investigate and diagnose him and then leave him to decay as a terminal case, as happened to the old man left in hospital. John responds to the discussion of the dream: 'You've got an uncanny knack of reading my mind or something. There you go again. I should have learnt by now, I'm fifteen years old.' Mrs E says that although he feels she may understand him, he also thinks she does so by pouncing into his mind, and that it may feel dangerous to be understood by a tiger-her.

THE SECOND AND THIRD TERMS

After a seasonal break John gets on the couch, exclaiming: 'Back to bed!' He sighs blissfully and expresses relief that Mrs E has not gone to Australia. He complains about her absence and his enforced loneliness during the break, but soon relates a fantasy of a patient with an 'Oedipus complex' who intrusively disturbs her and her husband by obscene telephone breathing. A little later, now speaking in a pitiful little-boy voice, he refers to childhood fears of his mother being a wolf dressed up when she sat by his bed. Mrs E points out that the lonely, frightened little-boy self is separated, split off, in his mind from 'a patient' him who obscenely disrupts her intercourse and breaks up her coupling when she leaves him for her husband. The child-him delights in her actual presence by his 'couch-side', but uses it to protect him from his fears about an image of her incorporating a vengeful wolfing Daddy rival by his bedside.

Mrs E is able to increase the sessions to two shortly after the break and John becomes more settled in the therapy, with some understanding of the pleasure with which the infant-him relates to it. A session begins: 'Thank God for this bed, couch, whatever you call it. Aah. I need a cool drink, two cool drinks.' Mrs E recognizes the feeling of need and relief emanating from his infant self for the two sessions to assuage his thirst and provide life-supporting comfort. John now responds: 'O God, I'm sick, I need a third session! Why do I always feel sick when I see girls? I'm a failure.' Mrs E wonders about the kind of failure. 'Failure to extract something else, a third session on demand!' Mrs E talks of the Jasper-baby who believes that he is a failure when his demanding tongue is not as powerful as an envied Daddy penis in getting what he wants, and he is in danger of throwing up what she gives him. John soon complains of seeing few patients in the clinic, although staff and secretaries go around with pots of tea and biscuits as if they were waiting on people. Mrs E suggests that he feels the clinic represents her Mummy body, felt to be full of unseen inner inhabitants, envied inside babies, who don't have to wait for sessions, but are fed and cosseted as he wants to be.

Sometime later Mrs E, to her double distress, is unfortunately called away from the clinic without notice just before John's session on account of a domestic crisis (fortunately not serious in the long run, but urgent at the time), and can only leave a message of apology for him. An unscheduled interruption is, of course, very disturbing to the work. John misses the next session, ringing up to say that he has a cold. He comes back for the following one with a sore, dry throat, which appears to have meaning for him as the dry mouth of the baby John when Mrs E was not there to feed him with his session.

John recounts bitterly how he felt his parents had betrayed him once when he was little by leaving him briefly with Grandmother, whom he could have killed. Mrs E suggests that this is what he feels she deserves for what he sees as her treacherous betrayal. John says he had once wanted to comfort a little girl who had an injection. 'Ha, ha! An injection, that's comfort! I don't believe it's a child in your domestic crisis!' (The receptionist may have indicated that this was the case, although Mrs E had not said so in the message she left for John.) He talks about what he calls a local French peasant ritual of pruning and manuring fruit trees to make them fertile. Mrs E says John appears to feel that she actually went to make a new baby with her husband in his time. He now speaks of the *au pair* who is about to come: he will have to hide in his room, because she will wear jackboots and suck his brain. Mrs E says he feels that this is the imagined revenge of the 'non-existent' child in her domestic crisis, the baby she is not to have, whose life is pruned away by a deadly injection and manuring – that is, by a now faecally manuring 'shitty' Daddy penis. She also comments that he may fear the presence at home of a 'not-born' sister. John now tells her his version of a joke from the then-current repeat of the 'Monty Python' television series: her domestic crisis becomes that of a fourteen-stone weight falling on her husband! His sadistic reaction to deprivation is apparent here, as it also was in relation to the previous break.

By the third term of therapy John believes that he is not a homosexual, but is scared of girls. Although he is still unable to approach them, he gives them longing looks and for the first time recounts a daydream about actually loving a girl, rather than about the sexual exploits of Sir Jasper. But it is girls who are felt to be imbued with a capacity for positive action (as are his mother and Mrs E in other contexts), and it is they who are meant to notice him and make the first move in the external world, as opposed to the Sir Jasper sexuality of omnipotent, infantile phantasy. A girl, however, can also be frightening: she can represent a vengeful, jackbooted little sister who is not allowed to be born, or a receptacle for unwanted parts of himself, such as his jealousy.

THE SECOND YEAR

I shall now summarize some of the work of the next year. Alongside the wish to relate to a girl, John's sadistic and domineering approach to Mrs E continues. He confuses what he marginally perceives as evidence of maternality and femininity in Mrs E with masochism, simply because she puts up with him. 'Did Hitler have psychoanalysis?' It might have helped him to be more powerful and deal with the opposition, he suggests. Mrs E points out that on this basis she should be a masochist, enjoy his sadism and work for Hitler too! He joins a group of boys at school to tell anal jokes at the expense of girls, whom he regards as a group of silly nymphomaniacs. His response to much of what Mrs E says in the sessions is also mocking. More than once he threatens domineeringly to come in the night and cut off each and every one of the leaves of the plants in her room: Mrs E speaks of the part of John that works for Hitler, who is determined to kill every single green shoot of life that she is felt to love: the good thoughts and babies that are felt to exist in the room of her mind during his absence are all to be liquidated.

John eventually refers to a film he saw about a Nazi concentration camp, and his deep sense of shock at seeing how some prisoners seemed to end up working for the guards as if they really liked them and would do anything for them, even willingly stoking up the ovens.[1] John also articulates fantasies of Jasper performing in the presence of an SS boss, as if seeking his admiration. John is now associated with a gang in the external world, possibly to a minimal extent only. In his inner world, however, there is a gang fuelled by powerful anal-sadistic, infantile sexuality. John is both a willing participator in, and a prisoner of, this sadistic concentration camp gang operating under the aegis of a destructive, Hitler-loving, SS 'Big Brother' part of himself, one from which he dare not seek freedom, but slavishly obeys (see above, Chapter 4, pp. 106–7). This part of himself perversely seeks to promulgate lies in the name of truth, to couple both Mrs E and the truth-seeking psychoanalytic thinking she loves with Hitler, and confound good with bad. It thus has much in common with what is conveyed in *Nineteen Eighty-Four* (Orwell, 1949). Here the lie is that 'Freedom is Slavery'. When this is raised by Mrs E, John acknowledges his conflict about working for this guard gang of his mind, and his cowardice in opposing them, the latter being linked with a fear of anal assault.

John is now in contact, and has some wish to contend with, his perverse state of mind. The raping sadism of Sir Jasper is clearly exposed. Such a state of mind is cruelly opposed to the recognition of any goodness emanating from Mrs E, and what are felt to be her desires for a good family – represented by, among other things, the green shoots in her room.

Immediately following on the delineation and recognition of his enslavement to the gang, and some wish for freedom from it, an aspect of John, which he calls 'Truly', emerges. Truly seems to represent the feminine aspect of his normal bisexuality, and to understand and identify with what Mrs E, now clearly seen in strong opposition to Hitler, is felt to want. This Truly part is at first experienced as existing separately from other parts of himself, and is reported by John as writing little notes reminding him not to be greedy, or to recognize the fact of separation. But John appears to fear reprisals by his sadistic mental gang if he is seen to be a Truly renegade, and there is also a pull to stay within the power of 'Big Brother' as a protection from having to confront these issues further.[2] The developmental impasse here is that Truly is not experienced as strong enough to take on the SS. For John to be able to challenge the gang, he would of necessity have to fight on behalf of his good objects, based in a loving, depressive position state of mind; cowardice is confronted not by narcissistic self-endearment, but by love of others.

An attempt to move forward developmentally and seek a loving relationship with a girl exposes John to envious internal assaults from the gang. Cowardice, combined with his problem of passivity and fear of failure, play into the impasse. The expectation is that his mother or Mrs E will take any necessary action on his behalf, and his problem in confronting his passivity is probably made more difficult in that there may be some degree of smothering by Mother which needs to be withstood. He now daydreams of the *au pair*, but avoids her company. It is his mother or Mrs E who is meant to demand that he takes the *au pair* to a dance, where he would apparently be welcomed by the other boys. These boys are clearly not in the same set in his mind as his anal internal gang, and there seems in fact to be some evidence of somewhat better relationships at school since he has become more in touch with the nature of his competition.

However, he tells Mrs E that she works only because her children no longer need her at home and she doesn't want to wash the dishes all day, with an implication that she is to enjoy the 'freedom' of being his houseworker-slave, although he also takes himself to task about such a view. He is also aware now that his occasional expression of thanks at the end of a session can be confused with expressions of dismissal. Truly tries to substantiate what has been received from therapy, and asserts that some degree of separation between what he wants and what he can have has to be recognized. There is some evidence that his major opposition is no longer to the actual birth of the baby girl whom the mother in his mind is felt to want, but rather to having to give up being the 'dog-in-the-manger' baby himself. His jealousy is now directed primarily to what he feels to be the mother's inside babies, her internal population that does not have to face separation (as exemplified earlier by the hidden clinic population being fed continuously with tea and biscuits). As the break approaches his growing appreciation of what he feels Mrs E has given him diminishes, and he sees her as prostituting herself with others during the holidays.

THE THIRD YEAR

John is now at the university of his choice. He has a number of friends, is making some attempt to mix with girls, and is looking forward to earning his own living in the future. On returning from the break, he is open to his pleasure in feeling 'poor little me', a lonely, sick little boy, and thus absolved from action. He is also aware of the dangers of his feelings of superiority. Sessions were previously seen as a way of life and a requirement to avoid any experience of loneliness. Now he talks about seeing them in terms of a drink (with the emphasis on quality rather than quantity) and a lamppost, and thus representing not only necessary ongoing refreshment but as something that can lead to the provision of internal illumination, succour and guidance.

Against considerable – but not total – resistance from John, it is accepted that the therapy will end after a further year. There is clearly much more work to be done in relation to John's recurrent recourse to sadism and tendency to passivity, but a part of himself is now actively joined in the struggle. Helped by the degree of internalization that has taken place, a co-operative adult aspect of John's personality can introjectively identify with internal objects, now felt to have some 'equipment' with which 'to modify infantile structure and curb infantile omnipotence' (Meltzer, 1967, p. 91).

Here is a thoughtfully presented weekend dream which occurred soon after the decision to end and about a month before the first holiday break in the third year. The perversity of the SS is clearly not defeated.

> It takes place in the students' café; boys and girls are eating. I am in there dressing, putting on my trousers. A boy is buggering another. One is bending down with a hole in his trousers; the other is leaning forward with approximately five inches of penis joining them. I think I musn't look at this flexible hose [the penis] joining them, but then think: 'Why not?' and the scene changes to karate. The instructor says, 'There's nothing wrong in that, it's good for karate, just go off and do it in pairs.' I feel I am about to have an ejaculation at any moment and try to change the picture to a girl, but can't quite make it.

John goes on to associate: 'I think I was too cowardly to finish the dream. I was upset because I had been reading about a psychological theory that you become homosexual by conditioning – that is, by a homosexual experience plus masturbation. I read it in a book, a bit before the chapters on Freud. I also had a fantasy of keeping a girl prisoner and inflating her breasts. Ever since I was small I always wanted to make things, but I don't. Perhaps you're verbally conditioning me. But I really can't argue. Now I feel I am speaking with a false voice.'

Discussion extends over several sessions. The setting suggests a view of the world where there is room for a number of boys and girls to eat and to learn together. For the baby John what seems to be unbearable is the removal of a feeding tube, the nipple, from his own mouth, and for this to be linked in his mind with the ejaculation of Daddy semen leading to the making of a new girl baby which will pair up with the breast-café. Despite some resistance, he joins in competitive boy pair fights in which babies are for the chop, 'buggered up'. The place of learning and feeding becomes a karate institution, linked with what goes on inside his trousers – that is, masturbation with perversity of intent. The karate instructor in charge functions on the lines of the earlier SS Big Brother figure, disseminating what is 'good' for the karate of the dream, and is linked with the 'gang' of his fingers in anal masturbation (Meltzer, 1973). The breasts have come to represent the source of what he receives from Mrs E in the sessions as well as what she can give to another patient, as a mother to a new baby. By holding them prisoner, the baby John not only conveys a 'dog-in-the-manger' attitude, but by blowing them up, inflating them (with his bubbly baby spit), conveys his competition with the idea of a daddy filling them up with love for a new baby. Mrs E now represents for him this mummy with the captive breasts, who in his mind may be filled up with spit instead of milk. He thus cannot feel at all sure about the status or intent of what she will say to him: whether she feeds or conditions him. A further consequence of what, for him, has become their joint unreliability is that he cannot estimate his own sincerity towards her.

John says that when he left at the weekend before the dream, he decided therapy was a load of rubbish, and he would do it himself. 'Oh, I can't talk to people,' he moans. Mrs E suggests that he may feel he has lost an internal version of a mother who helps him to talk. She reminds him how at the end of last session what was being addressed was the feeling of loneliness, the coming break and later ending, and also the idea of a new girl patient-baby for Mrs E. What he seems to be talking about is a feeling of being rubbished by her, together with his response that it is the therapy which talks both of ending and of a mother with a new baby that needs to be rubbished, and that he can do this himself! But there does seem to be some argument with this view in the dream. He is in conflict. The baby John wants to make things, like Daddy does, but perversely spoils his own creativity. Perhaps what he feels is 'queer' is his acquiescence in the conditioning by the gang to a form of 'homosexual' hate which does not let him understand his own 'Freudian' wishes to make things, to make babies, and by indulging his pleasure in 'chopping' the new baby, he doesn't let himself learn about love.

A feeling about being more hopeful about really growing up is now frequently conveyed, but not always sustained for long. John speaks of how he had hoped to be all right before finishing in the summer, but when his driving instructor told him he was to drive unaided for the next half hour, he went to pieces! 'I hate my parents going out on Saturday night and I hate you! I have these terrible daydreams, such as this one of shaving your head, cutting it off from your body, chopping it up, putting it on a spit thing and grilling and eating you; delicious!' An air of embarrassment and some concern, however, accompanies the bravado of the account. A friendly girl has suggested that he join others on a holiday trip, but he can't accept this contact from girls. Mrs E suggests that he cannot accept friendly advice from a mother-her that he should join others as a step forward in his own life, and also allow her a Saturday night contact with her husband. Instead, the baby-him cruelly chops off and cannibalizes her head, the head-breast part of her that feeds him with her thoughts, leaving her husband with the dead body, but also feels that this is terrible.

John says he has read an article which, he fears, could be true. In it the author meets a girl, and in the course of having intercourse she bites his penis and leaves him crippled for life, with the result that the article has to be written from hospital! Mrs E talks of his fear of vengeful talion punishment, in this case a penis for a breast-head, and that the part of her that he has grilled, tortured, bitten up and cannibalized in revenge for going out with her husband at the weekend bites back castratingly at him from inside, and leaves him fearing that contact with girls may be on this model.

He complains about his father making him take an umbrella, although he knew from the radio it was going to be sunny. Mrs E suggests that John feels that his contacts with hopefulness and pleasure are spoilt. She recognizes that he feels that his parents are fussy, but tries to show him that whatever the nature of his external parents may or may not be, there is an internal situation which influences him. She refers back to his hatred of being left alone on

Saturday nights when it seems that in his mind a potentially sunny parental intercourse between his parents, or between her and her husband, may be rained on – perhaps urinated on by the baby John; or an umbrella diaphragm cap may be mentally inserted to stop the fertilization of the next baby. It is the version of internal parents in his mind in consequence of these activities that spoils his unencumbered enjoyment of the sunshine of life, makes him go to pieces and cuts up his aspirations.

John sighs, and associates to a 'Monty Python' sketch with a baby with a huge teat. One woman says, 'Oh, take the teat out', the other woman says, 'Oh no, you'd better leave it in'. They took it out; it was like taking out a plug, and the baby swallowed up everything in the room, all the furniture and the people. John says that he thinks he will never, never grow up. Mrs E recognizes the clear current distinction between John's infantile and adult feelings, and refers back to the old dispute as to whether it was his or her job to monitor his mouth and the greed of what had at one time been called the wolf-baby.

One can see from this material how important it was to allow plenty of time between planning a date for an ending with John and the ending itself, in order to relate to his resentment.

The last week before the break shows evidence of increased depressive concern. John recounts that while his parents were having a party on Saturday evening, he went to see a commune to think about whether he might want to live there. He was amazed that instead of just getting involved with the couple, whom he called 'the parents', who ran it, he felt both concern for the troubles of some of the inhabitants, and in touch with the wish to help others conveyed by a woman worker there, whom he associated with Mrs E. He thought he must be getting all Freudian or something! He is aware that what he now calls 'big-boy' him had to be taken out on Saturday night by a more adult self because 'big-boy' him kept sabotaging things his parents wanted to do. Mrs E recognizes with him that she and her husband are thus implicitly allowed to get on with their own intercourse on Saturday night, and Mrs E's wish to help others apart from himself is acknowledged.

What John calls two 'weird dreams' follow:

The first dream: It takes place at the karate club where I was sparring with a girl. She was still wearing her karate suit but had to put on two transparent 'cup' things, such as people have when fencing. These cups went over the nipples only, and were screwed on, followed by black things screwed on top, leaving just a little transparency.

The second dream: There is a circle, around which there are ten or twelve figures. A little girl is born into the middle. Something hard is done to the girl, but not too hard.

The baby John sparring with Mrs E for possession of the breast is 'foiled'. The cup of weaning is there, and the black cap of the 'death of the breast' (Meltzer, 1967) is being screwed on for him as an active experience, although the breast remains light and illuminating, and is shielded for the new baby. John has to take his place along with Mrs E's other patients, perhaps ten or twelve in number, who have to accept the birth of the new 'baby sister' patient and of the breast coming alive again for her. But the little girl must accept some expression of the accompanying jealousy and hard feelings. John associates to a daydream of masturbating with his penis against the breast and obtaining an erection, but it was no good. There is thus also a call for recognition that in internal reality only Daddy can screw life into the breast for the next baby, the new little sister.

The term finishes with John's expression of enjoyment of a particular course. A girl has asked for his help, and he feels that he must give up being 'poor little me' or the unapproachable intellectual 'wonder kid'. On reflection he feels that he went to the commune not just to see how he felt, but to try to see how he looked in the eyes of others. It was very frightening to say, but it didn't seem that he looked too bad. He feels that he will just have to struggle. But how is it, he asks, that after driving badly and doing karate badly, both teachers say he has improved? Mrs E says that he may feel that he is painting a weirdly opposite picture to the one he often presents, and he needs her to understand how doubtful about it he is. She helps him to see how, in the instances he now quotes, his driving force and karate fighting (in contrast with the first karate dream) seem to be linked with some concern for the wishes of parents in his mind. He now has some guiding light from internal parents who are allowed to 'do their own thing' of making a baby girl, while he does his, which seems here to be about trying to drive along the road of his own life and grow up.

John's contradictory emotions are more accessible to himself. In the external world he passes his driving test (for an automatic car) and gets the karate belt he wants. He thinks of setting up flat with a girl to whom he feels close, but can't make it, and she leaves, saying he is not loving enough. He feels remorseful for his tantalization of her and considers that he has been behaving like the SS.

His relations with his parents improve. In contrast to his usual complaints about his father's ineptitude or absurd bossiness, he expresses appreciation of his help, as on an occasion when he drove wildly and crashed a light and his father told him to reverse, which he did. It had never occurred to him, he said, that he could put the brakes on. His father appears to have acquired some authority. He is pleased for his mother's sake that she is working more. He complains about his pleasure in hurting, and regrets upsetting her. He is sympathetic to his father, saying that he wished his parents had had more children and appreciates sacrifices he has now learnt they made for him in infancy. He can't understand how his parents' friends at home can treat him as if he were grown-up. It seems that by means of the internalization of work done in the transference, especially in relation to his infantile demands and negative feelings, his internal parents become better endowed, leading in turn to a more positive perception of his external parents and to the expression of some kindness towards both their needs and their perceived defects.

His internal situation remains volatile. He tells Mrs E he should stand on his own two feet and then, dismayed to hear what he is saying, complains that he is being turned out from therapy too soon, and that he will be able to survive only for a week. 'Well, if you don't make something of me, we are wasting each other's time!' Time, it seems, is no longer to be wasted, but the argument remains as to whose responsibility development is. A little later he asserts that if Mrs E persists in this weaning, he will smash up her office and take her stuff away! Mr E is also vanquished in a fantasy karate fight. Shortly afterwards he blames himself for being such a leach. He becomes grumpy for a time and complains about the sessions, which 'used to be everything'; it seems here that he himself now blackens the nipple and briefly attempts self-weaning to shield himself from the beauty of the breast that is gradually dying for him as an external object.

But he also worries that Mrs E is ending, not because he is ready, but because she is dying of breast cancer, which Mrs E relates to the feared effects of his greed. This links with recurrent anxieties about Truly's ability to stand up to an SS officer, and that his karate belt is just a toddler's badge in this respect. Mrs E suggests that it may be difficult for him to allow her to represent a mother who can also be supported by a non-Hitler husband. John puts Truly on trial for not being good enough, and the SS on trial for their harshness. 'I've been so stupid!' he exclaims. 'But how can the SS and Truly be integrated – its impossible!' The difficult drive for integration is apparent.

His dreams have had an increasingly reflective quality, and the unconscious thinking in them is apparent. John, partly in preparation for his future self-analysis, now sometimes talks about them in the past tense, conveying how he himself is trying to think about them, as opposed to being part of the action. Here is one from the middle of the penultimate term:

> The place was a jungle but also a learning place, my university. People were jumping into this lift thing, which wasn't a proper lift, but open, more like a room being lifted up and down. There was this black girl, pretty, but with a short white dress. At the top, which was also our house, a girl looked in, a white girl in long black trousers, and then a boy jumped in, and she followed, they were going down. The black girl cuddled up to me, which I liked but I also didn't like. The boy was saying something about integration, to do with an integer under a curve. I couldn't understand and queried it. Oh, it's second-year work, he said. The lift then changed into a proper lift and we were in the basement, and I had to get out. There were figures on the floor and there was a big fire.

This dream helps us to understand something about John's current response to ending therapy. In association to it, he tells Mrs E how he had to wait for a lift back from the club on the Saturday night before the dream, so he went to a party with a group of people, mostly couples, where he was one of the odd guys. He recounts how he gazed pathetically at the waitresses as if to say: 'I'm not with them, I'm a baby, smile at me, pick me up, have pity on me!' One response to the demand for integration is thus of the 'poor little me', the baby who claims that he should neither be weaned nor left to witness couples until his wedding day, and pleads to be the ongoing baby at the breast, lifted up by Mrs E's waitress arms.

In the dream, links are indicated between the internal world, his own home, and the clinic world of Mrs E. The composite setting of jungle and university implies a need for learning and integration. John uses the clinic lift to go up to see Mrs E and goes out downstairs past the Records Department, and the limited occupancy of this lift-room, his time for being lifted up and carried by a Mrs E mummy, is already acknowledged in the dream, showing greater integration in his dreamlife than in the preceding external situation. In internal reality the nipple has acquired a black cap, as in the earlier dream, and now the pretty white dress-breast is getting shorter for him. Although time is running out, and the death sentence on the external breast has been pronounced, the breast remains cuddly, to which he is ambivalent: it is nice, but difficult, to be friendly with Mrs E when the ending is in sight. An aspect of the breast (the white girl with the long black trousers) also seems to be going down following the boy and becoming one of a couple, followed by the presence of a whole new 'integer' baby under the curve of Mummy's tummy-house. He is asked in thinking of the dream to integrate the idea of a lift-room with no ongoing place for him with one that contains a couple and an embryonic baby.

When John becomes a second-year university student he will just have finished therapy, and the resentment about being left to do second-year work on his own outside the clinic becomes unbearable. When he has to go down by the lift and out via the basement/ground floor for the last time, the fire appears to be stoked by the burning resentment of his SS self. It is clear from the recent material, however, as well as the material of the session itself, that the problem is not now one of having had nothing or being rubbished by Mrs E; a diminishing breast-Mrs E remains friendly and available for internal integration. It is rather one of relinquishment, with a couple in occupation and a new baby to come.

DISCUSSION

We can now reflect on some of John's difficulties as seen in therapy. A baby John has made ongoing demands, verging on parasitism, for possession and control of the breast. In such circumstances an image of a free, loving breast or mother cannot be internalized, and he passively remains 'poor little me', without the inner resources to grow up and find a girl of his own. He is also scared of girls; they could be vengeful unborn sisters he has kept from the breast, or they could simply leave him feeling a poor little failure. He has also entered into projective identification with the daddy or penis, in the form of the – often sadistic – Jasper superman-boy, with consequent confusion as to identity, the superman-boy being confused with the daddy or penis. The development of depressive anxieties has been restricted.

John's 'queerness' and questioned homosexuality can be thought about in various ways. His very early reference to wanting to be stroked with his head in another boy's lap has not reappeared, and may have its basis in a normal 'homosexual' turning to the penis in the femininity phase of infancy and love for the parent of the same sex within the Oedipus complex (discussed in Chapter 4), reinvoked in puberty with the re-emergence of overt sexual drives. A normal single-sex quasi-gang, quasi-group of pubertal life may be expected to encompass some expression of physical sensuality among the confusions of pubertal sexuality. Such a group in John's school environment would also probably include the boys by whom John would like to be liked if he took a girl to a dance. But John's extreme rivalry seems to leave him friendless and initially outside such a group. He has thus missed out on some of the normal pleasures of adolescent life which might also have provided some containment for his splits and projections. The strength of John's earlier fear of the group was not based simply on external rivalry among schoolfellows, but on the underlying fear of those whom he has omnipotently surpassed, triumphed over and dealt with by tooth and claw in the tigerlike presidential drive of the jungle of his inner world. His possibly brief membership of an external gang helps contact to be made with his membership of an internal pubertal gang informed by anti-life perversity, as shown in the Hitler material and the dream of the 'buggering up' of the new baby. This is accompanied by a related anxiety of being attacked anally, as punishment for seeking to leave this gang. Much of John's emotionality in these groupings has to do with possessive jealousy, hate and fear, not love.

Changes are clearly taking place. John does have better contact with boys, with a suggestion of better inner relationships. There is also evidence of introjective identification with a 'good-enough' father, accompanied by a lessening of projective identification, so that little more is heard of Jasper, who may reappear in a less virulent, more openly infantile form as 'big boy'. John is becoming more manly in aspiration and braver in facing his anxieties about girls. This links with the emergence of a Truly part of himself, a representative of his bisexuality, in introjective identification with Mrs E and what are felt to be her maternal aspirations. There is also evidence of recognition of parents whose coupling needs to be protected.

THE FINAL TERM

John now lives in a hall of residence and tries to make friends there. He struggles with the ending. He says it would be easier to say Mrs E has given him nothing than say what he really thinks; if she would just spout Freudian theory and not do him any good, he could just complain instead of having to feel grateful. He clearly perceives her to be unique, and senses that she also recognizes his uniqueness, and finds this hard to bear. He is aware that he has introjected goodness, but, as he says himself, he wants the breast all the time. The problem of possessive jealousy rather than envy interferes with his gratitude (Klein, 1957) and the problem of relinquishment remains.

Here are two dreams from the middle of this final term:

The first dream: It is a place like a university. There are flats. Father is there. We have an *au pair*, not beautiful, quite small, but intelligent and a good worker and able to learn. I tried to get her to latch on to me as 'poor little me' and then cut her, but she wouldn't accept it. She went out with a lot of young people and made friends. There were lots of flat carts, such as they have at market stalls, with roofs on, and some were empty. The girl did not seem to want to be especially friendly to me. But there were two fat black girls, side by side, pretty, and they were quite friendly to me and talked.

The need to relinquish is being worked on. The breasts are getting flatter for him, and perhaps bearing his sadness, which he would like Mrs E to do for him. The empty carts, the final sessions, are on the way. The new *au pair* seems to represent his little-girl bisexuality, with which he is now able to get more closely in touch, probably because he is able to relate more positively to the mother's (represented by Mrs E) wish for a new girl baby. A now strengthened Truly-girl part of him seems able to enjoy a healthy social life and does not go along with any tantalizing sadomasochism in relating to his pain of ending, nor does she get into collusion with his little-boy self into forming a little couple to avoid the pain. Father is there in the background, felt to be a presence behind both the weaning and also the fattening up of the breasts, represented by the two fat black girls, with their black caps on for him, but plump for the new baby. Despite the weaning, the breasts remain friendly to him. This gives some hope of maintaining an internal relationship with Mrs E after the ending.

> *The second dream*: It is at the university and in the jungle. There are two girls, a bloke and me. The bloke has a lion on the lead; he is frightened it is going to munch us all up. It is grazing. I go out of the room to a counter like they have in the hall of residence and demand a rifle because I am a Vice-Admiral, although I do realize that at seventeen that's a bit doubtful. A girl gives me some kind of stamps [associated with an idea of environmental protection], and I go on to another girl, who asks for my international driving licence (which I could get for the Volkswagen this summer, though it's not really any good if there's trouble because I haven't passed the non-automatic test). I try to pull my rank: it's ridiculous not to give the rifle to a Vice-Admiral, etc., etc., but to no avail.

The lion-baby John is now on the lead. The university predominates over the jungle, and there is a fatherly super-ego man who is not going to let him munch up others, or himself. The lion, which can now graze, contrasts with the tiger in the first jungle dream, and the present fatherly man also contrasts with the earlier vengeful or decaying fathers. The inhabitants of John's inner world have clearly changed. Both the breasts (the two girls) and the intercourse (the Volkswagen, especially in the summer) are protected environments which are not to have unlicensed intrusion; they are not to be rifled. The baby John puts up his counter-claim, acknowledged as dubious – that of indulgence for his 'admirable vice' (the Vice-Admiral, and a would-be successor to the earlier President of the Jungle). An adult part of John is also apparent; he sees through the fraudulent claims of the baby who is kicking against the strength of the inner objects he now possesses, and is aware that this baby will need to have his jungle vice internally supervised in the summer.

The session ends with an account by John about a delinquent child who had refused to have fewer than five sessions of therapy and wouldn't stop, implying that that aspect of himself is on the lead. He has also seen a little girl who might be Mrs E's patient. Of course he wanted to bash her up, but she did seem quite nice.

He expresses concern about the strength of his loving feelings for Mrs E, and of his Truly self. In another session John recounts how tears came into his eyes when contact lenses were fitted at the oculist's, but he clearly conveys that he is in contact with his sadness about the ending. He reports a dream in which Mrs E tells him to go to the director's office and finish fitting together the difficult jigsaw which she has given him. Thus he now has an internal mother who expects him to finish 'putting himself together' with the equipment he has received from her, under the aegis of the director-father, bearing the pain this may cause him: no splitting of the parents is allowed, and there is a call for introjective identification with this inner couple. In the external world he passes a second driving test, this time for a non-automatic car. 'There seems to be no way out,' says John, with a mixture of relief and sadness. 'It's up to me, all my life, it's like riding a tiger, and how do I know I won't make a mess of it?'

John is to ride the tiger, not to *be* it, but there is no guarantee of success. He can only try to do his best.

Mrs E, according to her usual practice, saw John for review sessions once a term over a period of time. He continued to do well in his studies and, with a considerable struggle, advanced in his social and sexual life, and in what might be called 'suffering love'.

7 EXPERIENCES IN A COUNSELLING SERVICE FOR YOUNG PEOPLE: AN EIGHTEEN-YEAR-OLD SAYS HELLO AND GOODBYE

We now turn from long-term work to think about one way in which a psychoanalytic approach can be used in individual brief work with young people. I follow an intervention with one particular client in some detail, and use this as the basis for a discussion of the method followed. I then reflect upon the usefulness of this approach, and consider its further application.

The work takes place within a service which offers brief counselling or consultation to young people from the age of sixteen up to the late twenties. It is thus available to young adults who may still be involved in the processes or aftermath of adolescence. The setting within which any service operates is likely to affect the way it is perceived by its clients, and may influence what is provided. This service functions as a separate unit within a clinic providing more intensive therapeutic services, most of which require a formal referral. The staff of the service are themselves primarily engaged in long-term psychoanalytic psychotherapy with children, adolescents or adults elsewhere in the clinic, but are concerned here to develop ways in which they can usefully share their understanding with a wider population who may not be candidates for psychotherapy. The service operates on an informal self-referral basis; the client makes arrangements with the secretary for an appointment, which can usually be provided fairly speedily. Up to four appointments are normally offered. If long-term therapy appears to be an appropriate outcome of the work, it can be sought either within the clinic, on the same basis as other referrals, or elsewhere.

LUCY'S FIRST SESSION

Lucy, aged eighteen, comes into Mrs D's office. She has quite a childish-looking face, with no make-up, and wears jeans. In accordance with the policy of the service, a client is not asked by the secretary why he or she wishes to come. Lucy tells Mrs D that she is in the midst of taking A levels, and has felt upset since being told things about herself with which she disagrees. She explains that, 'just for fun', she had taken up an offer of a free personality test by a certain organization, and was very upset at the outcome. She describes the test itself as containing questions which were quite straightforward, such as whether she enjoyed parties – which she does, and said so; however, 'the woman' who gave her the test made her feel awful and said that she needed their course on communication. Mrs D senses that Lucy is looking at her a bit defiantly, even though her voice trails away a little: 'she didn't know what . . . someone said come here'. Mrs D comments that Lucy feels she has had some kind of need put into her, and is distressed by it. On discovering from Lucy what the organization in question is, and aware that it is viewed by some people as seeking to find converts to a particular way of thinking, Mrs D recognizes this with Lucy as an aspect of external reality which may be relevant to her feelings. She goes on to comment that there may now also be some sort of question in Lucy's mind about what Mrs D's 'organization' offers or might suggest, and what sort of woman she herself might turn out to be.

Lucy bursts out forcefully that she hates therapy – she'd had some when she was ten, she didn't really know what it was, or why she went, she had just played chess with a man, it was at the time of the break-up of her parents' marriage, she didn't know what . . . Her voice fades and she starts to cry, but then firmly puts her handkerchief away. Mrs D comments that while Lucy seems to want help, and is trying to get it, she does seem to be afraid that Mrs D, rather than responding to her in a straightforward manner, may try to stimulate some need she doesn't feel, or try to involve her in what she regards as incomprehensible and disturbing therapy, which she associates with a clearly unhappy time in her life. Mrs D goes on to explore with Lucy how she had come to the service and whether whoever had suggested it had any particular outcome in mind. No, she had come at the suggestion of a friend's mother who had just mentioned the counselling service, not knowing exactly what it involved. Mrs D recognizes with Lucy that she seems to be aware that more formal therapy also takes place in the building, and goes on to differentiate and clarify the nature of the counselling contact she is offering. She adds that they can talk about whether Lucy wants to come again at the end of this session. Only if they should both eventually think that something further would be a good idea would Mrs D, with Lucy's agreement, try to see how this might be arranged.

After this clarification of the framework in which the work is held, Mrs D wonders if Lucy has any further thoughts about what might be troubling her, or what she might want to think about in relation to herself. Lucy talks freely, ranging from one thing to another. She has an obsession with her weight; she wouldn't mind losing a few pounds, although they both agree that she seems reasonably slim. Lucy says she normally eats fairly sensibly, but sometimes stuffs herself. She can't say what brings it on, but mentions that she doesn't feel she's doing very well in her A levels. Despite Mrs D's attempts to explore this, it is not possible to get further than simply hearing about Lucy's subjects and interests. Lucy goes on to say that she is glad to be leaving and going to Australia in the summer, and that she doesn't have all that many friends here. In response to an enquiry from Mrs D, she explains that both her parents remarried after their divorce, and she will be spending a year with her father in Australia. She speaks positively of her relationship with her mother and her own two sisters, and also with her mother's new family of younger children, but she does acknowledge some difficulties. She has applied to take a catering course in the UK on her return, with an apparent implication that her absence will be less emotionally important because it will be for only a year.

In this conversation Mrs D feels aware of a sense of loss which is not in accord with what Lucy is saying, and, using this countertransference reponse as a potential carrier of meaning, attempts to understand more about Lucy's feelings about those she will leave behind. Lucy talks in a matter-of-fact manner about a recent break with a boyfriend, saying first of all that she had broken with him, and then, on discussion, that the break could be said to have happened the other way round, as her boyfriend had also dated another girl. Her unwillingness to see him, even if he was not necessarily going out with the other girl, finally led to her abandonment of their shared group of friends. Mrs D, although she is also aware of the presence of some hurt pride and jealousy in Lucy, still feels a sense of loss as she listens. She attempts to explore the strength and variety of feelings underlying leaving the group, but Lucy pushes this aside as being relevant only to the past, and of minimal importance. Mrs D comments on the number of breaks and changes, in both the past and the future, that have been mentioned, including the break-up of Lucy's parents' marriage, and the clearly painful feelings it evoked in Lucy. Lucy responds by acknowledging some anxiety about next year, mentioning that Father is a successful, rich hotel owner, but that he has been divorced and remarried several times.

As the predetermined time of the end of the session is approaching, Mrs D reviews briefly with Lucy what they have talked about as a preamble to a decision by Lucy about coming again. In the course of this Lucy acknowledges, albeit without much emotion, how she has cut herself off from her group of friends, and also refers in a very detached way to her future absence from her mother. Mrs D talks about Lucy's departure for Australia, due to take place very soon, and suggests that Lucy may be trying to cut herself off from and lose some of the 'weight' of her feelings about leaving her home and having broken with her friends before she goes. Lucy now emphasizes her 'stuffing', which is currently worse and sometimes makes her feel sick. She contrasts happy, excited feelings when she is with the group, and adds that she does not have good relations with herself, in that she watches herself talking to Mrs D and wonders what Mrs D will think. Mrs D says that it sounds as if Lucy may be indicating that she feels driven to stuff by a feeling of inner emptiness, and that this may have something to do with 'cutting off' from friends and family, who now may not feel very friendly, and also with not feeling friendly herself; she also seems to be afraid that Mrs D might become unfriendly. It is apparent to both that the exploration is by no means complete, and Lucy seems pleased to come in a week's time.

This initial interview reveals that Lucy's feelings of disturbance were felt to be stirred up by persecutory action outside herself: namely, the comments by 'the woman' in 'the organization' about requiring their course on communication. As the interview progresses, Lucy, with Mrs D's help, is able to relate more closely to her own feelings of disturbance, with some indication that she may have difficulties in holding on to communications within herself. Mrs D, however, is left feeling very aware of holding pain relating to Lucy's break-up with her boyfriend and leaving the group, and that she has not yet been able to explore Lucy's underlying jealousy, persecution and sadness with her.

LUCY'S SECOND SESSION

Lucy, a few minutes late, comes jauntily into Mrs D's office with a cheerful 'hello', and a new hairstyle. She talks in a rush about having had her hair permed, having stopped slimming, how she had wanted to have something to tell Mrs D, and then, slowing down somewhat, announces that she is feeling better, and that Mrs D carries hope for her. Mrs D recognizes the change, and remarks that Lucy sees having stopped slimming as progress. Lucy says she agrees with an earlier comment of Mrs D's that slimming and stuffing felt like extreme opposites for her, but adds that she might regret not losing a few pounds more in order to have a new image of herself in Australia. Mrs D wonders about some kind of 'mental slimming' being involved in obtaining this new image, and what is to happen to the old one. Lucy talks excitedly about meeting new people. Mrs D refers back to last week's discussion about 'cutting off', and wonders if there is more to be understood about what Lucy wants to carry with her in her mind, or cut off and leave behind. She points out that she, a new person for Lucy, is felt to be becoming important as a carrier of hope. She mentions the briefness of their contact in the counselling service, and how it 'hopes' to help by gathering feelings together, and says that they may need to think about whether Lucy will be able to take this hopefulness with her. Lucy accepts this as making sense.

Lucy says she thinks she has done badly in some of her A levels. She knew *King Lear* quite well, but a question she found particularly difficult was something on the lines of: '*King Lear* is not just a play about relationships between parents and children'. She was puzzled because she saw others writing about something she felt she knew about, but couldn't answer well. (We can see here that Lucy is now more able to be in touch with her feelings about the examination than she was in the first session, seemingly after some containment and understanding of what she brings.) Mrs D says it sounds as if Lucy is describing having felt cut off from her own feelings at that time. She talks about Lucy's year in Australia, clarifies first of all that Lucy's own sisters are firmly settled in England, and acknowledges that Lucy has described her mother as having remarried happily here. She goes on to explore with Lucy whether, despite this, *King Lear* may raise questions for her about relationships between parents and children: Cordelia being asked to justify her special relationship with her father over that of her sisters, together with the absence of a Queen Lear in the play, may have some troubling inner meaning for her as she prepares to leave her mother and sisters and go to live with her father. Lucy seems to be about to cry, but asserts that she is determined not to, and that she doesn't want to look for sympathy. Mrs D, who has also been thinking about the possible presence of envy and jealousy between the sisters, feels increasingly sad herself at this time, and comments that Lucy might find it difficult to differentiate feelings of sadness from looking for sympathy.

Lucy now says, in fairly sombre tones, that there were not many people to say goodbye to here, and that she would like a great reception committee when she goes to Australia, but she had hoped for this last time she went, and didn't get it. There were also difficulties about her 'stuff'. 'Her stuff?' asks Mrs D. Lucy talks, now again moist-eyed, about having nowhere to leave her childhood possessions; on a previous brief visit she had deposited a box with a treasured collection of dolls and ornaments on her father's porch, and someone had turned it upside down and rifled it. Lucy asserts that it would be difficult to store these things at home, without being able to give any clear indication as to why this might be so, although she thinks there could be enough physical space. Mrs D recognizes the painful external reality of having divorced parents at either end of the globe, and suggests that Lucy feels that some of the treasures of her childhood may be at risk if she does not hold on to them herself. Mrs D tries to explore this further with Lucy, in the context of what is evoked both by the difficulties with *King Lear* and by the bearing of jealousy when she left the group. She discusses how hard Lucy finds it to leave the 'stuff' of childhood behind and store its treasures in her mind, inside her, where they perhaps also feel in danger of being 'rifled' – either by fears of not getting the reception she wants from her father in Australia, or, if she does, by sisters jealous of her becoming a well-received 'Cordelia' daughter with him. There is also the problem of her own feeling of jealousy and resentment in the context of there being younger children forming part of a complete, non-divorced family at home, which may lead to her feeling less treasured and also left out. Well, everyone feels like that, rejoins Lucy, adding something about the sadness of having been a great little kid, and having a feeling of being 'dropped out of your skin'. Mrs D says it sounds as if Lucy can feel 'dropped out' of feeling properly 'herself' when she is no longer a child in the 'skin' of a complete family.

Mrs D refers to Lucy's remark about there not being many people to say goodbye to here, and how she may want to cut herself off from the unpalatable feeling of the lack of a great goodbye committee from the group or from her ex-boyfriend, as well as from a feeling of underlying jealousy and envy of their continuing relationships. Instead it seems that she would like to replace such feelings by a new Australian image of herself, full of hope, meeting new people, and with no worry that she might feel in danger of being unhappy. Lucy acknowledges how low she felt on leaving all the group, and especially so before the plans about Australia were made. She describes how she had enjoyed the 'high', excited times with them (not due to drugs, Mrs D clarifies), although she had not been entirely comfortable with them, as she was more serious about education than the others.

Lucy now says that she does not know her father very well, having seen him only on quite brief visits in recent years. She says that he had hit her sisters and herself as children, although he was a good correspondent and a great financial success, as if this last point provided some antidote to her experiences and anxiety about the time ahead. On discussion she adds that he did, however, say nasty things about her mother. With some difficulty she recounts several scenes of violence at the time of the break-up of the marriage, stressing an occasion on which her mother showed signs of having been physically hurt, but maintained that she was all right, contrary to the evidence as Lucy saw it. Lucy contrasts these experiences with her early childhood, when they had all lived together in a luxurious annexe to the hotel where father worked at the time, and then of the exciting times, expensive dinners, and so on that she would have in Australia with her father. Mrs D now experiences herself as feeling very left out. She talks to Lucy about the picture she describes being like a story of a very special Princess being fêted by a king-like father, but in the background there seem to be painful shadows of a hurt mother and perhaps resentful sisters. She makes it clear that she sees this 'story' being told by a child aspect of Lucy, and the mother in it refers to an inner picture in her mind, and is thus differentiated from her own mother, now said to be happily remarried. Lucy concurs.

Mrs D attempts to put Lucy in touch with some of her emotionality from which she seeks to escape. She continues to try to help Lucy to think about and make links between different aspects of her feelings and her life, and uses the response that Lucy's communications evoke in her to further the work.

LUCY'S THIRD SESSION

Lucy buoyantly enters Mrs D's room at the appointed time. She tells Mrs D breathlessly that she can stay for only half an hour because she has promised to meet a friend for lunch; this friend, Lola, is in a mess and very depressed, and Lucy wants to cheer her up. She herself is feeling quite different – much better. Mrs D is aware that Lucy has come straight to her room, bypassing reception, and feels somewhat invaded, as well as being concerned about the proposed brevity of the session. She acknowledges that Lucy is sorry for her friend, but suggests that it may be easier for Lucy to look after the 'mess' and 'depression' in Lola, and feel that she, Lucy, is carrying hope for her, than to examine the nature of Lucy's own feelings of coming and going which are relevant to her departure for Australia, and also to saying goodbye to Mrs D. She suggests that Lucy's mode of entry to this session makes access seem very easy, with no thought of anything standing between them, such as a gap between sessions or an ending. By planning to leave early, Lucy seems to be making Mrs D the one to experience the shortness of time, and perhaps feel dropped.

Lucy responds quickly that she would rather leave feeling that she had more to say than feel that she had to fill out the time. Mrs D talks of Lucy's fear of encountering a space of time in which a feeling akin to emptiness extending into the future could be experienced, and feels that this might happen here. Lucy sits back, and says: 'OK, I'll tell you all about it', 'admitting' that the time has gone very quickly, and that she had thought about not coming to this session at all. She feels so much better now, so different from the time after the exam, when she felt she had not done too well. She has also now heard that she can take part in the entertainment programme in her father's hotel in Australia. She is moving her feet as she speaks and almost pulling her bangles off her arm (which she has not done before), and Mrs D comments on how Lucy now can't wait to dance off and undo the ties here. Lucy laughingly assents. Mrs D comments on the change from last week and suggests that Lucy now wishes to leave any anxieties about her future in Australia behind, and also does not want Mrs D to 'stuff' any awareness of empty time or space here into her.

Lucy now speaks more solemnly: she thinks she will be OK with her father's new wife; she must spend time preparing for the interviews next week for the catering course in England in a year's time, but finds it difficult not to stay with her feelings of excitement. Mrs D links this with Lucy's idea of a new Australian image, which they discussed last week, recalls the 'high' feelings experienced in the group, and wonders if an aftermath of feeling low or empty could recur, on the lines of the slimming and stuffing. Lucy says she thinks that it could. She admits that she feels over elated, finds it difficult to sleep and is all 'go'; she had to apologize to the depressed Lola for her bounciness. Mrs D talks about Lucy's apparent belief that at the moment she has more than her fair share of bounciness and feeling 'high', and that Lola has less, and that she is sorry about this. (Lucy nods assent.) Perhaps Lucy is anxious that some of her 'depressed' feelings are now located in Lola, and maybe in Mrs D herself, and feels that she needs to 'come down to earth', but that this could be painful. Lucy quickly reiterates that it is important to have plenty left to say at the end and not feel finished. Mrs D takes up Lucy's dread of an ending in which she could feel 'dropped', 'finished' and empty, like a kind of dead-end perhaps, and that this is the feeling she wants to avoid. Lucy may fear that Mrs D would give her some kind of empty time, already full of a feeling of having finished.

Mrs D goes on to think about Lucy's feelings concerning others left behind, such as her mother and her ex-boyfriend. Lucy talks a bit about the support her mother has given her, and says that she has done quite a lot of thinking between sessions; maybe she was a bit hard on her ex-boyfriend, taking pleasure in leaving him behind. She had even thought of sending letters which she really treasured back to him. She also had the fantasy of returning to the pub where the group met, having become a great 'success story', following on what would be her achievements in the hotel entertainment in Australia. Mrs D speaks of Lucy's imagined pleasure in getting her own back, and making someone else suffer and maybe feel something of a failure in contrast to her success.

By this time it is well past the half hour that Lucy had planned to stay, and Lucy says she is now sorry that she had made it such a short session. She talks again about how she has tried to cheer Lola up by encouraging her to make a cake with her. Mrs D says that she thinks that Lucy is aware of feelings, both of sadness and of being dropped, threatening to accompany her goodbyes. It seems that she is afraid of experiencing such emotions, and tries to mix them into the feelings of others, such as Lola. But she then seems to feel that in wanting to go off happily she is keeping too much 'bounce' for herself, and this doesn't feel comfortable either – there has to be some mixing of the ingredients of feeling depressed and feeling elated, as in mixing a cake. Lucy, with a struggle, seems to try to think about this a little in the context of what they have talked about so far in the session.

As Lucy does not yet know all the times of her interviews, they agree on a provisional time for their last meeting; Mrs D comments how difficult it may be for Lucy to come actually to say goodbye and risk the experience of 'finishing'. Lucy says she would like to see Mrs D on her return; maybe she will be a 'success star' by then. Mrs D points out that it is she who is being designated as the privileged one in these circumstances! Lucy adds that she would also like to see her ex-boyfriend. With some shyness she asks what Mrs D would feel if she *had* to see her again. Mrs D talks about the different ways in which Lucy feels she can deposit or evoke painful feelings such as depression, sadness, failure or envy of success in others which, she fears, could result in making her feel unwelcome on her return. Maybe Mrs D is to feel envious and resentful of Lucy's predicted success, as in the fantasied response of the pub group, as well as perhaps feeling intruded into and made into a compulsory 'reception committee' for her return. Lucy agrees, and also seems relieved when Mrs D comments on the possibility of her saying 'no'. Lucy is now much less ebullient. Mrs D says that she thinks it could make sense for them to meet and think together about Lucy's feelings on her return if Lucy wants it at that time, but wonders if this possibility of meeting again will make the 'finishing' seem different for Lucy. Lucy smiles, confirms the provisional time of her next appointment, wishes she hadn't arranged the meeting with Lola, and actually leaves having had a full session, on which Mrs D comments.

Lucy in fact rings to cancel the last appointment, leaving a message that it clashed with her interview times. An offer of a replacement time is sent, but it is possible that this does not reach her. Lucy does, however, personally hand in a letter to the receptionist for Mrs D. In it she conveys the factual information of having been offered the place she wanted for her course, but recounts that her marvellous feeling of well-being has gone, and she is quite troubled. She is particularly unhappy at not having seen Mrs

D to say goodbye, and to thank her. She ends by describing how she is struggling to understand her perplexing feelings, but also wants to dismiss them and put them aside. Mrs D feels very sad.

What particularly stands out in this third and last session is the painful issue of the ending for Lucy. Her letter, including her recognition of not wanting to attend to her difficulties, makes it clear that she is in fact attempting to relate to issues that had arisen in the work with Mrs D, although the actual 'goodbye' is not said in person.

LUCY: DISCUSSION

I should now like to think about Lucy's problems and what took place between her and Mrs D, and use this as a basis for drawing together some of the salient features of this kind of work.

Within this counselling service for adolescents and young adults a graphic picture is conveyed of a child Lucy feeling 'dropped out of her skin' and abandoned on the porch of life, ill-equipped for the continuing experience of adolescence and seeking to be rid of her pain. Lucy came in a state of distress which she regarded as being derived from her previous encounter with another organization. Her fears about what the counselling service could be like were apparent. Mrs D initially provided space to experience and think about Lucy's distress, and clarified what was available in the context of her fears. The opinion of the previous organization that Lucy needed some form of help with her communications may have been correct in the sense that Lucy was, as we saw, prone to cut communications with her own feelings, but she experienced the actual outcome as very persecuting. Any understanding that was conveyed by Mrs D to Lucy was transmitted not as an authoritative statement but as something which arose out of the process of ongoing interchanges between them, and thus appeared to be easier for her to assimilate. Mrs D, of necessity, offered containment for Lucy's initial anxiety and brought it into focus with what the service offered. She also related to Lucy's 'pre-transference' anxieties – that is, those arising prior to any actual meeting – about herself, the service and the institution in which it took place. To ignore these could leave the client feeling that what would be offered could, for her, only feel persecutingly unuseable.

Lucy's need for the physical presence of her childhood treasures spoke to a sense of inner insecurity and vulnerability. She tended to cut herself off not only from her own feelings but also from external relationships, such as her group of friends, when she felt hurt. Feelings – of sadness, for example – when she found them unbearable, were liable to be projected into external objects. Mrs D was certainly left feeling very sad. Following a process of cutting off and mental slimming, Lucy could be left with a sense of emptiness or the presence of vengeful 'cut-off' inner objects; she could then feel driven to stuff, or to become involved in an excited, manic flight to other relationships, to which she tended to latch on in an overoptimistic manner, as in the case of Mrs D herself. The degree to which Lucy found parts of her emotionality, such as her sadness, unbearable was based in her life experiences. Her inner lack of a unified parental couple may have made the adolescent group particularly important for her, but perhaps also difficult to sustain. Its loss left her bereft of wider containment for her splitting and projective identification, some of which is seen in relation to Lola.

Very primitive, catastrophic anxieties about feeling totally 'dropped out of her skin' were apparent. This graphic phrase, experienced together with Lucy's anxieties about feeling 'finished' on ending, suggests a very early primitive anxiety of dropping to pieces with no skin to hold her together (Bick, 1968), resonating for Lucy with the falling apart of her childhood family. A little-girl aspect of Lucy, parting from Mummy and her siblings and going to Daddy, was also met, and one can glimpse some painful ongoing oedipal phantasies relating to an acrimonious parental relationship and divorce. Although she did not specifically bring her troubled 'goodbyes' and future 'hellos', the issue of painful separations was paramount for her, and was related to in the work. Lucy's experience in relation to the goodbye from the counselling service spoke for that event in itself, as well as indicating others that had gone before.

One might well consider that Lucy would probably need therapy to help her to grapple with her deep-seated problems: her lack of inner containing potential for bearing persecution and loss was evident. The quality and quantity of dissociative, projective and hypomanic psychic activity and its consequences could clearly not yield in four sessions and would probably need the help of intensive work in the transference. But this was not the time to think about therapy, even if Lucy's earlier hatred of it were to be overcome, as she was about to leave the country.

How helpful, then, was this experience for Lucy? She achieved some insight into some of the troubling consequences of her external and internal personal relationships. Although some of this insight might be of a very fluctuating nature, she may have been left with something to struggle to be in touch with again. She also gained some awareness about problems she might have to face in Australia, so she had an enhanced potential with which to relate to them. Very importantly, a problem that came alive in the work, the dread of the ending with Mrs D, was experienced and thought about. In the counselling service Lucy had a first-hand taste of a brief therapeutic experience which related to her current needs, leaving the possibility of formal ongoing therapy open for the future. She may have been helped to have some space in which she could become aware that this was something she could actively want for herself. Mrs D later heard that this did in fact happen.

THE NATURE OF THE APPROACH

The worker tries to put together what she observes, hears, sees and thinks in a way the client may be able to use. Mrs D attempted to understand, in an emotional, experiential sense, what Lucy was conveying and what was happening in the room between them. This aspect of the work is based on the concept of containment (Bion, 1962a), as discussed in Chapter 4. The concept has its roots in infantile experience, but can be used to help the client to think about and relate to his or her whole-life situation.

Clients may come to the service not only with their own problems, but with anxieties about how they will be received. The first task of a worker may thus be the essential one of containing anxieties about the service and the worker herself, as was the case here. Anxieties that come alive in the actual work – in Lucy's case, for example, the dread of the ending – also need to be thought about, so that there is an ongoing experience of containment. We saw with Lucy how links can be made between past and current events, and put together with anxieties about the future. A client can be helped to differentiate external reality from internal reality, but also to see links between external events and the phantasies in the inner world – as, for example, in the case of Lucy's divorced parents and her internal parental images. An older aspect of the client can be helped to be aware of the way in which feelings emanating from a child part of him- or herself are relevant to current problems. Such differentiation, clarification and linking, within a framework of containment, are salient features of this kind of brief work. The brief intervention may help the client to feel that he or she has greater access to his or her own experiences: a kind of mental map or globe – limited, of course, but, as with Lucy, helping her to be in closer touch with herself.

The temporary nature of the relationship with the worker as someone who facilitates this kind of understanding is, of course, something that will need to be taken up openly, and was particularly important in this instance. In brief work of this kind it would be both unethical and inappropriate to attempt to draw out and use the infantile transference as the major tool of emotional exploration, as in the longer-term work discussed in Chapter 6. To do so could leave the client feeling teased and abused. Increasingly dependent expectations could be fostered within the relationship, and constructive termination would become threatened. On the other hand, it is necessary to clarify the transference element in the relationship with the worker when it is actively used by the client, or becomes relevant in the course of the 'here-and-now' relationship. This was particularly important with Lucy, one of whose problems was, as we saw, a tendency to latch on to a new object or to expect someone else to feel her emotions for her. Avoidance of looking at the implications of the relationship occurring in the room could have left Lucy feeling that she had not really been heard, and without an experience of having her projections contained and thought about. Mrs D was particularly careful to try to attend to negative feelings in relation to herself or the service, whether they were actually apparent or likely to have been present, as in the case of Lucy's initial anxiety about the service. Understanding of what arises in the transference in this way may be able to be used to see if it can illuminate the client's own relationship to her life's events. Mrs D's awareness of Lucy's latching on to her illuminated how this could happen in Lucy's mind in relation to her father. This use of transference understanding contrasts, of course, with attempts in long-term work to bring external issues directly into the ambit of the infantile transference. In this work Mrs D made extensive use of her countertransference. Thus, when she found herself at intervals becoming subject to a sense of abandonment and loss, she could, on reflection, become aware that this was emanating from Lucy, and could be used to inform her response to her.

The predominant emphasis, then, is on the provision of an accessible, thoughtful, containing space, which might be better conveyed in this context by the term 'consultation' rather than 'counselling'. The need to make an appointment and bear a brief wait may filter out some of those for whom such a reflective process might not feel tolerable. Mrs D and her fellow members of a staff workshop were aware, from shared case discussions, of the dangers of inappropriate development of infantile transference and unrealistic dependency expectations. Experience showed them that this was most likely to be avoided by keeping the contact – which is designed to be brief, but can nevertheless have an intense emotional impact – really brief. It became apparent that up to about four sessions was the maximum that could be offered at any one time, although this might occasionally be followed by a review session, or a further contact with the service some time later. The response to such brevity, however, needs to be firmly held in mind throughout the work; it has also been found that such attention results in fewer unexpectedly missed sessions. (Lucy's failure to attend her last session was to some extent monitored in advance, and was intrinsic to the subject matter of her difficulties, discussed by both Lucy herself and Mrs D.) Although some clients do not want as many as four sessions, some, like Lucy, may find the offer of limited time hard to bear. This can, however, be worked with as part of the basic experience of the sessions. Also, this is if appropriate, the client can be helped to obtain therapy.

THE USEFULNESS OF THE APPROACH

Clients can be helped to feel more aware of who they are, where they are in their lives, and what troubles them. A social worker, aged twenty-four, was beset by what she described as depression and lack of confidence, experienced particularly in her professional work with disturbed families. It became apparent that part of the client's way of relating to difficulties, in wider aspects of her life as well as in her work, had been to cut herself off from awareness of her own needy and childish parts. This had left her not only with a feeling of inner impoverishment but also with idealized – but unfulfilled – expectations of her own competence to help others. Through the contact with the worker she became more aware of her own needs, and also more hopeful about the possibility of their being met. Instead of only trying to help others, she decided to seek therapy which could help her in her personal life as well as her work. The brief engagement in the counselling service brought to light what had been a false solution to the adolescent process, and allowed the split-off, infantile aspects of the self to become accessible for further integration through therapy.

Problems, in themselves unclear, may be clarified. An ex-sixth-former of seventeen was surprised at himself for coming, and puzzled as to why he had done so. It emerged that he was a fairly happy young man who appeared to have made good use of what was available to him, but seemed to have better relationships with the inner parents in his mind than he currently had with his actual parents, and possibly they with each other. The worker helped him to identify and address his reluctance to leave home and go on to what he felt might be a better life than the one he felt his parents actually enjoyed. Anxieties about feeling both triumphant and guilty if he were to feel that he surpassed his parents were recognized. Some understanding was reached about his conflict between trying to face these feelings or to maintain a kind of status quo which would hamper further development. Fears of feeling out in the cold, coming from a child part of himself, were also recognized. He said he felt much freer to become more active in making decisions about his future.

A student of twenty had dropped out of a college of further education for a whole year after his father had died. He had felt he could trouble no one at the time, and although he had now managed to resume his studies, he wanted to understand what had happened. He was helped to unravel what had brought him to feel that he needed to step into his father's shoes and stay at home to support his mother. It became apparent that seeking to 'be' his father, by means of projective identification with an infantile basis, had become entangled with his more adult wish to help and comfort his mother. This had led to an inhibition of his mourning for his father, with a consequent deprivation of his own need for a mourned and reinstated fatherly presence in his internal world, who could help him to build his own life. He was much relieved at being understood, and felt helped over a hurdle.

The last two examples relate to difficulties hindering the resolution of the adolescent process. The developmental strivings within these clients could readily respond to the understanding available, and after two interviews both these young people felt able to continue the work themselves. A service based on this approach can often help to disentangle difficulties sufficiently within its own boundaries to allow ongoing development to continue. It can also help in allowing a need for therapy to become overt. The informal, self-referring structure, without any 'reporting back' to a third party, may help it to feel essentially private and useable. There is no complication, or even possible deterrent, of needing to become a 'patient' for people whose difficulties may feel essentially personal, and who may be uneasy in expressing their distress in a more formal setting. On the other hand, the service is also able to relate to ill adolescents and help them to be in touch with extended help. Clearly, the work described here cannot offer the depth of experience of long-term work, and its benefits will obviously vary with the client's ability to make use of it. But it may, as we see in the detailed account of work with Lucy, be regarded as a brief therapeutic experience in its own right, appropriate to a client's current needs, and with a possibility of being able to contribute to future development. It is also economical in the use of resources.

At one time the staff of this particular service undertook an intensive clinical (unpublished) review of all the clients who came to the service within a six-month period; this included some of the clients referred to here. Those who came to the service brought a range of depression, distress and dissatisfaction about themselves and their relationships with others. Some were very disturbed; others much less so. The outcome suggested that a considerable proportion of those attending had been helped at least to some extent. Exceptions included some very ill young people in flight from other forms of help, a few nominally self-referred clients attending under pressure from other people in their lives, and those looking for specific 'answers' to very specific problems.

The majority of clients recognized that they were coming to a service which offered brief intervention only, and in most instances they were not actively seeking long-term therapy as a further prospect. The review indicated that slightly fewer than one in five clients wanted, and were helped to find, subsequent individual psychoanalytic psychotherapy or group therapy. For the majority, such an intensive intervention would have been irrelevant to their needs. It was thought, in any case, that a considerable number of the clients would have been unlikely to be able to make a useful commitment to this kind of intervention. It is encouraging, therefore, that in a brief self-referring counselling service of this kind it is possible to find a way of extending the benefits of a form of psychoanalytic understanding to many who would not need, seek, or, in some instances, be able to use psychoanalytic psychotherapy as such, and to whom such understanding would not otherwise be available.

The work reported here reflects one way of offering a brief psychoanalytically informed counselling service. The way a particular brief service operates arises partly out of its own working experience. It will also be affected by the aims and resources of any sponsoring institution, including arrangements for ongoing therapy where this is thought to be necessary.[1,2]

FURTHER APPLICATION

In a more formal clinical setting, a similar approach may form the basis of initial exploratory work with adolescents who may be seeking – or are referred for – ongoing psychotherapy, and for whom a sequestered approach apart from their parents is desirable. (I use the term 'exploratory' in preference to the more commonly used 'assessment' because it lends itself more readily to use as a vehicle for joint thinking about whether therapy is appropriate; assessment too easily carries the possible connotation of a potential patient being assessed and found wanting.) There will, of course, be points of difference. In an exploration relating to ongoing therapy, the extent to which a patient may actually be able to use – rather than be felt, perhaps by a referrer, to 'need' – it does have to be thought about; here it may be possible to gauge the presence of motivation to participate in ongoing psychotherapeutic work by considering the client's responsiveness to some interpretative interventions within the exploration itself. The capacity and background support to sustain both the regularity and nature of the commitment, including the gaps occasioned by therapists' holidays, must also be considered.

Interviews taking place within a counselling or consultation service, or provided as part of a more formal exploration for therapy, may themselves function as valuable therapeutic interventions, irrespective of whether they currently lead to ongoing therapy. Some clients, however, such as Lucy, may be unwilling to take part in what they may see as a formal 'assessment' focused on entry to therapy, but can make good use of a separate, sequestered service. There is a link between the brief work described here and the family explorations discussed in the next chapter: both can have a valuable function as self-contained interventions but can lead on, if necessary, to different kinds of appropriate therapy.

8   ADOLESCENTS AND THEIR FAMILIES: FINDING SPACE FOR CHANGE

The process of adolescence leads towards that of leaving home, and the value of a family approach to therapy at this juncture may be questioned. A family intervention, even in quite late adolescence, can, however, provide a second chance for relating to family difficulties before separation, and through it an adolescent may come to feel more firmly rooted in the family of origin from which he or she may have felt estranged or extruded. The work may lead not only to external family support for further development, but to some benign change in the inner world of the adolescent and in the family itself. More generally, at any age within adolescence – owing, in particular, to the propensities for splitting and projection at this age – members of families with adolescents may be in some doubt as to whether some problem is specifically a matter for individual concern only. There may be some difficulty in thinking about whether help is needed at all; if it is needed, what it should consist of; and who in the family needs it and can use it.

A brief family exploration may provide a containing space for such issues to be addressed, and I start by illustrating the nature of such explorations and their value to a family. Therapists with a psychoanalytic approach who see some reason for a family intervention have to find a way of using themselves within it. With this in mind, I go on to discuss a vignette of clinical material, with an emphasis on the experiences of the two co-therapists involved. This helps us to think about the way certain psychoanalytic concepts – in particular those of containment, transference and countertransference – can be applied in family work, and about single and co-therapy in a family setting.

An example of longer-term work, also with co-therapists, in which some improvement of relationships within an alienated family takes place, comes next, and is followed by a review of the nature of family work and its contribution to adolescents and their families. In the subsequent chapter I discuss an account of long-term family work with a single therapist, providing a more detailed example of this approach and its applicability. The approach itself is based on that of a long-term clinical workshop studying a psychoanalytic approach to therapy with adolescents and their families, and is discussed more fully in Box *et al.* (1981).[1]

FAMILY EXPLORATIONS

Some young people are aware that they need help. Lucy (Chapter 7) went to a counselling service. John (Chapter 6) sought and obtained a referral to a clinic. Both needed an individual sequestered setting in which to explore their difficulties. In some circumstances an initial family exploration may be sought either by the family itself or by the referrer, or may be suggested by a clinic. Such an approach is particularly likely to be thought of where difficulties are predominantly experienced in the actual family relationships. Sometimes adolescents, at least initially, may not see any need for help for themselves, and maintain either that there is no problem, or that the problem lies with their parents, siblings or environment. The motivation for attendance may therefore lie with parents who are worried about the adolescent, although the adolescent may be willing to come to therapy with the family.

An exploratory period of approximately four sessions with a family provides space for some awareness of what the problems may be to develop between the family and the therapists, and for some thought to be given to what emerges. Sometimes a very active piece of brief therapy develops in this time. Such an exploration may in itself be all that is required or wanted at that particular time, and considerable movement may take place within or following upon it. On the other hand, it may be followed by individual therapy with an adolescent and/or work with his or her parents, or by ongoing family therapy. As with the individual counselling service discussed in Chapter 7, there are indications for keeping exploratory work brief, and for the family to know that it will be brief. Such brevity may make the best use of the limited motivation of some family members. It may also make it possible to respond to the needs of the situation without the development of deepening manifestations of transference which would be inappropriate unless longer-term work is going to take place.

RELATING TO LOSS

Adolescence is sometimes experienced as driving a wedge between the generations. The family of origin will probably remain 'home' for many adolescents for a number of years, but may at times no longer feel like it.

Doreen, aged fifteen, was the only child of the Plant family. Her rather elderly parents sought what they called advice, but felt so distraught that they wanted to discuss the possibility of some kind of boarding school for Doreen who, they said, was getting out of control. Doreen sat silently, with a sullen, withdrawn expression, for most of the first session. Both parents complained bitterly of her rudeness, her insistence on going out with boys they thought unsuitable, and how she came home far too late; she was so different now from the Doreen of childhood – a childhood which, they implied, had been happy for all of them. One night Doreen did not come home until considerably later than the deadline they had stipulated, and they had locked her out for a time, although they later relented; since then she had hardly spoken to them. They bemoaned the fact that she did not seem to be their child any more. The therapist was aware of a little shiver coming from the silent Doreen, and wondered aloud whether Doreen also had feelings about her parents not being her parents any more. Doreen first looked as if she would rush from the room, but then she started to sob, and soon both she and her parents were hugging and attempting to comfort each other.

As the discussion proceeded, Doreen's parents recounted how they, after several miscarriages, had almost given up hope of having a child when Doreen was born, and found her entry into adolescence, and the thought of her finally leaving home, hard to bear. It became evident that Doreen, who in some aspects seemed quite childlike, also found it hard to give up the protected world of latency, and her positive, defiant entry into adolescent activities also appeared to incorporate a counter-phobic attempt to deny any anxiety on her own part, as well as to override that of her parents. The therapist responded to the thoughts about Doreen eventually leaving home, and how this had been experienced between the generations. For the parents it had become linked with their earlier losses, as if it were some kind of deathly miscarriage in which a child was being taken from them, while the throwing of herself into her new life by the adolescent Doreen attempted to ignore any feeling of loss within the child part of herself.

The family felt that this exploration, which was stormy in places, drew their feelings about Doreen's childhood, adolescence and eventually leaving home into focus with each other. The parents no longer wished to send Doreen to boarding school, and no member of the family sought further intervention. Although the Plant family had certainly needed help, the dynamics of this intervention were reasonably simple. Through it, Doreen's apparently defiant move into adolescence was helped to come together with a meaningful recognition of the various feelings of loss within the family.

The forward drive in Doreen was apparent, but there are many complex examples within families where some combination of external difficulties, personality traits in parents or child, developmental problems, unrecognized anxieties, and complications of the projective and splitting processes intertwine to hold back development. In the background stands the end of family life as it has been experienced.

Sometimes loss takes the form of an actual bereavement, which leads families to seek help. Where loss is very differently borne by the various family members – as in the case of Martin and his family, below – an intervention may contribute to the containment of depressive pain, help a member or members who have difficulty in

mourning, and relieve others of the burden of excessive feelings of
loss that do not belong to them.

INDIVIDUAL RESPONSES IN THE CONTEXT OF FAMILY DIFFICULTIES

Thirteen-year-old Martin remained withdrawn and sad for some
time after his mother's death. He appeared to obtain no solace from
his considerable musical ability, an interest and skill which he had
shared with his mother. An exploration took place attended by
Martin, his father, and his older brother and sister. The other family
members suggested that Martin, as the youngest child, naturally
found the death hardest to bear; they also recognized that his
mother's death had affected his relationship to his music. Martin's
brother and sister were very active in adolescent life, and took a
somewhat denigratory attitude to the 'old-fashioned' music loved
by Martin and their mother. It became apparent in the exploration
that Martin's closeness to his mother in her lifetime, expressed
partly through their shared interest, alongside his siblings'
involvement elsewhere, had led to him being used to carry some of
their sadness about their mother's death. This was fairly readily
accepted when it was raised by the therapists. Martin's father had
been too downcast on his wife's death to be alert to the imposition
on to Martin of his siblings' pain, but had been glad to make use of
the referral suggested by Martin's music teacher, and said that he
now felt more able to help the family to share their sorrow.

Paul, aged seventeen, had been discovered to be taking drugs of
quite a dangerous nature. His parents had succeeded in getting him
to go with them to a clinic in the hope that individual therapy might
be arranged, but when they were there Paul protested that this was
for their sake, not for his: 'You only care when you are frightened
of trouble with the law'; 'You've never paid any attention to what
I want.' Considerable recriminatory abuse was present in the first
exploratory session with Paul and his parents, although both the
therapists felt aware of deeper bonds. This led them to suggest that
a younger brother, Alex, not yet adolescent – who had not been
brought to the clinic for the first interview, with some idea of saving

him from an acrimonious atmosphere – should now attend. Despite the fact that he was only eleven, he seemed to have the capacity to allay some of the abuse with evidence of better times. Thus: 'But don't you remember, Paul, Mum and Dad did get you those things you wanted, which was quite difficult for them'; and 'But Dad, Paul came and got me from school all these times you asked him to, when Mum went to look after Gran.' Alex asked to be excused from further sessions to get on with his homework and hobbies. Paul did come to want individual therapy for himself. The intervention had both made use of, and enabled the family to use, its own assets.

One member of a family can be specifically used as a receptacle for the unwanted emotionality of others; Martin's siblings located much of their own feelings of loss in Martin by projective identification. Family members may disseminate unwanted or negative emotionality to the general detriment of others, but may also have positive capacities from which other members benefit. Meltzer and Harris (1986, pp. 158–60) describe eight emotional functions within family life which members may perform either as part of a general tendency or at a particular time: generating love; promulgating hate; promoting hope; sowing despair; containing depressive pain; emanating persecutory anxiety; thinking; creating lies and confusion. Functions may be assumed by the individual, or imposed upon him or her by others. What is often a normal or expected function of parenting can be expressed at times by an 'adult' capacity in children, as in the case of Alex. He was able to use his own capacities to restore some sense of proportion into family life, enabling more loving aspects to be experienced amid the vituperation and so enabling the exploration to develop with greater hopefulness at a time when the parents may have been worn down with worry and strife; he did not, however, try and get into an inappropriate parental role. While it may not be necessary for all siblings to partake in family work as a rigid requirement, brief participation by a member who does not otherwise attend may be able to make a contribution.

Divergences of cultural expectations can beset adolescent development. Ahmed, aged sixteen, in the course of taking his GCSE exams, took a marginal overdose of aspirins and promptly sought help. The only son of a successful immigrant family, he had found it impossible to tell them about his wish to train for an independent professional career, as opposed to fulfilling their expectations that he should now leave school and enter the family business. A family exploration took place which allowed the divide between Ahmed's aspirations and those of his family to be addressed, bringing the 'unspeakable' conflict into the area of thought and discussion. As an outcome of this, some time for reflection was agreed upon, during which Ahmed could study for A levels and also undertake individual therapy.

THE FAMILY, THE THERAPISTS AND THE INSTITUTION

Starting to work with families can sometimes seem bewildering to therapists – not only because of the impact of contributions coming from different members, but also because of anxieties which can arise in the relationship with a co-therapist. The following small piece of clinical material, brought to a workshop by troubled co-therapists, highlights such problems.

This family exploration took place in a Child and Family Clinic in a small university town. The clinic was located in a modern building, and the waiting area was shared with dentistry and other local health services. The two therapists were experienced in individual psychoanalytic psychotherapy, but new to family therapy and to working with each other. The first session with the Branch family was brought to a workshop for discussion. The father was a local lawyer; the mother was a nurse. Eva, their only child, was thirteen, and had difficulties in sleeping. The referral had been made by the family's general practitioner, who had indicated that Eva was attending only on the insistence of her parents. In the light of Eva's reluctance to come, the clinic staff thought that an initial family exploration would be the most useful response.

Eva sat at a table where some drawing materials had been placed, and started to use them. Her major contribution to the discussion was to say, as if she were tired of having to repeat it, that she was all right as long as there were no rough or sharp noises; this left the therapists feeling that they had been somewhat intrusive in asking.

It was mainly her father who gave a clear, factual account of the difficulties; these were of fairly recent origin, although both parents recalled somewhat similar sleeping problems in infancy. Voices or movement of doors within their flat could be more disturbing to Eva than traffic noise; storms were also frightening. Once she was unsettled, Eva remained irritably restless for hours. Father had initially thought that earplugs could have dealt with the problem, but Eva had not been able to bear wearing them. She did well at school and had plenty of friends, all girls, some of whom, unlike Eva herself, were starting to be more involved with boys. Yes, she had started to menstruate around the time of the onset of the trouble. Mrs Z, the female therapist, tried to draw Eva in, but received only brief monosyllabic responses.

The therapists described to the workshop how this conversation actually took place between the four adults (with practically no comment from Eva), and also what they themselves felt at the time. Mr Branch addressed what he said largely to Dr Y, the male therapist, and Mrs Z experienced the two men as participating in a quasi-medical dialogue about Eva's symptoms, lengthily discussing how long they were likely to last and whether medication might help. She felt that ongoing eye contact between them made it difficult for her to catch Dr Y's eye, and found herself resenting what seemed to her to be 'their' conversation, from which she crossly felt excluded. Meanwhile, Eva's mother directed her conversation mainly to Mrs Z. She talked at some length about what she described as the wearisome but necessary job of trying to get and keep Eva settled, which she called 'soothing Eva down'. This sometimes involved a prolonged stay in Eva's room until Eva was asleep, and avoiding opening the parents' bedroom door until late in the evening, particularly if Eva had already been disturbed. Yes, it was like babyhood all over again, in contrast to the relatively trouble-free intervening period. Dr Y, to his consternation, felt quite cross about the length of time he felt Mrs Z was devoting to hearing Mrs Branch's account. But both therapists felt helpless to intervene; they did not know what to say, and felt that in any case whatever they said could only be experienced as an interruption by their colleague and the parent to whom he or she was talking. They recognized how burdened they felt by their own unpleasant responses to their therapeutic partner. They both said that they had felt some relief when Dr Y had managed to turn to talk to Eva and look at her drawing. He commented that the sky in her painting looked as if there were gathering storm clouds in it. Eva's response – 'Suppose so' – left him feeling, however, that his remark was unwelcome.

Workshop members discussed this difficult situation. While they were sympathetic to the therapists' predicament, they took up what could have been problems for the family, affecting the contact from the beginning. They recalled that Eva had come only under pressure, and also questioned whether the family, although they were seeking help, really understood what the therapists were offering. Questions for the family about the significance of a Child and Family Clinic could be relevant to their feelings as to whether they had come to the right place, and affect their ability to use the service; some feeling about attending a clinic in a small town, based on their professional identities, may also have been present. On the other hand, the dental and quasi-medical ambience in the waiting area may have had some association with Father's thoughts about medication and the length of treatment. It was also questioned whether the largely separate communication of the three family members could indicate some anxiety about meeting as a family, however reasonable this approach seemed to be to the therapists. From the beginning there may have been unease about what could feel like 'rough' or 'sharp' input for all the family arising out of coming to the clinic.

Lucy (Chapter 7) came to the counselling service with her own expectations and pre-transference anxieties; a similar situation exists for a family coming to meet therapists at a clinic. Making space initially for open recognition of such pre-transference anxieties and doubts about the nature and meaning of where they are, who they are with, and what is going to happen may be necessary to enable a family to feel that there is a containing space available for them, and for the intervention to be viable. A clinic staff may consider that an offer of a family intervention is the most appropriate approach to the family problems, but it may, nevertheless, raise anxieties for the family. In retrospect the therapists thought that it could have been useful to have talked with the family about their expectations of the clinic and themselves, and to explain the exploratory nature of what they were offering, as Mrs D had done with Lucy. They thought with hindsight that they had become so silenced by the way the session proceeded that they gave less attention to these matters than they might have done if they were working individually.

Separate but intermingling strands relevant to understanding the family's problems could be seen within the presentation. One strand was conveyed by the accounts of what the family said, by what was observed as happening in the session, and by the content of Eva's drawings. From early on the therapists were aware of the presence of an underlying sexual current among the family, as portrayed in the context of the closed parental bedroom door, and perhaps about Eva growing up and going out with – or not going out with – boys in adolescence, but at the time they felt silenced in relating to them.

The second strand lay in the interaction with the therapists, some of which can be observed only through the therapists' own countertransference feelings, based not only upon their observations of the family and their direct communications with them, but also on what was projected into them in the session. We can sense that something of the unvoiced dissatisfactions and feelings of being out of touch with each other within the parental couple was conveyed into the therapists by projective identification. Keeping their voices down in conversation with each other so as not to disturb Eva formed part of the parents' account; now the therapists felt themselves silenced and in difficulties. They were burdened with the antagonism Mr and Mrs Branch had towards each other around settling Eva, probably compounded with some of Eva's own demands to her parents; we recall how the therapists, when they asked Eva about her sleeping difficulties, were made by her to feel intrusive, as if they were linked for her with noisy, intrusive, non-soothing parents. The feelings experienced by the therapists of being excluded and silenced, and made to feel cross, jealous and intrusive, were evidence of similar difficulties within the family about exclusion from pairing relationships within it.

The therapists' experience illustrates what it is like to be in direct receipt of projective identifications, and the difficulty of being aware that this is the case. Each therapist had to struggle with a feeling that they were being excluded by the other. As a result of what had been projected into them, each of them felt not only individually cross at being excluded by a couple, but also in danger of actually being intrusive. The effect of such projective activity makes it difficult for therapists – particularly those who are new to the work – to be in touch with a part of themselves that is not dominated by it, and thus to be aware that the crossness with their working partner is in fact very probably (but not always necessarily) the result of this activity. In the workshop Dr Y said he felt he had something in common with the wedding guest who 'cannot choose but hear' when the Ancient Mariner 'holds him with his glittering eye' (Coleridge, 1798). Bion (1961, p. 149) describes how it may be difficult to be in touch with being the recipient of projective identification, as this may be accompanied by an experience of strong feelings which seem to be justified by the external situation; only when this response is shaken off can the experience of 'being manipulated so as to be playing a part, no matter how difficult to recognize, in somebody else's phantasy' be appreciated.

If the feelings of which the family wish to be rid – here to do with being left out and made to feel jealous and intrusive – are stirred up in the therapists' countertransference, and can be contained and thought about by them, there is a possibility that the projective identifications, although not necessarily primarily intended as such, can be understood as a communication, and thus be used to further understanding. As recipients of the projective activity, the therapists can recognize with the family not only how painful it is to be jealous when one feels excluded from a pair relationship, but also how anxious they are that if this is openly acknowledged, as opposed to being 'soothed' away or 'plugged' out, some form of emotional thunderstorm may ensue. Despite functioning in a thoughtful, containing manner, the therapists must also be aware that they themselves could be felt to be responding in a manner with intrusive, storm-laden potential, and willing to recognize this with the family.

Within this family there was a problem of the containment of Eva's anxiety about being intruded into by something rough, sharp or stormy. Eva herself seemed resentful that the situations recurred.

Father's approach – by way of earplugs or medication – appeared to act as a barrier to the experience of anxiety, rather than containment of it. Mother's approach of 'soothing down' suggested that she used herself as a quasi-container functioning in the mode of 'sponge' or 'nappy', emolliently soothing and removing rather than thinking about and responding openly to Eva's anxiety and irritability. Once the therapists felt able to intervene, they would be able to explore the different responses of individual members in the context of the family themes of jealousy and intrusiveness in the session as a whole: Mrs Branch's 'soothing down' of Eva to avoid her feeling left out, resulting in Mr Branch feeling left out; his possible preference for 'plugging', not hearing, anxiety; resentment from a stormy Eva about both some form of intrusion and feeling left out. This might then have led into exploration of issues around the bedroom door and anxieties about adolescent sexuality.

The workshop heard later that the therapists had been able to be in touch with the feelings about exclusion and intrusiveness within the family, and to give some recognition to anxieties about Eva's entry into adolescent life. The attempt to hear and think about manifestations of anxiety and the stormy response to feeling excluded, rather than to 'plug' them out or 'soothe' them away, paved the way for Eva to become more open to her own feelings and willing to accept a referral for individual psychotherapy where issues around her sexuality could be related to with some privacy. The parents also agreed to meet another worker so that they could think about the differences between them. The family exploration, including the containment of the anxieties and hostility that it may have aroused, paved the way for more sequestered contacts – which, certainly as far as Eva was concerned – would not have been acceptable earlier.

This vignette, together with the earlier examples, illustrates how containment in family work needs to be an active process. Different – maybe antithetical – views or actions within the family, whether these are expressed verbally, by projective identification or even by silence, need to be gathered in and thought about. Some development of understanding may follow. Individual feelings can be attended to in this way, but held within a family context. An exploration of this kind may enable members of a family, sometimes with an initially marginal degree of commitment, to decide with the therapists if, and how, they want to go further. (The nature of containment in family work will be further enlarged upon in the next chapter in connection with the Rose family.)

TRANSFERENCE ISSUES: SINGLE AND CO-THERAPY

Pre-transference will probably be relevant to any beginning, and therapists will always draw on their countertransference experience in any kind of therapy. When a family come with a general expectation of finding a helpful response to what is troubling them – as was, for example, largely the case with Martin and his family – minimal reference to the nature of the relationship between family members and the therapists may be necessary. On the other hand, as we saw with the Branch family, negative feelings – whether directed towards the therapists themselves, or to the providing institution – do need to be recognized to avoid the danger of contact being broken off. Painful issues around the ending of a contact, however brief, in which there has been a growth of positive feelings in the 'here-and-now' transference, may also need to be reviewed openly, so that some containment can take place. In longer-term therapy, as we shall see in the next chapter with the Rose family, changes in the relationship to the therapist or therapists will probably need to be followed both in their positive and their negative aspects, allowing the deepening implications of what the relationship represents to be understood, and separations to be contained.

Many therapists work as a couple, often with a co-therapist of the opposite sex, in both exploratory and longer-term work. This may assist work around oedipal and other issues involving two parents. As we saw with the Branch family, it can be meaningful for family members to feel that they can communicate something specifically to one of two people; a difference of sex between the therapists may help to clarify underlying meanings about who or what is being addressed. Two therapists in receipt of projective identifications may often be 'programmed' differently by the family, and thus can make use of their separate countertransference experiences in their interactions with various family members, enriching the understanding of family dynamics (A.H. Williams, 1981). With the Branch family, although both therapists were made to feel intrusive, Dr Y was led to feel more of an authority; Mrs Z more of a 'soother'. As both these therapists discovered, to make active use of a countertransference response in this instance of feeling intrusive can be difficult and painful; Dr Y and Mrs Z did really feel hostile to each other. Sometimes therapists, confident in their partnership, may feel it appropriate to make use of their different reactions more openly in the session, as Dr A and Mrs B did in sessions 4 and 14 of the group therapy discussed in Chapter 10.

Some therapists find that working on their own allows them to be more responsive to anxieties with an infantile basis affecting all the family, and prefer to work in this way, at least with some families (Copley, 1983). The economy and availability of professional time may also be relevant here. Whether or not a therapist has a therapeutic partner is, however, likely to have meaning for the families with whom he or she works, as we shall see in further examples in this and the next chapter.

Co-therapists clearly need post-session discussion time in which projections can both be recognized and disentangled, and also separated from any actual differences of opinion arising between the pair. A containing workshop, seminar or consultation, which has tolerance for the therapists' responses to the projections and difficulties with which they are working, can be useful to both single and co-therapists.

RESTORATION OF FAMILY LIFE AND INNER ENRICHMENT

I shall now summarize a piece of longer-term therapy which contributes to the thinking about a number of issues in this chapter and in Chapter 9. It adds to the discussion of co-therapy, and portrays a different outcome to the question 'Don't you think it's natural for a son to want a father?' raised in the Rose family in the next chapter.

In the Forrest family it was questionable in psychic reality whether Tony, a boy of sixteen, really felt he belonged within his family – at least at that time. After his parents' divorce and subsequent episodes of stealing and violence at home, he had spent some time at boarding school. His learning was a long way behind his assessed intelligence. He now lived with his father, new stepmother and fifteen-year-old sister, Samantha. Two older step-siblings were mostly away from home. After violent episodes at school and an escalating threat of violence at home, a further removal from home was mooted, this time into care. There was a menacing atmosphere at home. Tony had threatened to steal from his father, and to attack him when he was with his stepmother – both events to involve stealth and actual, bloody violence. His father had reacted with the threat of bloodthirsty reprisals against Tony. The family, with considerable doubts, had been persuaded to seek therapy, and a family exploration took place.

The exploratory period was experienced as gruelling by the solitary female therapist, Mrs J, whose male co-therapist partner had unfortunately been unable to take part as planned. Only Tony and his stepmother came to the first session, Tony claiming that he had come to assess the suitability of the therapy. He also provocatively presented his arrival with his new young stepmother as some form of successful, forbidden intergenerational triumph, and mocked the idea that it could be meaningful to make any reference to an absent father and male co-therapist. The possibility of Tony being 'taken into care' was referred to in the session. Mrs J was aware of a quite maternal approach from his stepmother towards Tony, and questioned the presence of some form of 'care' which was neither cynical nor custodial. Tony's response was that this was not relevant to what they had come to talk about: his stealing and lying. He implied that firm adherence to such an agenda was required and, with some pride, proceeded to give examples of some uncaring, delinquent exploitation on his part which had made other women appear foolish, and which the therapist took as a triumphant display of the power of delinquency over the possible presence of caring women within the family or here in the clinic.

Tony's father came to the remaining exploratory sessions, and his sister came to some of them. In this exploratory period Mrs J felt that she and her inner good objects were subjected to a form of mental assault from both father and son. She took up with the family whether this could be intended to find out if she was a worthwhile opponent in a cynical game, or to make her undergo an ordeal to prove that she and her approach had both something to offer and a capacity to survive. The exploration clearly carried meaning for the family, and ongoing therapy with Mrs J, together with Dr K, her male co-therapist, was arranged.

Blood and knives formed part of the expressions of hatred, menace and violence between father and son, focused in the area of parental sexuality. Revenge for being excluded, coming from a split-off baby part of Tony, was rampant, and was probably exacerbated by actual experience of violence in childhood. Feelings of dearth existing amid a display of plenty, forming a stimulus to jealousy and envy, were taken up by the therapists as relevant to Tony's threatened attacks on his father, and his perception of his parents' rich sexuality. On the other hand, was he felt to be too dangerous to the family's image of itself to have a place within it? Father's business, which had a somewhat glossy image, had a branch in France, and some members of this 'jet-setting' family, the parents in particular, sometimes flew back from a Parisian weekend to their weekly Monday session. (A relative cared for the children if they remained in the UK.) The therapists commented on how they themselves were invited to envy what was often presented as the superiority of the family's glamorous, suggestively provocative and exciting world, as opposed to what was indicated as being their dull one, with out-of-date values. The family initially saw Mrs J's wish for a co-therapist as representing her feeling of needing protection. This was in fact true, although her predominant thought was that the presence of a male co-therapist was strongly indicated for this delinquent boy. Her motivation was later mocked and cynically designated as being merely her means of working in a bigger and better room.

It was important for the therapists to find a way in which they could relate constructively to the family; dangers abounded. There were attempts to seduce them into collusion with the manic, envy-provoking, delinquent currents of the family if they entered into discussions in close detail; there were also attempts to lure them into a more excited confrontation with this world. To respond from an anti-delinquent, 'super-egotistical', 'establishment' position would have been experienced as disparaging and unhelpful. To avoid this they found a method of working which allowed them some space to think together in the session. They always sat in the same chairs, leaving a little distance between them and the family. As well as talking to the family members directly, they also talked to each other openly about the family communications in a thoughtful but low-key manner; what they said was sometimes taken up by the family, sometimes ignored. This allowed a world of concern for their mutual good objects to be apparent in the session without seeming to attempt to impose them on the family. It also provided the therapists with the opportunity of cleansing their own minds by means of their shared discussion, particularly if they felt they had strayed into some manic current of family interaction.

Recriminations about past and present abounded within the family. Painful and violent instances in the children's early life were brought up, initially expressed largely as complaints between Tony and his father or his sister. These included grossly divergent views between Tony and his father as to why Tony had been sent away from home: because of Tony's violence according to Father; because of the violence towards him according to Tony. The past was kept alive as a form of weaponry. Squabbling between the children over present privileges was rampant. Tony frequently failed to carry out tasks entrusted to him, and was sometimes treated as if he were a living-in odd-job boy as opposed to a family member. Provocative rivalry was also expressed by the father and the son towards the therapists, Dr K in particular. But sexuality was also often represented by Father, with an expectation of support from Tony, as a male-dominated activity, in relation to which the men could get together and, with mutual pleasure, regard the women in the session – especially the stepmother and Mrs J –

merely as inferior sexual objects. There was also some testing out to see if Dr K could be drawn into this state of mind. These attempts were followed in the thoughtful conversation of the therapists, without directly engaging with some of the provocative dialogue or colluding with the denigration. On many matters, the daughter, Samantha, tended to emphasize her conformity to her father's wishes, frequently adopting an air of provocative superiority to Tony. Sometimes, however, she treated Tony as if he were her partner, leading the therapists to raise the question of Tony's roles – odd-job boy; Father's male anti-feminine support; sister's partner – and to wonder about the nature of a son's part in the family. Softer, more maternal currents emanated on the whole from the stepmother, often initiated by eye contact with Mrs J.

As the therapy progressed, there was an increasing interest in the therapists' contributions, and more tolerance of their relationship. Tolerance amongst family members also increased. Following on the therapists' attention in the sessions, unhappy and violent experiences of the past became more recognized for what they were, and less used as weapons with which to attack others. Current problems, such as complaints about Tony's failure to work and lack of achievement at school, also began to be addressed with less acrimony. Amid an accompaniment of some mild 'clashing of antlers', evidence of growing admiration for the male therapist, tempering the envy, could be observed in both Tony and his father. More normal rivalry between Tony and his sister for love, attention and some form of positive valuation from their father gradually became apparent.

Changes took place alongside each other, both within the family and in Tony himself. While the possibility of 'something happening', and the tension surrounding it, still remained, a reciprocal place for a father and a son which was not based on violent – particularly sexual – rivalry, and an equally violent response, became established in the family after nearly a year of work. The family, without any change in their general outlook on life, came actually to function as a family. With greater shared recognition of family membership, Tony's flaunting of delinquent and menacing behaviour, particularly against his father, subsided, and he gradually granted his stepmother some motherly function. Alongside this, the 'outward hideousness' of his way-out clothing and hairstyle – which had been understood as carrying a provocative function against his father, as well as being a general mark of his identity – diminished into less outrageously flamboyant adolescent gear. He became more able to study, and started to achieve in his school work. His peer-group life began to sound as if it carried some interest and friendship for him, as opposed to being represented as a means of support around his delinquency. He also, on his own initiative, made contact with his own mother after a long gap. His earlier clinging to the identity of a stealer and liar could now be seen as a means of holding himself together as an outsider to the world of family life, unable to risk loving without some hopeful belief in its reciprocation. This therapy helped Tony to find the place in his family that he needed, leading to a more benign representation of family life in his inner world and allowing introjective identification with good internal objects, able to support further adolescent development.

FAMILY EXPLORATIONS AND THERAPY: A BRIEF REVIEW

A brief family intervention can not only serve as an introduction to individual therapy, as with Eva and Paul, or family therapy, as with the Forrests and the Roses (Chapter 9), but contribute to the acceptance of such help. It can also help a family which finds itself in difficulties amid the sometimes bewildering processes of adolescence to gather itself together and relate to problematic issues within its membership. Understanding of enactments based on emotional ties between the generations which are no longer appropriate in adolescence can serve as a considerable relief to developmental strivings within the family. A move towards independence and adulthood could be hindered or stultified by unsevered ties of infancy on the part of parents or children (Doreen), unchallenged and worked-through assumptions (Ahmed) or intrusive projective activity (Martin).

Longer-term family therapy is different from an exploration in that it provides an opportunity for considerable change and development within the family, as we have just seen in the case of the Forrests. It is probably the treatment of choice when the difficulties are largely experienced as being within the family interaction itself; these include indications of family mythology, as was the case with the Rose family (Chapter 9); excessive splitting; fusion or non-differentiation between family members; or where scapegoating occurs (Copley, 1981).[2]

In considering the nature of this approach, it may be helpful to think about it briefly in the context of other family therapies with which readers may be familiar; some understanding derived from one may in fact be applicable to another. The cluster of what Minuchin *et al.* (1978) describe as transactional patterns of a family process encouraging somatization – namely 'enmeshment, overprotectiveness, rigidity and lack of conflict resolution' (p. 30) – can be seen in the Rose family (see Chapter 9). Similar features can be present within different approaches, but be answered differently within them. Minuchin *et al.* write: 'In the systems paradigm, every part of a system is seen as organizing and being organized by other parts. An individual's behaviour is simultaneously both caused and causative' (p. 20). The psychoanalytic family therapy described here also stresses the interpersonal, interactional nature of family dynamics as understood in psychoanalytic thinking, drawing in particular on the use of projective identification described in Bion's work. It is also indebted to the writers quoted in the context of group dynamics in Chapter 10. As, however, a major emphasis is placed on the psychic reality of the inner world and unconscious phantasy, a sense of causation within a family will be experienced and related to differently within this approach.

Minuchin *et al.* require the therapist to act at times in the modality of a director, and at others to affiliate and enter coalitions against some members of the family to unbalance the system (p. 106). Prescriptions for family action are also given by other family therapists including Selvini Palazzoli *et al.* (1978). In contrast, the psychoanalytically based family therapy described here needs, by its nature, to be non-directive, non-affiliative and non-prescriptive (Box *et al.*, 1981). To be otherwise would be incompatible with the provision of space in the therapists' minds for containment of the family processes, and allowing families the opportunity of meaningful change based on their own experience.

9 AN APPROACH TO PSYCHOANALYTIC FAMILY THERAPY: A HOUSE AND ITS INHABITANTS – A FAMILY DRAMA

Work with the Roses, a South American family, took place on a weekly basis for about a year. Miss F, the therapist, saw the family alone. The family presentation was often dramatic, evoking in Miss F a sense of witnessing – and indeed, at times, being asked to take part in – a family drama in which the members had overlapping parts. Miss F attempted to encompass family members' dramatic enactment of their mythology, and to bring this into the area of thought where its meaning could be addressed.

The external 'stage' on which the drama was portrayed as taking place was often the family house. An internal stage was frequently glimpsed, on which family phantasies about the inhabitants of a 'house', often bearing some relationship to a mother's body, were played out.[1] To bring a live experience to the reader is always difficult; here I seek to retain something of the dramatic element in Miss F's account. It is a pity that it is not possible to present such an interaction in operatic form! By means of such a medium it might be more feasible to convey the impact on Miss F of the various family voices speaking at the same time, and perhaps even to pick out their separate content – the latter was sometimes a problem in the sessions themselves. One might also enable the audience to experience the drama and the 'music' of the communications more closely. Additional voices could convey not only some of this family's external background, but also some of the phantasies sensed in their mythology.

A medical referral arrives at the small-town Family Centre where

Miss F works. Bella, the referred patient, youngest daughter in the family, is described as an emaciated anorexic of about sixteen. She is said to have become withdrawn over the last three years or so, to have 'lost' her periods, and is only just managing to attend school on a part-time basis. The older sister, Carla, aged twenty-one, works, and is described as having difficulties which bear some resemblance to those of Bella, although they are much less severe: she eats in binges, has become thinner, and is much less sociable than previously. Father has a small ranch-style farm; Mother is at home. The family have made two previous attempts at therapy (neither psychoanalytically based), but soon withdrew from the first and are being referred on from the second. The referring therapists (who had 'prescribed', without avail, that Father should become more involved with Mother) are unwilling to work further with the family because of Father's sporadic attendance and Carla's refusal to continue, and suggest that a psychoanalytically based approach might be appropriate.

A long letter from Mother dramatically amplifies the referral: Bella will not eat unless Carla eats the same food at the same time, which Carla refuses to do; Bella says she hates Carla, but rings daily from school to check that Mother is cooking enough food for her. Apart from going to school, Bella refuses to go out and stays in her room for hours, often inside her wardrobe in the dark, banging and crying; she will only wear old clothes and is altogether unlike her cheerful, more friendly self of a few years back. Could the service help Mother with 'her' daughter? Miss F – with the support of the centre, and despite serious misgivings related to the apparent severity of the difficulties, the failed interventions, the reported limited participation by Father, Carla's non-attendance and Mother's very personal approach – offers to see the family for a series of exploratory interviews.

THE EXPLORATORY PHASE

Carla does not come. The initial impact on Miss F of the three family members who do attend is considerable. They frequently talk at once. Bella, to Mother's distress, looks dishevelled and neglected.

She is dressed, at her own insistence, in baggy, shabby clothing, with no particular style, asserting that she does not deserve better. She conveys a sense of illness, but is very active in the session. She screams and shouts (for example, rudely to Father: 'Who wants to hear you?'), and sometimes hits or pummels Mother, claiming that she favours Carla. Mother frequently appears not to notice this, but at other times she complains (often correctly) that Father does not notice, and that he did not attend the previous therapy. Father says morosely that there is no place for him. The impression is of a non-listening, shouting, blaming mêlée. As the exploration proceeds, anxieties and complaints pour out, voiced particularly by Mother to Miss F. These largely recount, in considerable detail, the week's events, many of which are detailed variations on the recurrent topics mentioned in the initial referral. Bella won't come downstairs; Carla – who, according to Mother, 'can' eat, and according to Father is not really anorexic – won't eat what Bella might eat, so Bella won't eat. Bella complains that Carla binges and then won't eat, and says she will make Carla suffer. But Bella also continues to check that Mother cooks enough to feed Carla properly. All this continues alongside – but separate from – a quite amicable agreement that Mother cooks more than enough, and enjoys doing so. Both Mother and Bella also insist that Carla and Bella are not jealous of each other.

Father complains that holidays and outings are arranged around the girls, that he does not get Mother to himself, and he looks forward to the children leaving home. Bella tells Father off for neglecting Mother and leaving it to Carla to help her to look after one of the ponies when it is sick, but she also complains bitterly that holidays and outings are arranged for Carla's convenience. She refuses to accompany Mother and Carla when they go shopping, with what may be threatening undertones of a suicidal response when she is left behind. Mother, however, stresses that she begs Bella to come, and is anxious about her when they are out. Miss F finds all these complaints painful; the hardest of all to bear are the parental accounts of how Bella shuts herself inside her wardrobe in the evenings and screams and shouts with no explanation.

Despite the noise and complaints, a feeling of closeness within the family is also apparent. Mother and Carla regularly return home from their shopping trips with little gifts for all the family, often including something for the ponies which the children used to ride when they were small. The parents indignantly insist that Bella is not mentally ill and so, of course, they have refused hospitalization for her. Father in particular asserts that they are a 'normal family'; the first therapy was abandoned for suggesting otherwise. But Bella histrionically calls for Miss F to rescue her, as if she is caught in some abnormal place with a prison-like quality.

Miss F feels the overwhelming impact of these dramatic outpourings, and the absence of space for thought. Her attempts to intervene thoughtfully are frequently interrupted by interjections from Mother of 'Just let me say this' as Miss F is about to speak – Mother is usually attempting to recount even more of the disturbing events which have occurred since their last meeting. Miss F ends the session at a time known in advance to the family, and Mother, after Miss F has indicated that this time has come, often begs for advice (the giving of which, Miss F has already clarified, is not part of the way she works). Miss F feels that she is used in the session as a receptacle, on the lines of a toilet which is in continuous demand, but insufficiently available. She recognizes with the family that Mother, as family spokeswoman, voices the urgently felt need for her to hear what they feel to be their constantly accumulating, unbearably painful complaints, often directed at each other, which arise between and during the sessions. When the end of the session comes, and they feel that some of the experience of the painful events is located in it, they want her, quickly and separately from it, to tell them something that will ameliorate matters for the coming week.

Miss F also gathers together and comments on what appear to be the dramatically voiced but only marginally heard anxieties about death within the family: Mother and Father anxious about Bella starving, Bella anxious about Mother starving Carla, and Mother anxious about something happening to Bella if she and Carla go out. The family, sounding amazed, agree, and there is some lessening of the degree of noise with which complaints are hurled in the session. Actually being listened to with attention, and what is conveyed actually being thought about, is clearly an amazing – and helpful – experience. Miss F also indicates that she has taken in both sides of the family argument as to whether Father is a paternal 'dropout' from the family, or whether there is no room for him within it. Following on this, Miss F raises for examination in the transference whether there may be divergent views within the family as to why she herself does not work as one of a pair of therapists, on the lines of their previous experience, but in response she is simply told that they are happy with her.

After four initial exploratory sessions Miss F undertakes a review with the family, and thinks about future contact. With this particular family she also sees Bella and her parents separately on one occasion each; Bella wants this, and the parents also ask for it, saying that Bella is the one to be 'treated'. Miss F also needs sequestered space with Bella to think about how disturbed she may be. Seen alone, Bella speaks fairly calmly, but can only focus fairly repetitively on family aspects of her problem. She cannot relate to her statement about not deserving better clothing. She admits to some appetite, but insists that Carla must not be slimmer than she is. Although she lacks insight as exemplified by her comment 'You're not suggesting that I'm jealous of my sister, are you?' – she seems able to tolerate Miss F's affirmative response.

The degree of splitting and intermeshed psychopathology within the family – manifested, *inter alia*, by the diffuse recriminations of the sessions, the shared involvement in not eating by the girls, together with the nature of the parental response – suggests the appropriateness of at least some further family work. The absence of Carla is worrying, however, especially as the family emphasis has now moved from Carla herself not wanting to come, to the insistence, voiced by Bella and protectively acquiesced in by Mother, that she must not do so, implying that harm could come to Bella if she did. Miss F wonders inwardly whether this absence would make family work impossible, and whether intensive individual therapy for Bella might prove more feasible, but dismisses the latter plan; there is no clear indication for individual work coming from Bella, and in any case it would be unlikely to be sustained without family support. If Bella were to be seen separately as 'the' patient, Miss F has some doubts about the extent of active family commitment, despite the needs of Mother in particular for containment; breaks could also be more disturbing. The provision of more than one worker would also stretch limited resources. Therefore Miss F, after consultation with her colleagues, proposes a continuation of family work, initially for a term but with further extensions by agreement as necessary. The family accept. Miss F, while she recognizes that there are family anxieties about Carla's attendance, reiterates the therapeutic desirability for it. Miss F always provides a chair for Carla, and makes it clear that she is held in mind throughout the therapy.

Where work is to continue, as here, the preliminary exploratory process provides a useful background for decisions about management issues; the centre confirms with the general practitioner that he will continue to monitor Bella's physical health, and also ascertains that in-patient treatment facilities could be available, if needed.

THE APPROACH TO THE WORK

The process of containment (Bion, 1962a), as described in Chapter 4 and discussed in relation to family work in Chapter 8, underlies this work. Miss F pays attention to the constellation of family communication. Holding in mind what the family is conveying does not yield immediate clarity of meaning, but provides mental space in which to treat the communications as potentially meaningful. This family appear to use Miss F as a kind of toilet container into which they can evacuate their pain. Although they refer to fears of death from the beginning, members do not seem able really to experience them and understand that they have them. Miss F, by bearing and thinking about the dramatic and evacuatory material poured out in the sessions, is gradually able to experience and reconvey elements of its contents so that they become more meaningful and available for thought by the family, as in the case of these anxieties about death. Here Miss F has much in common with the mother who uses her maternal reverie to contain the anxieties her infant conveys to her by means of projective identification (Bion, 1959, 1962a).

Miss F, in contrast to the family's 'not noticing', actively gathers together and comments on varying individual impressions and views: views of being left out; differing views on Father's role; anxieties about death. These are attended to in a family context:

Father's doubt as to whether there is a place for him in the family is both held together and contrasted with Mother's and Bella's criticisms. The provision of this thoughtful attention appears to lie behind the diminution of the family 'noise', and may have had something to do with the wish to continue, particularly on Father's part; he now attends regularly, with increased involvement in the sessions themselves, much to Mother's surprise. Holding together the varying contributions of family members helps the understanding of themes which are important for a family. Any understanding that may gradually arise in the course of the work is presented not as a 'solution' to a problem but as a response to the family's feelings. This, of course, is similar to what happens in individual psychoanalytically based work.

Miss F's containing function in thinking about the family's interaction is paramount; although she actively notices the destructive aspects of their behaviour to each other, to make this a major focus could be experienced as a hurling back of abuse such as occurs in the family's own interaction. When she is about to speak after a particularly acrimonious family exchange, Miss F sometimes senses that Mother's interruptions convey a fear that Miss F will hurl something back. Miss F then speaks to the fear that she would not take in what the family want her to hear but, instead, would return to them the painful recriminations that they felt had been disposed of in the session, just as, they feel, they do among themselves. In other words, while she attempts to function as a container, she speaks to the family fear that she could do the opposite. Within herself she thinks of this as an anxiety that she might function as a leaky or overflowing toilet. As the work continues we shall see how it is possible to find greater meaning in the material, and actively to explore the family's responses to any understanding.

ONGOING WORK

A large part of the weekly sessions consists of an account of the awfulness of the preceding week, in which complaints and blaming are very apparent. Nevertheless, more periods of comparative calm follow the decision to continue, and the family members begin to speak of their history. (The therapist herself tends to raise questions of history only in the context of a need for further understanding at any particular time.) Mother is an only child; her father left home when she was a baby. Mother's mother died when Bella was twelve, having spent the last years of her life in a home, senile and confused, but she was visited regularly, apparently with considerable affection, by both Mother and Father. Miss F questions whether Bella's chosen shabby, ill-fitting clothing, which could be evocative of a confused old lady in dressing-gown and slippers, has some link with this, but the family all agree that this is not so. The parents have said that they are a Jewish family, and Miss F questions if there can be some reference to the Holocaust, but the parents maintain firmly that both families were settled in South America before the war, and had no active European connections. In contrast to what seemed to have been both parents' real affection for Mother's mother, Mother speaks vituperatively against Father's mother, his sister and the latter's children, whom, she claims, his mother favours. She resents Father's regular visits to his mother (his father is dead), and complains about how Father took on responsibilities for his sister's wedding, and also for their own, occasioned by Father's own father's meanness and non-involvement. Miss F, unaware what significance this may or may not have, simply recognizes that she has noticed what might be preoccupations within the family, such as those of absent, opting-out or mean fathers within their families of origin. The parts played in the life of the Rose family by some of the relatives they mentioned became clearer later. They all remained somewhere in Miss F's mind during the therapy and, with hindsight, might be portrayed in our imaginary operatic set, to convey some additional element in the underlying family preoccupations.

As the sessions continue, Miss F becomes aware of graphic and recurring imagery in regard to the family within the family house. Mother, by daytime, is seen cooking in the kitchen and, in the evening, alone in the living-room or, more often, upstairs in one of the girls' bedrooms, watching television with Carla or preoccupied with Bella, frequently attempting to cajole her from her wardrobe. Father, in the evening, is often seen isolated in the kitchen, watching television alone, or going back out through the kitchen door to the ranch. The existence of a parental bedroom in this 'set' is not apparent, although Father is sometimes disapprovingly described by Mother as going to the bathroom unclothed when the girls are around. A little French window in the living area, through which the girls sometimes slip out and feed the ponies, is frequently depicted.

Father complains on more than one occasion that his job in the family is relegated to being the 'money-bags'; Mother does not allow him to try to get Bella to stop banging and crying in her wardrobe and to come downstairs in the evening. Mother maintains that in doing so he would be violent; Bella shouts her agreement. What would happen if Mother died is often brought up: Father says he would leave home, as he could not look after the girls; Mother says she would not want the girls to quarrel over what was left. (Mother is neither particularly old nor in poor health.) On one occasion Father says he does not want Mother to draw on her savings now, in case he dies.

Miss F shares with the family what she understands at the time in relation to these anxieties concerning death, although she is aware that she is only beginning to glimpse something of their possible meaning. She spells out how they describe their house and the activities within it as if it were made up of separately occupied compartments, and how in this context they portray a picture of a house of living death, a cemetery-house, linked with the image of the body of a dead mother, with fighting daughters, not getting enough or greedily wanting more, within it. There is an isolated father, potentially violent (according to Mother and Bella), or leaving home (according to Father), but in neither case with any capacity to maintain life within the house. Miss F links this with a possible fear of some disastrous sequence to a coming together of the compartmentalized family, as they believe could occur if Carla came to the clinic. She reminds the family of Bella's earlier plea to be rescued, and wonders aloud if Bella's screaming and shouting from the wardrobe, which causes so much distress to them all, may represent for the family some idea of being locked in an emotional cemetery tomb, from which they want her help to escape. A somewhat softer atmosphere gradually becomes apparent in the room. As the end of the term approaches, the family and Miss F agree to an open-ended continuation of the therapy.

Considerable change has also taken place. Father is heard to say that he has tried to refrain from an adverse comment about Bella to please his wife. Bella admits openly, though briefly, to some appetite, and to being troublesome at times. Her constant ringing up and checking on whether Mother is feeding Carla has stopped. She no longer spends the evenings banging in the wardrobe, although she still often cries on her bed, where Mother's attempts at comfort may end with Mother herself joining in the noisy wail. Miss F talks to them about the forthcoming seasonal interval, when they will not be meeting, and what she considers to be their doubts as to whether she will keep them alive in her mind, and her mind alive for them, over the coming separation. They wonder if Miss F has ever worked with a family as difficult as themselves, and smile at her suggestion that members may feel that she has a relationship to an 'easier' family at home, which may be relevant to their feelings about the time when they will not be meeting. (The family are aware that she wears a wedding ring, although she works professionally under her maiden name.) From this they go on to talk of earlier, happier days when the children were little, and they were a more expressively loving family. They recount how they used to send birthday cards – not only to each other, but also to and 'from' the children's ponies.

The lessening of the symptoms and the noisy evacuations follows the thinking space and attention the therapist provides in her mind for the family. Miss F, initially probably experienced as providing much-needed containment on a somewhat part-object basis, now represents someone more personal for the family, linked with an idea of parenting. The family may have some wish not to be so difficult, and are able to share memories of happier days. Miss F recognizes with the family the changed emotional feeling in relation to herself in 'here-and-now' transference terms. We are aware that a therapeutic process, with a clearly discernible relationship to Miss F, is under way.

Unforeseen building work is undertaken at the centre during the vacation, and when the family return, furniture is stacked around in the passage, as if ready for removal. Mother asks Miss F in dismay:

'Are you packing up and leaving us?' Miss F talks about members' feelings of being abandoned by her in the interval, and their doubts that she might not be able to keep them in mind, but would just disappear, which they take as being confirmed by the activity in the centre.

The atmosphere within the family has also deteriorated during the vacation, and rows take place at home and at the centre. Father complains that he is excluded from the kitchen at times when Bella, who refuses to be observed eating, might eat, and Bella responds: 'Who wants to see you?' Mother wails: 'Let her eat!' Bella, weeping furiously, cries: 'Only five minutes alone!' Bella's screaming on her bed has become worse during the break; Father admits to having entered her room and turned on the light when he felt he could no longer endure a particularly lengthy bout. Mother and Bella threaten to call the police if there should be a repetition. Mutual accusations of selfishness abound, and Miss F wonders aloud if eating is felt to be selfish. But the ponies have been bought new ribbons and given treats of sugar. Bella claims that people are treated like animals; Miss F adds that animals may be treated like people, and used as recipients for the love which it seems difficult to express within family life.

After some weeks the sessions are again calmer, and a lessening of Bella's screaming at home is reported. Miss F links this with the resumption of therapy and feeling attended to by her. In one session there is a sharing of their daydreams of being a nice family: this is depicted as being able to sit round a table and all eat together normally. Bella says she doesn't want Carla to die; she also says that she is ashamed if she herself is seen eating. Carla is reported as saying that she won't eat 'Mother's rubbish', and claiming that the good food goes to Bella. Mother says she nearly brought Carla, who is now willing to come. Bella protests. 'Sorry, Miss F,' says Mother, reassuring Bella that Carla won't be brought.

Miss F comments that the family seem afraid to experience the presence of Carla, representing someone who is left to eat rubbish, together with Bella, represented as getting the good food, believing that this could harm Bella; the wish to be a nice family and eat together may feel unrealizable because of what is experienced as a harmful imbalance between what different members get and want.

Miss F adds that it is she, Miss F, however, who is to feel the loss of
Carla at the 'therapy table' and, in the sessions, is not to have the
nice, complete family they believe she wants, thus making it clear
that the pain of not being the 'nice family' is being split off from the
family's own experience and projected into her. Mother now
speaks of being too fat herself. Father says he likes this, and
cheerfully claims that he feels this gives him his money's worth!
Mutually vituperative blaming about selfishness in relation to some
expenditure now takes place. Miss F follows the theme of
selfishness and greedy possessiveness that she experiences as being
portrayed within the family: she contrasts beliefs about dying of
starvation or being given rubbish on the one hand, with being seen
to eat or being too fat and embarrassed about having had good food
on the other, and suggests that shame and potential guilt about
eating seem to lie behind the family rows on this subject. The family
agree; Bella adds that no one in their family, including herself, can
think.

The theme of feeding the children's old ponies comes up again;
Miss F comments that they seem to be allowed to be fat with
impunity. Father describes how he had actually wept over the death
of a much-loved male pony some time ago; after this he had
watched the birth of another one, checking to see if it was male –
only to see whether they should call it Juan or Juanita, he adds.
Another male pony is mentioned as having died in the vet's
'hospital'. Mother, in commenting warmly on their shared affection
for the ponies, says they are a small family. Miss F, who recalls
having already made such an enquiry some time earlier and met
with a negative response, asks again about a possible miscarriage
in the family. She is told – somewhat dismissively, as if it is hardly
worth mentioning – of a quite early miscarriage between the births
of Carla and Bella.

Miss F refers again to the warm, human feelings attributed to the
ponies within the small family, and wonders about this missing
baby. Drawing on Father's weeping for the death of the loved male
pony, the death of another male pony in 'hospital', and watching
for the sex of another at birth, Miss F says it sounds as if the family
feel that the miscarried baby would have been a boy. Father
describes how he helped to clear up after the sudden miscarriage,

called the doctor, and left the bundle for him. He had never thought to look for or ask about the sex of the child. He agrees to the suggestion of sadness, but insists that this has nothing to do with whether the baby was a boy. Mother says that Bella knew nothing of the miscarriage, which occurred about three years before she was born; Bella, however, says that she has known about it for as long as she can remember, and also that she had heard that Father was furious that she herself was not a boy, with which Mother agrees. Miss F wonders whether Father had been expected to dispose of most of the bundle of feelings around the miscarriage for the family, including his own, but also questions whether Bella's banging and wailing in the wardrobe is relevant to feelings about a non-live birth of a possible son to continue the name in this Jewish family. Father then tells her that he changed his surname because his father objected to his marriage to Mother on grounds which, he felt, had to do with his father's financial selfishness.

Miss F clarifies with them that Bella's illness started when she was about thirteen, and wonders about any link with the missing family joy of a boy's Barmitzvah. Yes, says Father, but what would it have cost! Miss F comments on the apparently 'money-bags' nature of Father's response, as financial spokesman for the family, about the cost of a Barmitzvah, and goes on to ponder what could be an emotional cost for the family in the context of the giving up of the family name, whereby a link between a father and a son is broken. Later, when the isolation and withdrawal of Bella and Carla are again referred to, Miss F talks about the emotional cost of thinking about a missing brotherly companion with a circle of friends who might have been in contact with the two girls, who had been described earlier as sociable and outgoing when they were younger.

It now seems possible to put together more formally some of the understanding that has gradually been developing with and about this family. It operates largely under female dominance, and could be described as having features of a matriarchal and especially 'girl-gang' family, as described by Meltzer and Harris (1986, pp. 162–3). In the latter families, an often greedy drive to possess what is regarded as necessary to fulfil the needs of weaker members is common, but without acknowledgement of any dependence, and with a tendency to project guilt. Drama, rather than thought, is the food of this family. The absence of thought referred to here is the absence of family members' ability to find space in their minds to become aware of – to 'K' – their own emotional experiences. Some change, however, has taken place during their attendance at the centre. Bella's earlier comment about no one in their family being able to think seems to indicate some feeling of being at least partially in touch with the situation.

A dramatic enactment of family mythology – predominantly orchestrated by Mother, but often in conjunction with the girls – is staged in the family house, itself representing an infantile phantasy of a mother's body and its contents as described in the work of Klein (1932). The substance of the myth is understandable in terms of shared, intermeshing individual psychopathology relating to this mother's body from which life does not emanate. There is a shared family notion of babies waiting to be born, but dying inside of starvation, unfed with proper food owing to the greed of others; it is thus shaming to be seen to be manifesting greed by eating and leaving others to starve. Central to the family myth is the miscarriage of the believed-to-be-missing son, and the guilt to be avoided about his non-birth occasioned by the greed and selfishness of the family members. Guilt, or its avoidance, is not directly experienced as such by any individual, but is part of what is projected and enacted within the family, without any mental impact. The family drama enacts the drive to keep alive, to blame others, and to avoid blame and guilt oneself. At a deeper level, however, it is Father's non-participation in the life of the family that is felt to deprive the dying children of proper fatherly internal food and care, and to contribute to the maternal house being experienced in phantasy as a cemetery. Implicit loving fatherly sexual activity, leading to the birth of a desired new baby and sustaining a mother, together with what are experienced as her internal babies, is a necessary aspect of a fatherly presence needed to provide containment at a deeply intimate level to the mother in the rearing of the children, with all its accompanying anxiety (Meltzer, 1973, p. 68). In this family, Father may be designated as the clearer-up of the mess of the miscarriage, but this is depicted as a physical action, without any real 'noticing';

hence it provides no possibility of real containment of its painful mental content. This is projected and enacted among the family.

As some of what is brought by the family gradually becomes more comprehensible in the process of therapy, Miss F shares further understanding with the members, session by session, in language appropriate to them. The indicated presence of the missing boy in the mythology enables her to address more openly how frightened the family are of not feeling a nice family, and how they feel their greed stood in the way of the birth of a further baby. As she gains understanding, she can show them how members enact various parts, change the actor, scene and specific content of the drama, project the greed and thus protect themselves from experiencing guilt individually: Bella can scream in the womb/tomb cupboard as the one imprisoned, waiting to be born; Carla may occasionally binge alone, but she is also said to complain that the good food goes to Bella, and she will not eat Mother's rubbish, with which she is left. Food, realistically only too available and rejected as far as Mother is concerned, is never felt to be sufficient for all who need it. Bella's shame can be avoided if Father, cast as the accusing intruder, does not see her eating. Bella can check if Mother cooks enough for Carla, and protect herself from feeling greedy. But this does not mean that Carla should necessarily eat the food; if Bella and Carla eat exactly the same food, and are equally slim, feelings of greed can be avoided, and both jealousy and envy can be felt to be non-existent.

Father can experience himself as wrongfully excluded from his share of the fat richness of the mother-house and its inside, but by others he may be experienced as selfishly seeking to appropriate the riches of its contents for himself, turning out the children, or alternatively as intruding violently into the compartmentalized 'privacy' of the mother and 'her' children, as depicted in the scenes around Bella's bedroom. But Mother can also speak of herself as if she were a dead house, with the girls fighting over the residuary contents, and Father can portray himself as unable to succour life. It is also possible to share with the Roses how the cosseting of the ponies may represent loving feelings towards representations of new babies in their family, but also serves to mask their actual absence.

These thoughts are conveyed to the family as seems appropriate in the context of their ongoing mutual complaints. Miss F perceives herself at times to be appreciated by one or other member – more often than not Bella – as attempting to think on their behalf. She acknowledges this as well as recognizing that the understanding she offers is not generally acceptable to the family, and that members are distressed by the links she seeks to make.

Father continues to remark that he is unconvinced that the miscarried baby was a boy. Miss F feels overwhelmed by sadness despite these disclaimers, and, making use of this sadness in the countertransference, comments again on how Father cleared up the miscarriage, and maybe was meant to have cleared any sadness away for all of them; now, perhaps, it is she who is asked to bear this for the family. Father now says that he always had bad relations with his own father; he died one month after Bella was born, and never saw her. Miss F acknowledges the painful complication of Father's relationship with his own father, and wonders if his father would have seen Bella if she had been a boy. Father agrees that his father would have wanted to have seen his grandson.

A MINI-DRAMA AT THE CENTRE

There is, however, a considerable and rapid change in Bella. She becomes calmer, much more cheerful, wears new, fitting, adolescent clothing and make-up, and appears plumper. Having left school some time earlier, she suddenly takes a full-time job, from which the family insist that no time off is possible; they ask Miss F for a later therapy time, which she cannot currently provide. A mini-drama now takes place at Miss F's centre. The parents discover that a few people are seen later than they are, and ring up the administrator demanding this facility for themselves with another worker. Without waiting for a reply, they leave a message for Miss F that they will not be coming to see her any more. Neither a change of time nor a change of worker is offered, and Miss F writes inviting the family to return; after a few weeks the parents come back, clearly with some pleasure. Miss F tries, without success, to engage with them in thinking about this mini-drama; they continue to stress that they naturally seek to do what is best for Bella. Miss F puzzles aloud about how she was expected to respond immediately to what was conceived of as the family's need when she was asked for a change of time, removing any needs of others from her mind. She also tries to explore how the family sought to replace her by another therapist; was she also to be dropped out of their mind? She suggests that either she was not expected to notice the 'miscarriage' of the therapy existing between the family and herself as a real event having meaning for them all, or, perhaps, was expected to bear all the feelings of loss about it. With hindsight, however, Miss F regretted that she had not sufficiently understood or taken up what she later thought was the family's negative response to her failure to provide a later time 'on demand' for what was perceived as Bella's need, and that in not doing so, she was probably experienced as being like Mother's view of Father's mother: someone who favoured another family in preference to theirs.

Work with the parents continues, punctuated by a further seasonal break. The relationship between the husband and wife gradually moderates. The 'set' of the family house now includes a parental bedroom, and the parents tell Miss F that thanks to her, there is a great improvement in their sexual relationship. (No overt work on this theme had taken place.) Mother reminds Father to wear a dressing-gown in front of the children, which seems to underline the differentiation between husbandly and fatherly aspects of family life. They tell Miss F that Bella, as well as holding down her job successfully, is somewhat better at home, and eating a little more. This improved parental relationship, with some recognition of quality of contact, contrasts with Father's earlier wish to have his 'money's worth' of the 'fat' mother (greedily) to himself, with the emphasis more on the quantity of contact. Miss F comments on how improvement in the parental relationship, with wider aspects of family life attended to within it, seems to be accompanied by some change in Bella.

The parents use the time more for themselves, but Miss F does not turn the contact into marital therapy as such. She maintains a family approach, with space available for Bella and Carla to attend, and gives ongoing attention to their absence.

A little later Miss F hears that Bella has now begun to menstruate again, and is doing well at work. The parents, however, are still worried about her minimal eating, and want Miss F to see her. Miss F, although she has some doubts that she may be being caught up in the family drama, does offer a later family appointment, as she can now do so without disrupting other patients. It is clear to the family, however, that this does involve her in some special arrangement. Bella attends. She looks well; she is quite plump, and smartly dressed. She talks belittlingly of what she refers to as Carla's jealousy (probably meaning envy) of her life, as if such a base emotion were foreign to her. She recounts how Carla now stays in her room excessively, and that she herself no longer needs to see Miss F. Miss F comments how it is Carla who is now represented, and also denigrated, as the 'shut-in' one, while Bella herself is represented as 'outside' and 'free'. But as the end of the session approaches, Bella loses her superior air, screams, and says she does not want to 'go' any more, and it is difficult to finish the session. Miss F takes up the ambiguity sensed in the 'go', linking it with Bella's claim that she does not need to come, yet she finds it difficult to leave. Maybe Carla can represent not only the iller and imprisoned one, as Bella herself used to do, but also someone who, at the end of the session, does not have to 'go', linked with the idea of a baby felt to be enviably existing in a cosier inside place, who doesn't have to 'go' out into the world.

The drama thus continues in different terms, indicating the need for more family work, essentially with the whole family. However, a phantasy of a baby inside a 'mother-house' – not shut-in and dying, but felt to be in an actually enviable place – suggests some emotional change and development with increased relationship to life. Although increased understanding of family dynamics was gained, and no other patients were displaced, Miss F felt, with hindsight, that it had been a mistake to make this special arrangement around Bella, as it fitted too closely into the family pattern requiring Bella to come and Carla to stay away, and also provided space for dramatization that could not be worked through.

I will comment on only some of the remaining work with this family. Bella does not come again. There is sometimes talk of Carla coming, but she never does. Miss F is told that she is either ill, or frightened to come because Bella has threatened reprisals if she were to do so. Miss F, recalling the earlier 'Sorry, Miss F' about Carla not coming, points out that the parents do not press either daughter to come, and talks of how it is she, again, who is to feel the loss of a wanted Carla in the therapy. She also links these accounts with what she sees as the family mythology of a missing baby, and wonders whether there is feeling that a baby, even though there is vacant place available, might be so afraid of greedy, envious reprisals for occupying it that it might feel frightened to be born.

One day Miss F hears about changes at the ranch, and of Mother's objection to a smelly, noisy tractor of Father's being parked near the house when Bella is trying to sleep. For Miss F this evokes imagery of a mother-house with a precious baby upstairs (in the area of the breast), and a father depicted as being full of mess, somewhere down below, and felt to violate a horizontal line splitting the house into separate upstairs and downstairs compartments. Father says again that he will leave the house and children if Mother dies; the image of an untended mother and baby, and either a helpless father or an attacking one – in this case by means of bad smells – recurs. Mother goes on to complain of Father's lack of interest in the apparent identification and possible extradition of a man who is locally believed to be an ex-Nazi, but who, strangely, is reputed actually to have helped Jews at times. She also mentions Father's unwillingness to see Anne Frank's house if they were to visit Europe. Following some exploration by Miss F, the existence of some distant European relatives in Holland, not direct forebears, some of whom perished in the Holocaust, now comes to light, but the family do not treat this as having any specific significance for them. Miss F reflects on different points of view: one indicating the wrongful bringing of mess to a special mother-and-baby sanctum by a violent, felt-to-be-Nazi-like father, and thus dangerous to the 'Anne Frank' child in the house; the other of a father to whom Nazi-like qualities are ascribed, who is kept away from helping the mother and children. Miss F talks about the difficulties of joint exploration of any co-existence within the family of 'ex-Nazi' qualities and helpfulness.

THE FINAL PHASE

Miss F's next seasonal absence is a short one, and the parents return asking expectantly if she is pleased to see them. Mother says she has hardly complained about Father's mother recently, with the implication that this should please Miss F. Miss F comments that they feel they have done some good 'homework' in the interval, and expect her to be glad; she wonders if both parents feel that she is pleased on their behalf about an idea of possible reconciliation between Mother and her mother-in-law. Father indicates pleasure; Mother concurs, but specifically excludes her sister-in-law from any possible contact, and goes on to revive old grudges about the non-provision for family weddings by Father's father. Father says that Bella and Carla are now more friendly with each other; he would like a holiday alone with Mother, and he would like the girls to leave home. Mother says she feels that the children would die if they were left. Miss F points out how Father's wish for this exclusive relationship with Mother seems to lead to the girls being relocated in the 'mother-house cemetery' in Mother's mind, isolated from fatherly thinking and care. She puzzles aloud, as she has puzzled before, about the recurrent theme of Father, instead of his father, having provided for his sister's and their own wedding, and how the family seem to be influenced by an image of a non-providing and also excluded grandfather. This leads to both parents talking with warmth of Mother's longing for grandchildren and overt curiosity about their presence in Miss F's family, with an expectation of this being the case. Miss F suggests that she represents in their minds an idea of family and generational continuity, with some implicit link to a husband who would want to be a grandfather.

In the next session Father says reflectively that he had never previously thought of the miscarriage of a son: 'Don't you think it's natural for a son to want a father?' Miss F adds: 'And perhaps also for a father to want a son', and ponders further about the unhappy relationship with Father's father. Father mentions somewhere here how Mother has tried to find her father, to no avail, and also talks about how he himself had thought of retaking the family name, but had felt unable to do so. Mother says she could not forgive Father's family and would not invite them to a wedding of the next generation. Father now recounts how his father had left his mother and sisters (that is, Father's grandmother and aunts; his grandfather had already died) behind in Europe, where they had presumably perished. Miss F talks of the painful failure of not being able to find a benign image of a father, here represented by Mother's missing father, and of the terrible sense of being made to feel unforgivably selfish if one is linked in name with a survivor of the Holocaust, a father who could not keep his family alive; this seemed to add to the difficulty of thinking about a son or father wanting each other, of a son being born, or of any forgiving link between generations. Father, in sombre tones, says again that he cannot retake the family name, and that any religious significance in so doing would be to please Mother. Miss F questions the possibility of religious help; Father says no. Father doubts if they are the normal family he believed them to be.

The parents' regular attendance falls away. Father sourly complains that he is not allowed into family life, and wants an immediate solution to their problems to be found. Miss F sadly recognizes the painful awareness of earlier history, which they had wanted to keep out of their family life, but now feel was brought into prominence by means of their contact with her. The parents talk of Miss F not having helped but of having been so kind, and indicate that they will not return. Miss F feels left to mourn the miscarriage of the work.

DISCUSSION

The suffering among survivors of concentration camps has been widely reported (Krystal and Niederland, 1971). Feelings of chronic depression, anxiety with a profound sense of hopelessness, alienation, loss of belief and sense of purpose are described as common symptoms. The children of survivors are frequently vested with extra value, in that they are felt to embody the last hope for family survival and are psychically required to replace the unfinished lives of those who perished. Sigal (1971) suggests that the demands made by such relationships may amount to an experience akin to parental deprivation for the children, and may have a further effect on the children's children. A research study (Sigal *et al.*, 1973) describes parents who were survivors of Nazi persecution expressing more difficulties over the control of their children than other parents. Their children also showed greater difficulties in self-control, and were more rivalrous towards their siblings than others in the study. The research was taken to support the hypothesis that such parents, preoccupied with unfinished mourning of their parents and siblings, cannot respond to their own children's needs and, further, that the children could be expressing aggressive responses which their guilt-ridden parents were unable to express. It was also suggested that such difficulties could be compounded by adolescent identity problems – adolescents becoming disturbed either by identifying with their parents' preoccupations, or by reacting against them.

The Rose family had earlier conveyed a sense of actual and emotional distance from the Holocaust. Father's father was said to have emigrated from Europe well before the war and the rise of Hitler, with no experience of being in a camp and, by implication, quite young. Both Father and Mother were born in South America. Early in the therapy the family had spoken as if no active European connections existed, in either external or internal reality. A meaningful link with the Holocaust, including the fate of Father's extended family, became apparent in the therapy only as psychic awareness developed in the work with Miss F, and the significance of a missing father–son relationship became more real. We can now be aware that Bella's wardrobe dramatization and the preoccupations with death within the family may be multiply determined, and convey something of the prison and cemetery quality of the concentration camp as well as of a baby not able to survive the experience of a tomblike womb more directly based on the mythology of the nuclear family. It is possible that in the phantasies within this family a child who does not eat may become akin to a concentration camp inmate in the mind of a parent; children who do thrive may feel that they can be blamed for others perishing in the camp; a mother can try to protect a child, projecting culpability for harm on to a 'Nazi' father.

The family discussed here differs from the families in this research in that neither Bella's parents nor her grandparents were themselves actual direct victims of Nazi persecution; it was members of earlier generations, Father's grandmother and aunts, who perished. One may wonder, of course, how difficult it may have been for Father's father to mourn his mother and sisters, whom he left behind in Europe, and how an uncontained, unmourned presence of their unknown camp experiences and deaths may have pervaded both Father's childhood and again that of the next generation, Carla and Bella. In this context one may also wonder, but no more, about what might be called Mother's 'overvaluation' of Bella, and her fears that the children could die. Father cannot bear to continue the family name and tolerate the cross-generational link with his father, who left his own mother and sisters in a world which became that of the Holocaust. To notice and mourn the miscarriage of one baby boy seems, for this family, to be involved in an impossible guilt-making demand to notice and mourn multiple Holocaust deaths in the context of an unrecognized feeling of greedy survival.

THOUGHTS ON THE NATURE AND EFFICIENCY OF THE WORK

Two previous therapies had broken down. The opinion that the Roses were not a 'normal' family, attributed to the original therapists, lay behind the critical withdrawal from that therapy. It was now painfully raised by Father himself in the context of the withdrawal from this one. The therapeutic desirability for Father to be closer to Mother was specifically 'prescribed' by the second therapists. In the therapy under discussion the nature of the fluctuating experiences of closeness and non-closeness between the parents, together with the painful feelings underlying them, were the very stuff of the work itself.

Within the therapy, Miss F was initially experienced as a container who could receive what the family felt to be intolerable, and then as someone who could help the family to think about their anxieties. As she gradually attempted to make thoughtful links within the family drama, she was varyingly perceived in the transference as helpful or intrusive. Later she was experienced as a good linking figure between the marital couple, and as a mother/grandmother supporting the birth of new life, but finally as someone asking them to think about what they felt to be unthinkable. In the course of the work Miss F tried to acknowledge with the family when she was being perceived negatively by them, such as in the way they felt unattended to by her in the seasonal breaks. She found it less necessary to comment specifically on an ongoing experience of containment but did, however, find it useful to verbalize implicit positive transference experiences in regard to herself which implied some change in the family's perception of her, so that its underlying significance could be thought about. She thus acknowledged a belief, occurring towards the end of the therapy, of a wish to please her, and an implicitly positive transference view of her as a happy member of a family of three generations; this did in fact help to carry the work forward, however sad its outcome.

With such onerous and painful work, Miss F was grateful for thoughtful support from colleagues. On reflection, in view of the difficulties about father's place in the family, Miss F wondered if she could have attempted to explore further, in the transference, feelings about why she worked without a partner. She also wished she had been been able to make more active links in the transference with the severe splitting and hatred in the family, as indicated by Mother's non-forgiveness of Father's sister and the latter's 'spoilt' children, who were believed to be favoured by his mother in contrast to their own; for example, how unforgivable was she initially believed to be at the time of the clinic mini-drama in favouring such children with the session time they wanted?

Some therapists working in a family context insist on the attendance of all the family. Miss F had doubts about working without Carla. But it is clear from what transpired that work was done which was helpful for Bella, the indexed patient, although its extent was limited. Without any understanding of the meaning of the material – which, of course, Miss F could not have had when she started working with the family – it would be difficult to be dogmatic about demanding full attendance. When it does become clear, as it did here, that the attendance of a missing member is central to the family's problems, the position about continuing to work without them becomes more debatable.

How can one assess the outcome? After some containment of the family distress and anxieties, Bella no longer spent her evenings crying and banging in a dark wardrobe. Following developments in the understanding of the mythology, she put on some weight, started to menstruate again, and her outward appearance changed to that of a 'normal' adolescent. She sought and obtained a job which she was said to be holding successfully, and which probably embodied some escape from the painfulness of ongoing family life. A degree of physical and external change in this anorexic girl, within the eight months during which she herself attended the therapy, is clear, and one must assume that there was some minimal accompanying emotional movement to enable this adolescent development to take place. Major difficulties, however, remained. At least some of the food she did eat continued to be obtained by 'stealing' unobserved into the kitchen, and thus involved the psychic as well as physical exclusion of others; the collusive exclusion of her sister from therapy by her mother and herself continued. There was also some massive projection into Carla, although the sisters were latterly reported as being on better terms. A considerable improvement took place in the relations between the parents at one time, but could not be sustained.

Work with this disturbed family, even without the desirable and probably necessary presence of Carla for more substantial results, also led to some movement from drama to thought within the members themselves. It gradually became possible to be in touch with the meaning of some of their difficulties, culminating in the sad recognition of not feeling themselves to be a 'normal family' after all. The magnitude of the task that they felt might achieve this was also revealed, but could not be approached.

We saw in Chapter 8 how psychoanalytic family therapy could help Tony to rejoin family life, providing a basis for ongoing individual development and a happier interaction. Here it could help Bella to make some individual steps forward, away from the anti-developmental prison of the shared family mythology. Such therapy can be seen to have a contribution to make to understanding and possibly alleviating quite severe disturbance; the capacity to relate to, contain and possibly alleviate primitive emotionality held within a family may make it, in some cases, the therapy of choice.

10   Psychoanalytic Group
Therapy with Adolescents:
A Journey
in Psychic Reality

Psychoanalytically informed group psychotherapy, even if it is brief, may be able to offer a valuable experience to adolescents, some of whom would be unable or unlikely to seek individual therapy. I shall begin by giving some indication of the theoretical and practical background before describing therapy with a group of young people over a period of twenty-two weeks. It is in the minds of the therapists that the contributions of the group members are attended to as a whole, and I make considerable use of the responses of the therapists, Dr A and Mrs B, throughout the life of the group. In this way I hope to be able to present the members' experiences in the context of the container offered for them. I use the experience to amplify and reflect further on the nature and usefulness of the approach, before going on to think about some of its applications.

THE THEORETICAL BACKGROUND

Bion's understanding of group dynamics underlies and informs a Kleinian approach to psychoanalytic group psychotherapy. His descriptions of basic assumption and work group activity (outlined in chapter 1, pp. 10–11), have helped us to relate to many social groupings, ranging from those described in *Romeo and Juliet* to others in contemporary adolescent life. Bion, as well as introducing these concepts, paid particular attention to the detailed manifesta-

tions of basic assumption processes in his discussions of the therapy
groups he himself conducted. His later work in the field of
projective identification and containment (Bion, 1962a) now also
helps therapists to try to follow the way emotions may pass
between, and become redistributed among, group members in a
clinical setting. Clinical use of these new developments is
supported by his earlier understanding of the fundamentals of
group dynamics.

Developments within a wider field, some of which amplify Bion's
work, are also relevant. Gosling (1981), Hinshelwood (1987),
Jaques (1955), Menzies Lyth (1988, 1989a), Miller and Rice (1967),
Rice (1965) and Turquet (1974, 1975) are some of those who have
broken new ground in the understanding of group dynamics in
therapeutic, institutional and social contexts. Their findings
illuminate the need for therapists to be in touch not only with the
emotionality of the group as a whole, but also with the interactive
processes between the group and the institutional setting in which
it meets.[1] We shall see at the end of this chapter how this extension
of understanding is of value to those who want to widen the social
application of clinical interaction.

Psychoanalytically based group therapy, under the initial
stimulus of Foulkes, has also developed over a similar period, with
some degree of similarity to that based on the above thinking.
Within this latter approach, 'all communications and relationships . . . are seen as part of a total field of interaction: the group
matrix' (Foulkes and Anthony, 1957, p. 28; original emphasis), and
thus also involve the whole group. In this approach more emphasis
may, nevertheless, be placed on the individual member as the
object of treatment (p. 57), together with the part played by the
small group in 'taking on its own therapy' (de Maré, 1985, p. 112),
while many of those influenced by Bion's work have made 'more
systematic use of the group situation in their interpretations than
have most other therapists, in the sense of trying to base these on
the here-and-now dynamics in the group situation as whole'
(Sutherland, 1985, p. 62). In the group work described in this
chapter the therapists certainly worked 'with group processes and
the individual as related to them, and not with the individual
separately' (Menzies Lyth, 1974, p. 2).

SETTING UP THE GROUP

Dr A and Mrs B set out to offer a therapy group for eighteen-to-twenty-one-year-old patients; no group for this age range was currently available in the department where they worked. Experience had shown that some young people who clearly needed help had been unable to remain sufficiently in touch with their needs to sustain a commitment to individual therapy. The therapists, aware that in adolescence a sense of need, as well as of a self able to respond to it, can be fragmented and projected into others, hoped that if such projections could be held and thought about in the here-and-now of the therapeutic group process, members might be helped to become more aware of themselves and their own needs. They also bore in mind that in following this understanding of a fragmented sense of need, they might be offering some places to those in whom the degree of commitment was problematic, and that there could be risks of patients dropping out as well as acting out. It was also recognized that members of this age group, while seeking to fulfil their external adult status, might have left home and be without any form of direct family support, and thus in particular need of containment, much of which would have to be provided within the therapy.

The therapists envisaged including some isolated individuals who found themselves unable to take part in the ordinary social groupings of adolescence, together with some young people who were active participants in social group life, and in this sense 'naturals' for membership. Some potential members were likely to be geographically unsettled, between school, further education or work, and unable to make a long-term commitment. This, taken together with the need to have firm boundaries of time and place within which the group processes could be contained, indicated that the group should be a time-limited one. Plans were made to start a closed group with about eight members sometime in the autumn, finishing in the summer, and thus avoiding a long summer break during which some young people could be on the move. It was thought that this experience might be sufficient for some members. Others, having become more aware of their own needs, might seek, and be able to use, more therapy. Such an approach could also conserve therapeutic time.

There were, in fact, considerable difficulties in getting the group started at all. By the time eight patients had been gathered in the late autumn, some of those who had been waiting withdrew – sometimes no reason was given; others said they felt sufficiently helped by the exploratory work. As the group would have to finish in July, it was decided to make a start in February with six members who were currently waiting, and with whom the therapists had kept in touch about the delay. The therapists recognized that to increase numbers it would now be necessary to have an open membership in the initial phase. These initial arrangements will be discussed later in the light of the therapists' experiences in the group.

THE MEMBERS

I shall now give some information about the members and the way they joined the group.

From the First Session: *Ian*, aged twenty: a university student with problems concerning drugs, alcohol and sexual relationships. He was first seen in the clinic counselling service, and then by Dr A. *Bill*, aged twenty-one: an outdoor worker, who felt unsettled and appeared confused. He had left university after one year and had some rather unorthodox individual therapy. He came to the group after a consultation in the clinic. *Mary*, aged twenty-one: a university student, worried about her relationships, particularly with men, with whom she found it easier to have sex as opposed to what she felt were more meaningful personal contacts. After an exploration with a colleague in the clinic, she was seen briefly by Mrs B.

From the Second Session: *Sheila*, aged twenty: a student, going abroad at the end of the summer, and in the long term possibly seeking individual therapy. She was concerned mainly about not liking herself and her inability to keep her boyfriends. She was first seen in the counselling service. *Derek,* aged twenty-one: a shop assistant. He had previously been seen by Dr A in the course of a family exploration on account of his difficulties in mixing.

From the Fourth Session: Hamish, aged twenty-two: a postgraduate research student. On consulting his general practitioner about what he saw as a physical ailment, he had been surprised to be referred to the clinic, where it had been suggested that the group, to which he felt 'sent', might make him more psychically aware. *Annie,* aged eighteen: an intelligent girl who had dropped out of education and was living in a squat and subsisting on a mixture of temporary work and social security. She had seen Mrs B in the counselling service, and had become very involved in the experience.

From the Fifth session: Gordon, aged twenty-one: an outdoor worker. He was referred by an external counsellor specifically for group therapy in order to help him with mixing socially, and had been described as being of 'lowish IQ'. He was seen briefly by Mrs B before joining.

THE GROUP

To try to share the experience and the approach, I shall follow the group session by session, 'warts and all', but in the latter half describing only the main themes and events of some of the sessions.

The First Session: The therapists had arranged a room with a circle of eight chairs for the six expected members and themselves. Their hearts sank as only two people, Bill and Ian, joined them. (Some potential group members replied to their invitation later, saying they were feeling better, had been helped by the exploratory interviews, or had work commitments.) The therapists clarified the arrangements for the group: it would last until a specified date in July, there would be no Easter break, although Mrs B would be away for two weeks at that time, and each session would last an hour and a half. They explained that six invitations had been sent out for this beginning, and that the group would be open to new members for a time.

The two members spoke to each other about why they had come. Bill talked reassuringly about group therapy being OK and things being OK if you waited. Ian talked dismissively of his drug problems and claimed that things weren't much different in a group than in a pub. Mrs B remarked that nothing much seemed to be actively expected of the therapists, and Ian wanted to know if they were going to do anything. A third member, Mary, arrived, and commented on the empty chairs. The men said something about a babble of voices, and Mary said too many members would make her jealous. Mrs B commented on the presence in the discussion of the absent members.

Bill spoke lengthily and disjointedly, referring to his previous therapy, his mother's incurable illness, his carelessness with money and how the group was fine as long as no one was violent, but in too jumbled a form to comprehend. Attempts by Dr A to punctuate this monologue by pursuing the fear of violence made no impact; Bill continued to talk unclearly about past experiences, and said that he was relating to Mary by 'turning her off'. Despite this, some warmth came through, and Dr A suggested that Bill was keeping the group warm. Mary wanted to know what was going to happen, provoking immediate protests from Ian that it was their group and they could make it what they wanted. Mrs B took up the notion of group power, and possible anxiety about absent members. Mary giggled and suggested that the absent-member theme could be a plant. Ian asked where the tape-recorder was (perhaps with an implication not only of suspicion but of a need to keep the therapists 'taped'), and continued to protest that it was the members' group and they could do what they wanted. Despite these flares of verbal activity, the atmosphere was largely desultory. *Waiting for Godot* (Beckett, 1956) came to mind.

The therapists discussed the group after this and every subsequent session. They were dismayed both by the poor attendance and by the form of the session, and indeed felt that they had not 'done' enough, as Ian had implied. In retrospect, they thought it would have been better to be more open about Bill's jumbled flow.

Comment: The therapists may have wished they had been able to point to the conflict between the contemptuous dismissal of them as unimportant and possibly fraudulent on the one hand, and a feeling of passive demands from them on the other, suggestive of a dependent basic assumption that they must totally provide or be seen as worthless. Some intervention on these lines might have helped members to function more as a work group (Bion, 1961), which in this context would imply using the parts of themselves that were able to co-operate in the therapy as actively as possible.

The Second Session: Sheila and Derek joined the group. Dr A read out a letter from Ian saying he found it pointless to keep coming. Mary and Bill spoke of their 'pub group' meeting with Ian after the last session, in which Bill had said the group was worthwhile, and Mary had taken a 'wait and see' approach, with some implication of patience rather than passivity. Mary quizzed the two new members. Derek just managed to bring out a sentence about his difficulty in mixing, and was left alone for the rest of the session. Sheila spoke of not liking herself and losing her boyfriends. Bill talked in a rambling manner about boys and girls understanding each other, followed by some reference to a wireless in the night and ending with an egg, forgotten in the cooking, exploding and becoming malformed. Dr A, who momentarily lost contact with what he was trying to say (and thus tended to validate his interpretation), responded to anxieties about whether the therapists would be able to understand what was brought to them and hold it in mind, or would lose touch with it, with fears of an explosive, 'malformed' outcome. Sheila wanted to know if the therapists were talking realistically, and this led on to conditions necessary for adequate group work being pondered: one view favoured cosiness; another asserted that past events were inappropriate. It was also questioned whether the group was only a concept in the minds of the therapists which they might discuss together. Mrs B said the therapists were now seen as a pair, who might think about the group, but possibly just for their own interest.

In their post-session discussion the therapists shared their relief about the increased membership.

Comment: The therapists were able to use themselves more actively as containers, while recognizing group anxieties about their not being able to do so. The membership were clearly engaged in the work group activity of attempting to relate to their problems.

The Third Session: All four current members came, two slightly late. Remarks about the waiting room led the therapists to comment on the meaningfulness to the group of the wait between sessions and waiting for latecomers. Sheila and Mary contrasted the ease of a sexual contact as opposed to a 'relationship'; Sheila said that no relationship lasted longer than three weeks. Mrs B responded actively, taking up anxieties arising in this third session about the group not lasting, fears of self-exposure and the risks of loving. Dr A pointed out the different responses to the material: Derek looked and watched; Sheila risked and exposed: others contributed or appreciated that their problem was voiced or shared. Afterwards both therapists felt that they had responded in a 'mothering' way to those who had 'exposed' themselves. Dr A, very aware of the way Derek had seemed to watch voyeuristically, had felt filled with despair. Mrs B had felt freer, and probably was freed, to take a more active role by the holding of despair by Dr A.

The Fourth Session: Hamish and Annie joined the group. The women, including Annie, discussed difficulties in relationships, with some comments about how men might react, while there was a dead sort of feeling among the men in the room, including Dr A. He pointed out how the women spoke as if the men were not there. Mary now succeeded in prising a response of 'Just shy' from the silent, and obviously reluctant, Derek when she asked if he ever spoke. Mrs B also pointed out how Bill now seemed to be pushed into becoming male spokesperson against his will. Whether the individuals, or the opposite sex, were 'used', as opposed to being related to as people, was now discussed. Hamish, quizzed about relationships, just seemed able to say that he had not gone 'that deeply' into them. Risks of exposure, and now perhaps the need to scapegoat someone else who was not taking such risks, were raised and linked with themes of the last session.

Comment: The projection of inadequacy into the men was used by the male therapist to inform his response, and we can see some similarity to the use of countertransference in family therapy discussed in Chapter 8.

The Fifth Session: The final new member, Gordon, joined, and remained silent throughout. Hamish volunteered to 'kick off', and 'introduced' himself in this, his second session; others followed suit, then there was silence punctuated by the odd desultory comment. Mrs B suggested that only the therapists were felt to know the rules of the game. Conveying disaster, Bill gave a jumbled account of how he had lost his job, partly through taking Valium, and was thinking of going to Mexico. Dr A took up both the feeling of despair and the escape from it. Mary led the group in trying to 'help' Bill, claiming that he would be better treated in individual therapy, and that the group should meet twice a week; it was, after all, 'their' group. Dr A, referring to the original 'kick off', said it was no longer 'kick the football' but 'kick the therapists'. Bill ventured that others understood what he said, though he didn't himself. This led to pondering by the therapists about the nature and utility of group processes: could others be aware of something about you that you were not, and was this helpful? What about silent members? Mary objected to Derek's silence, as she did to that of her flatmate, with whom she shared a sink, but not communications. Mrs B, aware of Annie's difficulties, and her own, but also with Derek and Dr A in mind, took up the possible pain in the group setting of members who had had a previous relationship of a different nature with a therapist. Dr A referred to the greasy blocked-up sink aspect of the group's mentality. Sheila said they could just say unpleasant things about each other. Both therapists thought afterwards that they had been active in elaborating and containing despair.

Comment: Such containment probably helped the group to work with some of its pain. 'Going to Mexico' now became a piece of group vernacular, sometimes with changing geographical connotations, for shared escapist phantasy which now carried meaning for the group.

The Sixth Session: Sheila and Annie were late, and the group seemed to be preoccupied with the unspoken question of whether it could manage without them. Hamish complained of the therapists' failure to spell out their supposed rules: that there should be no absent members, the therapists suggested. Mrs B was reprimanded for her 'interruptions', and she talked about the group's experience of her as a bad presence, a non-therapeutic therapist. Annie arrived, followed shortly by Sheila. The therapists' 'interferences' were reverted to: Dr A said members were being asked to declare if they were 'therapist-bashers' or not. Sheila proposed an extension of group time, with favourable group responses, especially, it seemed, because it was thought that this might interfere with the therapists' – implicitly shared – supper time, or with their time for other groups.

Comment: An atmosphere of children against parents was very apparent in this session. Themes commonly occurring in individual psychotherapy can be seen, such as greedy demands for more time for the group, and envy of time phantasied as being spent by the therapeutic pair feeding themselves in some kind of 'oral intercourse', or with other 'children'. The absence or lateness of members clearly affected those present.

The Seventh Session: Only Sheila, Gordon, Hamish and Derek were present. Mrs B gave the dates for her two weeks' absence. Hamish wanted to know if she would be replaced. Mrs B suggested that feelings about today's absences and her own future absence were being replaced. Silence followed. Sheila wished she could eat instead of coming to the group. Various demands for extra group time followed. Comments on the therapists' silence led to interpretations that they kept their best talk for their supper hour. Hamish implied that the group would be an interesting topic of conversation for the therapists, but wanted to know if others thought that group therapy was any good. Dr A suggested that it was felt to be a way of therapists filling their time before supper. Sheila angrily attacked the pointlessness of the group. Mrs B took up the despair about members' listening capacity (Gordon was asleep) in the context of the three absences today, and hers in the future. Complaints were made about Mrs B's 'interruptions', and some unclear idea about shuffling around group membership arose. Mrs B thought this might refer to pleasure in getting rid of herself, when she 'interrupted' the group by her absence. Some – also unclear – ideas about group disintegration followed, but accompanied by pleasure in looking forward to more of Dr A. The group ended with feelings of impotence and despair.

Comment: The importance for the group of the parental transference that was at times carried by the therapists is apparent, as is some pleasure in splitting the 'parents'. The 'presence' of the missing members and the importance of the going-away Mrs B are also clear.

The Eighth Session: Only Sheila and Hamish were present to meet Dr A at the beginning. Sheila said she thought the group was breaking up, and Hamish smiled as if he was pleased. Dr A puzzled about what one might do about, or learn from, the 'group is breaking up' sort of feeling; the implication of the present response being that all one could do was to leave it oneself, and good riddance. Derek and Bill came in, and Bill spoke in rambling fashion about a job he had got. Mary followed, and took up her now traditional role *vis-à-vis* Bill: keeping him going. The group became relaxed, and the entrance of Gordon, who settled himself down in a state of semi-sleep, was barely noticed. Dr A took up the mood: 'Thank goodness Bill and Mary are at it again – we can relax', thus avoiding feelings of the group breaking up and absentees or latecomers contributing to its downfall. Mary now talked of her forthcoming holiday, which she might have given up if the group was worthwhile, and invited Hamish's contribution to this topic. Hamish said he had hoped to receive medication for his (specified) complaint, with the added implication that he was still waiting for it. Mary criticized his unconstructiveness towards the group. Dr A linked Hamish's comments, with their implication that the group did not deliver the goods, with Mary's proposed absence on holiday for a similar reason. Mary, somewhat shaken, accepted this and asked Hamish about his life. Hamish said he did not like the fact that his parents had separated recently, nor his mother being away on holiday. Sheila asked if outside material was relevant, and Dr A wondered if there was a feeling of uselessness in the group linked with Mrs B's assumed holiday. Sheila now owned to some feeling of responsibility for the break-up of the group when she had been denigratory at the beginning, and was able – with help, and close to tears – to link this with her behaviour with boyfriends and the break-up of relationships. Other members now seemed to support the relevance of bringing in real-life situations. Sheila now thought the group was better, and they were getting more from the therapists. Dr A recalled how the therapists' supper time was felt to be better than ordinary time, and wondered if what they experienced was time being stolen behind Mrs B's back. Oh no, it would have been just the same if Dr A had been away instead, was the rejoinder.

Dr A, reflecting afterwards, felt that there had been a seductive attempt to enrol him as one of the group: 'When the cat's away, the mice will play.'

Comment: The interchanges between Mary and Bill seemed to be experienced by the group as basic assumption pairing activity which would ideally produce something new and save the group from its anxieties about breaking up. This, however, yielded easily on interpretation, and was followed by work group activity.

The Ninth Session: Mrs B was still away, and Mary was on holiday. Dr A read apologies he had received from Annie about her non-attendance and wondering if she should continue to come. Sheila said she and Mary had told Annie last Thursday that the group was better, and she should do so. Dr A tried to elicit feelings about these absences, with responses from Sheila and Bill that it did not affect them. Bill and Gordon became involved in a lengthy 'man-to-man' conversation about their similar work, finally concluding that there was little point in working because they would end up paying tax. Dr A pondered if this also applied to the group, which felt very dragging. Sheila and Hamish engaged in some talk about difficulties with their fathers, and the group went on to the topic: does one keep out of their way and keep quiet, or confront them? Dr A pointed out that some members of the group had met at Annie's at the time originally requested for an extra meeting, and how facial expressions and smiles in the room indicated that people were actively keeping quiet about this. Derek grinned and remained silent; Bill went into a lengthy perambulation about his dead father. Members accepted Dr A's link with the last session, and the difficulties of the whole group membership openly confronting the meaning of time felt to be taken behind 'Father' and 'Mother' therapists' backs.

The Tenth Session: Only Bill, Hamish, Mary and Derek attended. Mrs B was back. Sheila was on holiday. Bill wanted to know if people felt better in the spring, and Mary said she wanted to feel different, but without success; both contributions were jointly linked by the therapists to the persistence of 'wintry' feelings associated with missing members. Mary spoke of the earlier visit to Annie, who had wanted to go dancing rather than talk and who, Sheila and she now thought, had been a little superior in the group. Hamish made several bright-sounding remarks which appeared to divert from thinking about the 'wintry' feelings, and was challenged on why he came; in response, he made a scathing joke about group therapy being a cure for his physical condition. Mary spoke of missing a woman friend, and feeling criticized by her mother and flatmate for smoking too much. These interchanges led to remarks from the therapists about the difficulty of exploring the wintry feelings among the group; had Mrs B gone away for two weeks to escape them? Hamish, referring overtly to Mary's difficulties in her flat, said she was silly not to leave a house with bad relationships, and Mrs B wondered if the missing patients in the group were now felt to be the sensible ones. Mary recounted how the house she lived in now would soon be pulled down, and Dr A drew attention to the ending of the group. This was followed by a fairly clear account by Bill of how he felt infantilized by his landlady and her husband, who wanted tenants kept in their place; they were not issued with keys, or allowed to order milk. Mrs B related this to how therapists may be felt to 'let out' a bit of the clinic and themselves briefly for their own good, but not according to patients' needs – or demands.

Comment: The transference to the therapists has become very obvious in recent groups. Some struggle to stay with the 'wintry' feelings and not do the equivalent of 'going dancing' with Annie, or 'into spring' with Hamish on the lines of the earlier 'going to Mexico' is apparent.

The Eleventh Session: Only Hamish and Derek were present for most of this session, much of which was spent in silence. Hamish claimed that it didn't matter who was absent, and that replacement was easy. An anticipatory look of excitement from Derek on Bill's arrival was commented upon in the context of there now being three members to 'have a go' at the two therapists.

The Twelfth Session: Gordon (absent) was described as a non-participator, and Derek (present) as only a 'taker'. There was some attempt, in a fairly sad atmosphere, to think about what 'missing' the group meant when one was absent oneself, and to explore resentment and guilt accompanying an unequal 'give-and-take' process between members themselves and between members and therapists. Bill said he was saving rather than frittering his money, and a link was made with the idea of something worth saving in the group.

The Thirteenth Session: At the beginning there was speculation about Annie having left; Mary described this in terms of being the first to jump off an aircraft. In a grumpy atmosphere, Sheila asked Mary if she wanted to shake the silent Derek. In an ensuing silence, Gordon draped his coat over the chair which had been left vacant for Annie, and the therapists drew attention to the camouflaging of absence and ending, with perhaps others silently preparing to bale out. Bill said he must get his relationship with his mother improved or he was finished, indicating an urgency to get work done to avoid dying with the group.

Comment: There is a flight from the forthcoming ending, but a need to work is also recognized.

The Fourteenth Session: Mary said that Annie had left. Mary and Sheila lengthily discussed their relationship, including problems of mutual envy and also rivalry for Bill (who was away), although Sheila said she was no longer interested. The therapists reacted very differently to the interchange: Mrs B thought inwardly that the women might really be working, and that perhaps Dr A was falling asleep; Dr A, meanwhile, felt that he had gradually been put to sleep, and found it hard to participate. The two women had moved on to saying how they could get angry with girls, but not with boys, even horrible ones. Dr A rallied himself and spoke of the 'horrible boys' in the group who were not participating. (Derek, uncharacteristically was looking out of the window rather than behaving voyeuristically, and Hamish was looking into space with a glazed look.) Dr A wondered what this meant in terms of the group, and checked with Mrs B how she felt. Mrs B, relieved by his intervention, spoke to the feeling of having been cut off from Dr A as a consequence of the divisions made between the sexes in the group, which had been experienced within the therapeutic couple. The group now became less polarized.

Comment: The splitting of the therapists here resonates with what happened in the Branch family in Chapter 8; we can see how it was useful for the therapists to relate to it directly in the session.

The Fifteenth Session: Several members came late and Hamish remarked, with apparent pleasure, that groups got smaller. Sheila said that when people were missing it always made her think about what had happened in the last group. Bill came in, and held the group spellbound with his account of how he had skipped the last session for a football match. Gordon then took the group's attention with a long account of the iniquities of a fellow worker. The skipping off by the group to watch Bill's show and follow Gordon's 'Whodunnit' in preference to the previous topic were taken up by Dr A and linked to the 'going to Mexico' of an earlier session. Gordon and Bill then talked about their similar occupations, continuing to keep out the idea of the ending. When this was commented upon, Bill said how much he had got from the group.

Mary was crying by now, and Bill asked why; Mary said she wasn't any better outside, but could use the group more.

Comment: Moves to avoid attending to the pain of ending were evident, but there was also some attempt to work with more depressive anxieties: feelings of personal responsibility for what happened, and the pain of failure to achieve as much as one would have wished.

The Sixteenth Session: Bill excitedly got members to change places, leaving a gap next to Dr A. Mrs B wondered whether this was a version of musical chairs in which Dr A had to be 'out' as a result of some supposed harshness the previous week. Bill replied that he did not think that 'Dr B' (referring to Dr A, but using Mrs B's name) was more beastly than the other therapist. Mary and Sheila had a long, friendly exchange, and Mary then said she couldn't come for the last sessions because of an unavoidable work commitment. As this was questioned Mary looked appealingly at Bill, who responded that he had thought of taking a bus to Egypt. Sheila now announced that she was going to the States on the fourth of July for the work assignment she had previously mentioned, and would miss the ending. The therapists pointed out that whatever the external reality, the pairings of 'Dr and Mrs B', and then of Mary and Sheila, followed by the 'going to Egypt' in the style of 'going to Mexico', and further accompanied by a 'Declaration of Independence', suggested an avoidance of feeling dependent on a group that was ending, with fears of beastliness breaking through. Hamish said that as there were only four more sessions he did not find it necessary to miss any, in the process cutting out two sessions of group life. When this was pointed out, he dismissed it as meaningless. Bill spoke wordily about whether he was repeating a pattern of living, and how he wasn't sure if he was working in the group or showing off. Mrs B wondered if he was now attempting to contemplate the meaning of the ending for him, as opposed to continuing previous patterns, such as 'going to Mexico', and, if so, what he might be indicating for the rest of the group.

Comment: The importance of the ending became more and more evident, together with the attempts to deny it.

The Seventeenth Session: Confusions on the subject of ending abounded. Times when Mary and Sheila might be leaving were mixed up. A feeling that there wasn't anything else to do but just pack up and go was interpreted by Dr A. Bill inexplicably 'explained' his lateness with an account of a train journey, which seemed to be a further journeying away from the group. Sheila doubted the importance of knowing in advance about the ending, and when Hamish questioned how she would feel if it was to take place that day, she asked excitedly if it was going to do so. Mrs B commented on the pleasure of being part of an apparently exciting piece of action, 'News is being made', as an alternative to the experience of loss.

Bill gave a lengthy but incomprehensible version of what was meant to be happening: the therapists gradually grasped that a 'parcel' with unclear contents was being passed around the group. They suggested that Bill was both being used as, and acting as a receptacle for some of the muddle in the group about ending, which was being voluntarily recirculated within it to keep the experience at bay. This seemed to lead to some awareness of the end. Members asked if people had been helped. Bill insisted that Mary had changed; Mary thought she might be firmer with her flatmate, but that kind of change wasn't good. Bill claimed to have been helped by the group, and said that in a social situation no one would listen to him for more than five minutes. Mary spoke of not knowing what to do after the group: she wanted individual therapy, but would probably try encounter groups which, she thought, would probably not be good for her. Sheila spoke of not knowing how to replace the group, and wasn't sure if she needed to. Mrs B took up a fluctuating sense of experiencing the actual ending of the group as an intrinsic event, with a risk that any sequel would be seen as a bad version of the group.

Comment: The ending became more real, and was accompanied by persecutory pain.

The Eighteenth Session: Bill spoke movingly of his feelings of loss, and how he would feel paralysed when the group finished. Discussion followed about what the therapists would do after the summer; perhaps have a new group, someone suggested. A massive, confused account from Bill about a taxi ride and the number of 'p's' (pence) in the tip followed. The therapists felt confused and thought, on reflection, that they might have failed to understand or verbalize some painful feeling about the group being tipped out, probably in favour of a new one, and that some of the 'pee' and confusion about the ending had been tipped into them.

Comment: Loss was acknowledged, but ended as confusion tipped into the therapists.

The Nineteenth Session: There was an outburst from Mary that she should be offered more – rather than having to ask, Dr A suggested. (It had been said earlier that anyone who wished to think about having more therapy of any kind, or wanted an individual review session, could write to the therapists and would be seen soon after the group had ended.) Sheila wanted to know why Bill didn't join another group. Mary sobbed and complained about relationships with someone who had been her friend, and agreed with Dr A that this had some reference to Mrs B, who had seen her before the group and, she felt, would now be involved with others. Dr A related this to the group as a whole. Bill blamed himself for not listening sufficiently to Mrs B and the others, but only to Dr A. Mrs B spoke to some sense of awareness that could be a spoiling aspect of one's own behaviour in an unwillingness to think about further help. Sheila said she had found the group of value, though it hadn't been what she expected. Mary concurred. Hamish said he had got nothing: the group had just become a habit, although that afternoon in the week might feel a bit odd at first. Sheila thought she might get private therapy during her time abroad. Dr A and Mrs B brought together various theories about further therapy: the group was all that was available; therapists were too busy with others; the actual therapists were powerful, but neglectful. Bill thought Mrs B wanted them to help each other. Mary wondered if Hamish had been left out, and the therapists wondered if he embodied for the group an 'I care for nobody' attitude in the context of an ending of active group care.

Comment: Some constructive reviewing was attempted.

The Twentieth Session: Hamish said he had spoken to Derek, who told him he had got nothing out of the group: the therapists must have been there for a reason, and should have helped Derek, and also himself, more. Derek, speaking with difficulty, was persuaded to confirm this. The therapists took up the puppet/puppeteer aspect of this interchange, illustrating how members of the group could speak through each other, and the pleasure in the mutual attribution of failure. Mary said that what people got was their own responsibility. By now Sheila was crying; she talked of saying goodbye to a friend outside the group. (It was her last session.) Mrs B spoke about the difficulty of sharing sadness among the members within the group. Sadness about the ending, while at the same time trying to think about the future, was now conveyed by Sheila, Bill and Mary.

Comment: Acrimony vied with responsibility and sadness.

The Twenty-First Session: Hamish said that Derek had told his boss he wasn't coming any more. Dr A clarified that this had not been said in the group. No, going downstairs, said Hamish. Maybe the 'boss' in the group had been told, said Dr A. Gordon gave an uninsightful account of some driving 'accidents', involving police questioning, all of which were presented as the total fault of others, followed by a further account of a threat of the 'sack' for work he had not done when he was upset. The therapists puzzled about the possibility of some negligence, and wondered whether this spoke to undone work in the group. Mary thought Dr A was harsh; Dr A said he was now felt to be the policeman in the group. Mrs B spoke of his heavy cold as well as what was felt to be his cold attitude. Mary complained of Mrs B's protection of Dr A. Dr A talked about the resentment of the relationship between himself and Mrs B, which was felt to continue in the context of the dispersal of the group.

The Twenty-Second and Final Session: Bill phantasied the therapists sitting in a room with no patients; Mary said she had not thought of the therapists having a life apart from the group. Hamish complained that the group was too short, and was ending suddenly.

The truth that the date of ending had been known from the beginning was somewhat reluctantly admitted by Mary. Both she and Bill spoke of wanting more therapy, with an implied difficulty in asking for it. The therapists recognized that a feeling of being left out could lead both to spoiling of the experience itself, expressed within the group by Hamish, and to the difficulty of actually asking for more, expressed by Mary and Bill, and reminded members that they could ask for a review meeting with this in mind. Gordon came in, rather out of tune with the group, saying he was sorry for missed sessions, and it would have been better if he could have spoken more. Both he and Hamish sat looking somewhat downcast, while Mary and Bill continued to participate with a feeling of sadness.

GENERAL REFLECTIONS ON THE GROUP'S FRAMEWORK AND METHOD

The start of the group was delayed: this not only led to the loss of some potential members, but also limited its life. This, in turn made an Easter break inadvisable, depriving the group of what might have been a helpful experience in preparation for the ending. An individual exploration around the nature of group membership between one of the therapists and a potential member, which might have related to some pre-transference anxieties and helped a member to join the group, did not always take place, again largely due to constraints of time, and was regretted by the therapists. Prior contact might also have provided some awareness for the therapists about what it might mean to accept someone like Bill, who was not seen by either of them. The plan for closed membership, which had been thought of as contributing to an experience of a firmly bounded space, also went awry. However, the entry of new members proved perfectly feasible, and may even have been fruitful. This is in accord with the experience of Sinason and Kirtchuk (1985), who, working with a group of adolescents in a similar setting, found that the introduction of a new member could be experienced as contributing to the group's working potential. Despite the changes, the basic requirement of a stable external setting with clear time boundaries was, however, still provided for the group experience as a necessary adjunct to the space in the therapists' minds.

During the life of the group, various meetings of group members took place outside the sessions. Although this was a form of acting out, their existence – apart, perhaps, from the 'pub group' after the first session – had an adolescent flavour, and it seemed to be possible and appropriate to acknowledge such events, and try to relate to and make use of what they conveyed for the group in the sessions.

The therapists followed the experiences of group members, session by session. In their responses they attempted to give due recognition to each member's contribution, but to attend to it in a manner that was relevant for everyone in the room, avoiding a personal focus suggestive of what Bion (1961) called 'psychoanalysis in public'. This method of group work is particularly relevant to the splitting and projective processes of adolescence. Such therapy, in gathering and thinking about projections, as well as being interpretative, has a containing function and can be seen to have something in common with the family work described in Chapters 8 and 9.

THE CONTEXT OF THE EXPERIENCE

[*The numbers in brackets refer to sessions which illustrate the discussion.*]

The members' place in the therapists' minds was fundamental to the group from the beginning. The therapists, in fact, offered thoughtful containment, but needed to explore anxieties within the membership – that they, the therapists, would not be able to hold in mind what was brought to them, or that it would become malformed (2). These intrinsic anxieties within the membership about the therapists' capacity could sometimes be linked to events in the group: fears of group disintegration followed the expressed hostility to the time the therapists kept to themselves (7). Many of the interchanges related to anxieties about the viability of the group as a working therapeutic space. Could it, for instance, withstand the risks carried by self-exposure within it, and what it did to its own membership, as in the episodes of deadening the male members (4, 14)? At times external events could be constructively introduced and worked on within the group and linked to occurrences within it (8), but they could also be used as a means of escape (16).

Two major, recurring, interlinked themes were the importance of absent members to the group, with concomitant anxieties about its survival, and the importance to the group of the actual, planned ending. There was considerable resistance among the membership to the recognition of both these themes. The intrusive 'presence' of potential members who had not come was dramatically conveyed at the beginning (1). The actual absence of members in the ongoing sessions, or fear of it occasioned by lateness, could be understood as representing the lack of working potential in the membership, leading to despair and fears of the group breaking up (6, 7, 8). Attempts to avoid the impact of such feelings took various forms – a manic response of 'good riddance' (8), 'going dancing' (10) or a flight into spring away from winter (10). At times these reactions overlapped with those relating to the ending, around which numerous phantasies arose: the therapy 'house' was being pulled down because of the bad relations within it, or the ending was due to the therapists conducting the group as a selfish landlord and landlady (10). Members could also take flight from its impact in various ways: go off to a football match within a session, follow a 'Whodunnit' (15), 'take a bus to Egypt' (16), support a 'Declaration of Independence' from group dependence (16) or escape into the excitement of 'News is being made' (17). The ending could also be camouflaged (10); understanding about it could be muddled up within the membership (17) or tipped into the therapists (18). A wish to save and internalize what was worthwhile in the group also became apparent (12); some grappling with the more persecutory features of mourning was undertaken (17), accompanied by a gradual recognition of loss and with the emergence of more depressive feelings by some of the membership as the ending approached (19, 22).

THE GROUP PROCESS

The group process itself is central to understanding. Members could use each other adversely (4), or another member might understand something one did not understand oneself (5). It was possible to indicate how one member's contribution could serve to carry emotion for most of the group, especially in the form of flight away from psychic pain exemplified by 'going to Mexico' (5); it could also openly evoke something similar from others – Bill's flight into 'taking a bus to Egypt' (16) followed a plea from Mary, and was followed by a contribution from Sheila. Here individual propensities of a manic defensive nature may have operated in conjunction with a basic assumption of flight within the group. Bill and Mary's basic assumption pairing activities could rescue the group as a whole from the anxieties of breaking up (8). Such shared group activity could be differentiated from the way in which feelings, particularly negative ones, could be disowned by means of projective identification and located elsewhere in the group; Mary, Sheila and Annie could keep lively feelings for themselves and project deadness into the men (4), and Mary and Sheila could put the 'horrible boys' to sleep (14). A 'puppet master' Hamish could use a puppet Derek as a means of spreading his negative thoughts, and could be used by Derek to speak for him (20, 21). A silent Derek could also convey feelings by his eyes (3). Mary, when she herself felt that the group was not worthwhile, could stimulate Hamish's negative response (8), then disown her own state of mind. But good experiences could also be taken in: Bill could introject hope from being listened to (17).

In the to-and-fro of the group activity and therapeutic comment, it was possible for some learning from experience to take place, leading to some differentiaton of individuality from group process – something that is highly relevant to late adolescent development. Members could discover more about their own identities and propensities, as Mary may have done by reowning a particular negative response rather than leaving it vested in Hamish (8). Bill could become aware of his own neediness, and how he was helped (17). Mary and Sheila could work with and assess their perceptions of their external relationships in conjunction with their experiences in the group (3, 8). Experience underlay the fairly crude categorization of Derek as a taker rather than a giver, and Gordon as a non-participator within the group (12). The envious destructiveness displayed by Hamish (20, 22) could be noticed, and the membership helped with the difficult task of differentiating themselves from the degree of cynicism promulgated by some of Hamish's assertions (7, 11, 20), but without disowning what he could be expressing on their behalf.

TRANSFERENCE AND COUNTERTRANSFERENCE

As in family therapy, the therapists were informed by their countertransference, but relating in this therapy to the minds of all those in the group. Its use is graphically conveyed by the occasions on which the therapists could extract themselves from having been caught in the divisive activity between the sexes within the membership, and clarify what was happening (4, 14). The transference to the therapists was responded to in terms of the 'here-and-now' of the group process, but with a recognition of its child-based content where this was relevant (6, 7, 8, 10). Sometimes family-type emotions were conveyed, and some of the content of the sessions bore a similarity to what might be seen in individual psychoanalytic psychotherapy. The therapists were often seen as a pair to the extent that on one occasion Dr A was called 'Mr B' (16). The envy of the therapists' supposed supper time together, and the jealousy of other groups of 'children', accompanied by demands for extra time, were major themes (6, 7). There was pleasure in splitting the 'parents', joining up with one therapist behind the other's back, and in stealing time behind the backs of the pair (7, 8, 9). The bad 'presence' of a therapist who was about to be absent could be felt (7). There was also hostility to therapist-'landlords' who provided only temporary accommodation, where milk could not be ordered or keys issued – a theme relevant to the changes of adolescence (10). In this context, painful issues about the feelings of those who had had more individual relationships with the therapists needed to be acknowledged (5). What Menzies Lyth (1974, p. 3) calls 'transference processes' also took place among the membership within the group process – for example, those referred to between Sheila, Mary and Bill (14).

THE EXPERIENCE OF INDIVIDUAL MEMBERS

Ian: His attendance was too brief for comment, beyond saying that he later returned for a consultation in the clinic and was referred on to a group elsewhere, which he also left.

Bill: The therapists initially felt that Bill's presence was a problem, certainly for themselves, but he clearly found being listened to and an attempt made to understand him within the group not only therapeutic but unique (17). On occasion he became able to make clearly meaningful statements (10), and his involvement contributed to the efficacy of the group. The 'pass the parcel' activity (17) in particular suggests that he may have suffered from being used as a receptacle for projections. He tentatively raised the possibility of joining another group, but did not follow it up directly. The therapists informed his referrer of his continuing need.

Mary: She thought she had benefited from the group, and the therapists thought so too. Her interactions with Bill and Sheila often showed active use of the group regarding her problems in relationships. She gained some insight into some competitive and unconstructive aspects of herself (5, 8), and perhaps also into her capacity for work in the group itself. In a follow-up interview, Mrs B thought she appeared to have a stronger sense of wanting to know about herself, and it seemed appropriate to arrange psychoanalytic psychotherapy for her at her request.

Sheila: She also used the group actively. She was able to make links with her responsibility for events (8, 15) and appeared to benefit in a similar way to Mary.

Derek: Although his relentless voyeurism and silence (3,13) were understandably irritating to other members, his presence did not

seem to overburden the therapy. The way he 'got into' others with
his eyes, and his use by – and of – Hamish to express hostility (20,
21), could serve in the understanding of group processes. He clearly
needed therapy, and did have the opportunity to learn something
about himself in the group, although he was unable to make any
active use of it at the time. How far this was influenced by having
previously been seen with his family by Dr A we do not know, but
his inclusion was probably a mistake on this account.

Hamish: His contributions were frequently cynical and envious in
that they denied the meaning of experience, seeking to stir
destructive and disintegrative forces within the group (7, 8, 11, 22)
and what was obtainable from it, as in the final 'puppeting' of, and
ganging up with, Derek (20, 21). He could be said carry what
Meltzer, in a family context, calls a function of 'promulgating hate',
which 'consists in attacking the living links within the group by
playing upon the feelings aroused in frustration' (Meltzer, 1986,
p. 158). What he conveyed could, however, be used in the group
process for enabling some members to be more aware of
destructive attitudes within themselves (8). Hamish himself may
have obtained some minimal awareness of the psychic reality of his
own life through this experience. It seemed that he was previously
largely out of touch with his loneliness (8), as well as the psychic
isolation which accompanied his pleasure in hatred. His protestations about attendance having become a 'habit' (19) may even have
carried some undertones of the approach of Professor Higgins in
Pygmalion (Shaw, 1916), whose claim that he had just grown
accustomed to Eliza's voice and appearance covered a deeper
involvement.

Annie: Her active part in the group of members meeting outside
the therapy (9, 10, 13), taken in conjunction with her absence and
withdrawal from it, suggest a degree of acting out detrimental to
understanding from the work. This may have been related to her
previous dynamic relationship with Mrs B, which appears to have
been a contraindication to her membership.

Gordon: His membership seemed marginal; his name could be
forgotten and his attendance or absence could pass largely

unnoticed (8,12) by others and also by himself; he was sometimes asleep. He did not seem to experience therapeutic need, or to project it actively into others, and appeared neither to benefit from, nor to actively burden, the group. His statement at the end of the last session (22) might, however, be taken to portray a glimmer of insight and psychic awakening, and he did, in fact, go on to join another group in the clinic.

THE EXPERIENCE OF THE GROUP AND THE USEFULNESS OF THE APPROACH

Group members, varying in extent from individual to individual, were helped to be in touch with psychic reality; in particular: 'to acquire insights and understanding, confront painful truths, extend their knowledge of themselves and their relationships' (Menzies Lyth, 1974, pp. 2–3). In addition to – and apart from – its formal therapeutic function and structure, the group may have had something in common with the social adolescent groups referred to in Chapter 4, in that there was some opportunity to experience a range of emotional life within it. The functioning of the group may thus also have responded to a developmental lack in adolescent experience – that is particularly relevant to Bill, Derek, Gordon and Hamish, who may be assumed to have had their own particular difficulties in participating in social group processes. It does seem clear that group therapy of this kind can have room for the participation of some members who are, to a considerable extent, unaware of their needs, as was initially postulated by the clinic and the therapists.

In contrast with individual work – and, to some extent, longer-term group therapy – an experience such as this clearly does not provide the opportunity for 'working through'. Nor does it provide any particular attention to individual problems as such. In contrast to brief dynamic work, there is no formal opportunity for members to look at the involvements of their earlier or current external relationships. But in this group steps were taken in both containing despair and recognizing the flight from it. Hostility, jealousy, envy and greed could be given some kind of mental shape.

Projective activity could be examined, and differences between people could be seen as real, so that some increase in self-awareness could take place. While experiences within the group are unlikely to be of such a complexity or depth as to become internalized in a way that will have a major effect on the quality of inner objects, such a group can offer an opportunity for some change, and open the way for further development to take place. The membership could include, and in some cases clearly benefit, those who are unlikely to be offered or be able to sustain individual therapy – as in the case of Bill. Others, such as Mary and Sheila, could get to know themselves sufficiently to recognize the need for further help, and to feel hopeful enough, certainly in Mary's case, to seek it. The acknowledgement of the significance of the ending of a meaningful emotional experience, which some members of this group were able to make, is in itself a piece of emotional growth, significant in adolescent development, and can serve as a building block for further internalization of developmental experiences.

APPLICATIONS

The group we have just discussed was planned as a formal therapeutic experience, requiring clinical skill, a selection of members and some degree of commitment from them to sustain it. The essence of the approach, however, lies in the gathering in and holding of the thoughts and feelings of the participants in the minds of the therapists, which means that applications of it may be able to take place in a variety of settings. In many instances an initial application for group membership may not even be sought. Ellwood and Oke (1987), for example, describe pioneer work undertaken (with parental consent) with some twelve- and thirteen-year-old, highly physically mobile, boys in a large comprehensive school whose teachers found them restless, and difficult to engage and motivate. The actual work clearly needed to be adapted in style to the nature of the participants; boys such as these are unlikely to sit down and discuss problems calmly! Staff backing, helping to provide a firm boundary, was also clearly necessary.

Professional workers may seek to introduce a psychodynamic

group approach into communities such as in-patient adolescent units or residential adolescent homes, where a number of the adolescents may have a distressed background. Containment may be needed, but the therapists may not – at least initially – be perceived as containers. Meetings may be attended by some of the membership in a desultory or cynical fashion, with the therapists needing to pay attention to their own countertransference in order to be aware of responses which perceive the contact as pointless or hopeless, and the therapists themselves, perhaps, as mere institutional figures, not motivated by real concern. If the therapists are able to gather in and attend to this kind of pain and provide space for feelings which members find it difficult to think about, spontaneous participation may increase. In such circumstances, sustained regular attendance by the therapists is clearly important. Where a therapist, or co-therapist, is a member of an institution which – in the case of a hospital, for instance – may have a normal policy of staff rotation, discussion is obviously particularly important. Therapists in all institutional work, however, need to be able to help other staff within the institution to understand the need for the provision of a secure boundary for the experience to be viable (Menzies Lyth, 1988).

The group work described in this chapter varies in the intensity of contact offered. If it is adapted to the particular needs of the setting, and has appropriate institutional support, it may be relevant to innovative approaches to some of the interactions discussed in Chapter 5. In common with other therapeutic work in this book, it can provide an opportunity to get to know oneself, and to be able to bear doing so. This in itself may support further change and development.

NOTES

INTRODUCTION

1   M. H. Williams and Waddell (1991) elaborate this development in their discussion of 'Literary origins of the psychoanalytic model of the mind'. Rustin (1991b) discusses psychoanalysis and aesthetic experience in terms which exemplify changes in psychoanalytic writing about literature.

I   STUDIES IN LITERATURE

1   A PLAGUE ON ALL OUR HOUSES

1   Occurrences of basic assumption and work group mentality in everyday settings are described by Turquet (1974).
2   Rustin (1991a) elaborates on the difficulties of thinking portrayed in *Romeo and Juliet*.
3   Earlier versions of this chapter were presented at the 'Psychoanalysis and the Public Sphere' conference organized by the Sociology Department, Polytechnic of East London, and Free Association Books in October 1986, and at the Bridge Foundation, Bristol, in March 1990.

2   ACHIEVING ADULTHOOD IN A WORLD OF DECEPTION

1   The theme of honour and the integrative nature of these themes are also stressed and elaborated in Mueschke and Mueschke (1967).
2   An earlier version of this chapter was presented at the 'Psycho-

analysis and the Public Sphere' conference organized by the Sociology Department, Polytechnic of East London, and Free Association Books in October 1987.

3 THE AGITATION OF INEXPERIENCE

1 An earlier version of this chapter was presented at the 'Psychoanalysis and the Public Sphere' conference organized by the Sociology Department, Polytechnic of East London, and Free Association Books in October 1988.

II ADOLESCENT DEVELOPMENT AND THE SOCIAL FRAMEWORK

4 ADOLESCENCE: A PROCESS OF CHANGE

1 I should like to acknowledge my particular indebtedness, in writing this chapter, to Meltzer (1973).

2 Those who are unfamiliar with the theoretical approach of Klein and Bion may find the following useful: Hinshelwood (1991); Klein (1963c); Meltzer (1967, 1978a,b,c); Segal (1964).

3 Regular weekly observations of infants in their family environment have contributed to the understanding of infant life, including the building up of the inner world of the infant. Miller *et al.* (1989) describe and discuss such observations in the context of object-relations theory, and compare them with the findings of experimental and behavioural forms of observational study; Stern (1985) also discusses the world of the infant in terms of psychoanalysis and developmental psychology.

4 Isaacs (1952) discusses the nature and function of phantasy. Riviere (1955) discusses the unconscious phantasy of an inner world reflected in examples from literature.

5 These differences are examined in detail in Hinshelwood (1991, pp. 57–67).

6 This subject is reviewed in Hinshelwood (1991, pp. 94–111).

7 Klein (1955) discusses a novel illustrating projective identification.

8 Variations in terminology relating to introjection, projection and identification are usefully discussed in Sandler and Perlow (1988, pp. 1–12) and in Hinshelwood (1991).

9 Joseph (1988) discusses clinical aspects of projective identification.

    10 Coleman and Hendry (1990) review this literature.

5   THE ADOLESCENT AND SOCIETY

1   I use the word 'society' loosely, hoping that its meaning will be clear in the contexts in which it arises.

2   Numerous changes are made in the care system by the Children Act 1989, but the emotional situation described here is still relevant.

3   Mr G's work with Kit is described in detail in Copley (1988).

4   Consultations to the staff of a school with adolescents with learning and emotional difficulties led to the setting up of a course (attended by Mr G), devoted to helping teachers to relate to such tasks while still remaining in a teacher role (Harris, 1968; Salzberger-Wittenberg *et al.*, 1983).

5   The family consultation with Dirk and his mother is discussed from a clinical point of view in Copley (1987).

6   Buford (1991, pp. 270–315) gives a detailed description of the development and escalation of an episode of violence between football spectators and the police. This, I think, is a graphic example of fight/flight basic assumption activity.

7   Countertransference and transference in a wider setting are discussed in Copley and Forryan (1987); Salzberger-Wittenberg (1970).

III STUDIES IN THERAPY

6   PSYCHOANALYTIC PSYCHOTHERAPY WITH INDIVIDUAL PATIENTS

1   Responses of concentration camp prisoners to their guards, including that of becoming a 'slave personality', are discussed by Hoppe (1971) and Krystal (1971).

2   The difficulties in daring to try to leave a powerful, perverse gang are described by Waddell and Williams (1991).

7   EXPERIENCES IN A COUNSELLING SERVICE FOR YOUNG PEOPLE

1   This particular service is also discussed in Copley (1976). It is heartening to hear of the introduction of a new psychoanalytically

informed counselling service outside London (Bridge Foundation, Bristol). This has a similar approach to the one referred to here.

2   Hurry (1986) describes a psychoanalytically based walk-in service for adolescents in which there is some difference, in both theoretical orientation and immediate objectives, from the work outlined in this chapter. Both further the application of psychoanalytic thinking to adolescent needs.

Adamo (1990), in conjunction with accounts of the services referred to above (Copley, 1976; Hurry, 1986), describes Italian experiences of this kind of work.

8   ADOLESCENTS AND THEIR FAMILIES

1   The object-relations family therapy described by D.E. and J.S. Scharff (1987) has much in common with this approach.

2   Indications and contraindications for family therapy are reviewed more widely from both psychoanalytic and systems approaches in Offer and VanderStoep (1975).

9   AN APPROACH TO PSYCHOANALYTIC FAMILY THERAPY

1   Meltzer (personal communication) has commented on the enclosed family atmosphere of the Rose family as bearing some similarity to Lorca's 'House of Bernarda Alba' (Lorca, 1940).

10   PSYCHOANALYTIC GROUP THERAPY WITH ADOLESCENTS

1   R.L. Shapiro, J. Zinner, D.A. Berkowitz and E.R. Shapiro (1975) draw on Bion's group theory (1961) in their approach to group and family work, and in discussing the impact of group experiences on adolescent development.

BIBLIOGRAPHY

All books are published in London unless otherwise indicated.

Abraham, K. (1924) 'A short study of the development of the libido', in Abraham, K. (1927), pp. 418–501.

—— (1927) *Selected Papers on Psycho-Analysis*. Hogarth.

Adamo, S.M.G. (1990) *Un breve viaggio nella propria mente*. Naples: Liguori.

Association of British Insurers (1991) *Life Insurance and HIV/AIDS – The Facts*.

Auden, W.H. (1975) 'Music in Shakespeare', in *The Dyer's Hand and Other Essays*. Faber & Faber, pp. 500–27.

Bayley, J. (1979) 'Introduction' to Pushkin, A.S., *Eugene Onegin*. Harmondsworth: Penguin, pp. 9–30.

Beckett, S. (1956) *Waiting for Godot*. Faber & Faber. 2nd edn. 1965.

Bentovim, A. and Boston, P. (1988) 'Sexual abuse – basic issues – characteristics of children and families', in A. Bentovim, M. Hildebrand, E. Tranter and E. Vizard, eds *Child Sexual Abuse within the Family*. Wright, pp. 16–39.

Bick, E. (1968) 'The experience of the skin in early object relations', *Int. J. Psycho-Anal.* 49: 484–6 and in Harris and Bick (1987), pp. 114–18.

—— (1986) 'Further considerations on the function of the skin in early object relations', *Br. J. Psychother.* 2(4): 292–301.

Bion, W.R. (1959) 'Attacks on linking', *Int. J. Psycho-Anal.* 40: 308–15, and in Bion (1967), pp. 93–109.

—— (1961) *Experiences in Groups*. Tavistock.

—— (1962a) *Learning from Experience*. Heinemann.

—— (1962b) 'A theory of thinking', *Int. J. Psycho-Anal.* 43: 306–10 and in Bion (1967), pp. 110–19.

—— (1963) *Elements of Psycho-Analysis*. Heinemann.

—— (1965) *Transformations*. Heinemann.

—— (1967) *Second Thoughts*. New York: Aronson.

—— (1970) *Attention and Interpretation*. Tavistock.

Blom-Cooper, L. (1987) 'Out of court', *The Guardian*, 1 December 1987.

Blos, P. (1979) *The Adolescent Passage*. New York: International Universities Press.

Boston, M. and Szur, R., eds (1983) *Psychotherapy with Severely Deprived Children*. Routledge.

Box, S., Copley, B., Magagna, J. and Moustaki, E., eds (1981) *Psychotherapy with Families: An Analytic Approach*, Routledge.

Buford, B. (1991) *Among the Thugs*. Secker & Warburg.

Bunting, M. (1990) 'Hostels are no answer for us', *The Guardian*, 19 June 1990.

Butler-Sloss, E. (1987) *Report of the Inquiry into Child Abuse in Cleveland in 1987*. HMSO, Cmd. 412.

Canter, M., Comber, M. and Uzzell, D. (1989) *Football in Its Place*. Routledge.

Chambers (1977) *Twentieth Century Dictionary*. Edinburgh.

Chasseguet-Smirgel, J. (1985) *Creativity and Perversion*. Free Association Books.

Children Act 1989. HMSO.

Children's Society (1990a) *Young People under Pressure*.

—— (1990b) *Annual Review* 1989–90.

Coleman, J.C. and Hendry, L. (1990) 2nd edn., *The Nature of Adolescence*. Routledge.

Coleridge, S.T. (1798) 'The Ancient Mariner', in W.M. Dixon and H.J.C. Grierson, eds *The English Parnassus*. Oxford: Clarendon Press, 1909.

—— (1812) *Shakespearean Criticism, Lectures of 1811–12*, Lecture VII, *Romeo and Juliet*, Signet Classic edn, ed. J.A. Bryant, Jr. New York and Scarborough, ON: New American Library, 1964, pp. 173–83.

Comedia Consultancy (1991) (for the Gulbenkian Foundation) *Out of Hours*.

Copley, B. (1976) 'Brief work with adolescents and young adults in a counselling service', *Journal of Child Psychotherapy* 4(2): 93–106.

—— (1981) 'Introducing families to family work', in Box *et al.* 1981, pp. 35–47.

—— (1983) 'Work with a family as a single therapist with special reference to transference manifestations', *Journal of Child Psychotherapy* 9(2): 103–18.

—— (1987) 'Explorations with families', *Journal of Child Psychotherapy* 13(1): 93–108.

—— (1988) 'Demands on the worker in therapeutic work with children and young people', *Midland Journal of Psychotherapy* (1): 16-26.

—— and Forryan, B. (1987) *Therapeutic Work with Children and Young People*. Robert Royce.

de Maré, P.B. (1985) 'Major Bion', in Pines (1985), pp. 108-13.

Deutsch, H. (1968) *Selected Problems of Adolescence*. Hogarth.

Doyle, G. (1991) 'Who cares about the children of the state?', in *Gateway*, Children's Society, Summer.

Dryden, J. (1668) *An Essay of Dramatic Poesy*. ed. T. Arnold; 3rd edn. revised W.T. Arnold, Oxford: Clarendon, 1903.

Ellwood, J. and Oke, M. (1987) 'Analytic group work in a boys' comprehensive school', *Free Assns* 8: 34-57.

Erikson, E.H. (1968) *Identity: Youth and Crisis*. Faber & Faber.

Foulkes, S.H. and Anthony, E.J. (1957) *Group Psychotherapy*. Harmondsworth: Penguin.

Frank, A. (1947) *The Diary of Anne Frank*. B.M. Mooyart-Doubleday, trans. Valentine Mitchell. Pan, 1954.

Freud, S. (1905a) *Three Essays on the Theory of Sexuality*, in James Strachey, ed. *The Standard Edition of the Complete Psychological Works of Sigmund Freud*, 24 vols. Hogarth, 1953-73. vol. 7. pp. 123-245.

—— (1905b) 'Psychical (or mental) treatment'. *S.E.* 7, pp. 283-302.

—— (1911) 'Formulations regarding the two principles of mental functioning', *S.E.* 12, pp. 215-26.

—— (1917) 'Mourning and melancholia'. *S.E.* 14, pp. 237-60.

—— (1921) *Group Psychology and the Analysis of the Ego*. *S.E.* 18, pp. 65-143.

—— (1922) 'Some neurotic mechanisms in jealousy, paranoia and homosexuality'. *S.E.* 18, pp. 221-32.

—— (1923) *The Ego and the Id*. *S.E.* 19, pp. 3-66.

—— (1924a) 'The economic problem of masochism'. *S.E.* 19, pp. 157-70.

—— (1924b) 'The dissolution of the Oedipus complex'. *S.E.* 19, pp. 173-9.

—— (1931) 'Female sexuality'. *S.E.* 21, pp. 223-43.

—— (1933) 'Femininity' (New Introductory Lecture XXXIII). *S.E.* 22, pp. 112-35.

—— (1936) 'A disturbance of memory on the Acropolis'. *S.E.* 22, pp. 239-48.

Goethe, J.W. (1774) *The Sorrows of Young Werther*. Harmondsworth: Penguin Classics, 1989.

Golding, W. (1954) *Lord of the Flies*. Faber & Faber.

Goodsir, J. (1991) 'Justice and the new drugs culture', *New Law Journal*, 21 June 1991.

Gosling, R.H. (1981) 'A study of very small groups', in Grotstein (1981), pp. 627–45.

Grotstein, J.S., ed. (1981) *Do I Dare Disturb the Universe?* Caesura Press; reprint, with corrections, Karnac, 1983.

Harris, M. (1968) 'Consultation project in a comprehensive school', in Harris and Bick (1987), pp. 283–310.

—— (1976) 'Infantile elements and adult strivings in adolescent sexuality', *Journal of Child Psychotherapy* 4(2): 29–44, and in Harris and Bick (1987), pp. 121–40.

—— (1978) 'Towards learning from experience in infancy and childhood', in Harris and Bick (1987), pp. 164–78.

—— and Bick, E. (1987) *Collected Papers of M. Harris and E. Bick*, ed. M.H. Williams. Perthshire: Clunie.

Health Education Authority (1992) *Today's Young Adults: 16–19 Year Olds Look at Diet, Alcohol, Smoking, Drugs and Sexual Behaviour.*

Heimann, P. (1950) 'On counter-transference', *Int.J. Psycho-Anal.* 31: 81–4.

Henry, G. (1974) 'Doubly deprived', *Journal of Child Psychotherapy* 3(4): 15–28.

Hinshelwood, R.D. (1987) *What Happens in Groups.* Free Association Books.

—— (1991) 2nd edn, *A Dictionary of Kleinian Thought.* Free Association Books.

Hoppe, K.D. (1971) 'The aftermath of Nazi persecution reflected in recent psychiatric literature', in Krystal and Niederland (1971), pp. 169–204.

Howard League for Penal Reform (1990) Letter in *The Guardian,* 14 September 1990.

Hoxter, S. (1964) 'The experience of puberty', *Journal of Child Psychotherapy* 1(2): 13–25.

Humphreys, A.R. (1984) 'Introduction' to *Much Ado about Nothing*, Arden Edition. Methuen.

Hurry, A. (1986) 'Walk-in work with adolescents', *Journal of Child Psychotherapy* 12(1): 33–45.

Isaacs, S. (1952) 'The nature and function of phantasy', in Klein *et al.* (1952), pp. 67–121.

Jaques, E. (1955) 'Social systems as a defence against persecutory and depressive anxiety', in Klein *et al.* (1955), pp. 478–98.

Joseph, B. (1988) 'Projective identification: clinical aspects', in Sandler (1988), pp. 65–76.

Katz, I. (1991) 'Talking sex in Somerset', *The Guardian,* 8 March 1991.

Keats, J. (1817a) in *Letters*, ed. R. Gittings. Oxford University Press; 1970; corrected reprint 1975.

—— (1817b) 'On first looking into Chapman's Homer', in *The Poetical Works of Keats*. Macmillan, 1899.

Kenward, H. (1987) 'Child sexual abuse' in P. Maher, ed. *Child Abuse: The Educational Perspective*. Oxford: Blackwell, pp. 127–41.

Klein, M. (1932) *The Psycho-Analysis of Children*. Hogarth. 3rd edn. 1949.

—— (1940) 'Mourning and its relation to manic-depressive states', in Klein (1950), pp. 311–38.

—— (1946) 'Notes on some schizoid mechanisms', in Klein *et al.* (1952), pp. 292–317.

—— (1950) *Contributions to Psycho-Analysis 1921–45*. Hogarth.

—— (1955) 'On identification', in Klein *et al.* (1955), pp. 309–45, and Klein (1963c), pp. 55–98.

—— (1957) *Envy and Gratitude*. Tavistock.

—— (1963a) 'Our adult world and its roots in infancy', in Klein (1963c), pp. 1–22.

—— (1963b) 'Some reflections on "The Oresteia"', in Klein (1963c), pp. 23–54.

—— (1963c) *Our Adult World and Other Essays*. Heinemann.

——, Isaacs, S. and Riviere, J. (1952) *Developments in Psycho-Analysis*. Hogarth.

——, Heimann, P. and Money-Kyrle, R.E., eds (1955) *New Directions in Psycho-Analysis*. Tavistock.

Kobbé, G. (1976) *Kobbé's Complete Opera Book*, ed. Earl of Harewood. Putnam.

Krystal, H. (1971) 'Review of the findings and implications of this symposium' in Krystal and Niederland (1971), pp. 217–29.

—— and Niederland, W.G., eds (1971) *Psychic Traumatization: After-effects in Individuals and Communities*. Boston, MA: Little Brown.

Lasch, C. (1990) 'Afterword: the culture of narcissism revisited', in Lasch (1991), pp. 237–49.

—— (1991) *The Culture of Narcissism* (updated paperback edn.). New York: Norton.

Laufer, M., (1975) *Adolescent Disturbance and Breakdown*. Harmondsworth: Penguin.

Lorca, F.G. (1940) *The House of Bernarda Alba*, in J. Graham-Luján and R.L. O'Connell, eds Federico Garcia Lorca: *Three Tragedies*. Harmondsworth: Penguin, 1961, pp. 150–201.

Meltzer, D. (1967) *The Psycho-Analytical Process*. Heinemann.

—— (1973) *Sexual States of Mind*. Perthshire: Clunie.

—— (1975) 'Adhesive identification', *Contemporary Psychoanalysis* 11(3): 289–310.

—— (1978a) *The Kleinian Development*, Part I, *Freud's Clinical Development*. Perthshire: Clunie.

—— (1978b) *The Kleinian Development*, Part II, *Richard Week-by-Week*. Perthshire: Clunie.

—— (1978c) *The Kleinian Development*, Part III, *The Clinical Significance of the Work of Bion*. Perthshire: Clunie.

—— (1982) 'The conceptual distinction between projective identification (Klein) and container–contained (Bion)', *Journal of Child Psychotherapy* 8(2): 185–202, and in Meltzer (1986), pp. 50–69.

—— (1983) *Dream-Life: A Re-examination of the Psycho-analytical Theory and Technique*. Perthshire: Clunie.

—— (1986) *Studies in Extended Metapsychology*. Perthshire: Clunie.

——, Bremner, J., Hoxter, S., Weddell, D, and Wittenberg, I. (1975) *Explorations in Autism*. Perthshire: Clunie.

—— and Harris, M. (1986) 'Family patterns and cultural educability', in Meltzer (1986), pp. 154–74.

—— and Williams, M.H. (1988) *The Apprehension of Beauty*. Perthshire: Clunie.

Menzies Lyth, I.E.P. (1959) 'A case study in the functioning of social systems as a defence against anxiety', *Human Relations* 13: 95–121, and in Menzies Lyth (1988), pp. 43–99.

—— (1974) 'A personal review of group experiences', in Menzies Lyth (1989a), pp. 1–18.

—— (1979) 'Staff support systems: task and anti-task in adolescent institutions', in Menzies Lyth (1988), pp. 222–35.

—— (1985) 'The development of the self in children in institutions', in Menzies Lyth (1988), pp. 236–58.

—— (1988) *Containing Anxiety in Institutions: Selected Essays, Volume 1*. Free Association Books.

—— (1989a) *The Dynamics of the Social: Selected Essays, Volume 2*. Free Association Books.

—— (1989b) 'The driver's dilemma', in Menzies Lyth (1989a), pp. 124–41.

Miller, A. (1947) *All My Sons*, in Miller, *Plays One*. Methuen Drama, 1988.

Miller, D. (1969) *The Age Between*. Cornmarket/Hutchinson.

Miller, E.J. and Rice, A.K. (1967) *Systems of Organization*. Tavistock.

Miller, L., Rustin, M.E., Rustin, M.J. and Shuttleworth, J. eds (1989) *Closely Observed Infants*. Duckworth.

Minuchin, S., Rosman, B.L. and Baker, L. (1978) *Psychosomatic Families: Anorexia Nervosa in Context*. Cambridge, MA: Harvard University Press.

Money-Kyrle, R. (1953) 'Towards a rational attitude to crime', in Money-Kyrle (1978), pp. 245–52.

—— (1978) *Collected Papers of Roger Money-Kyrle*, ed. D. Meltzer. Perthshire: Clunie.

Mueschke, P. and M. (1967) 'Illusion and metamorphosis in *Much Ado about Nothing*', *Shakespeare Quarterly* XVIII: 53–67, and in J.R. Brown, ed. *Shakespeare, Much Ado about Nothing and As You Like It*. Macmillan, 1979, pp. 130–48.

Myerson, S., ed. (1975a) *Adolescence: The Crisis of Adjustment*. Allen & Unwin.

—— ed. (1975b) *Adolescence and Breakdown*. Allen & Unwin.

NACRO (National Council for the Care of Offenders and the Prevention of Crime) 1990, 1991 NACRO Briefings.

Offer, D. and VanderStoep, E. (1975) 'Indications and contraindications for family therapy', in Sugar (1975), pp. 145–60.

Orwell, G. (1949) *Nineteen Eighty-Four*, Secker & Warburg. Harmondsworth: Penguin, 1983.

Pafford, J.H.P., ed. (1963) *The Winter's Tale,* Arden Edition. Routledge, 1990.

Pines, M., ed. (1985) *Bion and Group Psychotherapy*. Routledge.

Pushkin, A.S. (1979) *Eugene Onegin* (1831), C. Johnston, trans. Harmondsworth: Penguin.

Rice, A.K. (1965) *Learning for Leadership*. Tavistock.

Richardson, S. (1747) *Clarissa*. Harmondsworth: Penguin, 1985.

Riviere, J. (1955) 'The unconscious phantasy of an inner world reflected in examples from literature', in Klein *et al.* (1955), pp. 346–69.

Rustin, M. (1991a) 'Thinking in *Romeo and Juliet*', in Rustin (1991c), pp. 231–53.

—— (1991b) 'Psychoanalysis and aesthetic experience', in Rustin (1991c), pp. 199–230.

—— (1991c) *The Good Society and the Inner World*. Verso.

Rutter, M. and Giller, H. (1983) *Juvenile Delinquency: Trends and Perspectives.* Harmondsworth: Penguin.

Rycroft, C. (1968) *A Critical Dictionary of Psychoanalysis*. Nelson. Harmondsworth: Penguin, 1972.

Salinger, J.D. (1951) *The Catcher in the Rye*. Hamish Hamilton. Harmondsworth: Penguin, 1958.

Salzberger-Wittenberg, I. (1970) *Psycho-Analytic Insight and Relationships.* Routledge.

—— , Henry, G. and Osborne, E. (1983) *The Emotional Experience of Learning and Teaching*. Routledge.

Samaritans, The (1991) Appeal.

Sandler, J., ed. (1988) *Projection, Identification, Projective Identification*. Karnac.

—— and Perlow, M. (1988) 'Internalization and externalization' in Sandler (ed.), 1988, pp. 1–11.

Scharff, D.E. and Scharff, J.S. (1987) *Object Relations Family Therapy*. New Jersey and London: Aronson.

Segal, H. (1964) *Introduction to the Work of Melanie Klein*. Heineman.

Selvini Palazzoli, M.S., Cecchin, G., Prata G. and Boscolo, G. (1978) *Paradox and Counterparadox*. New York: Aronson.

Shakespeare, W. *King Lear*, Arden Edition. Methuen, 1972.

—— *Romeo and Juliet*, Arden Edition. Methuen, 1980.

—— *Much Ado about Nothing*, Arden Edition, Methuen, 1981.

—— *The Winter's Tale*, Arden Edition. Methuen, 1963; Routledge, 1988.

Shapiro, R.L., Zinner, J., Berkowitz, D.A. and Shapiro, E.R. (1975) 'The impact of group experiences on adolescent development', in Sugar (1975), pp. 87–104.

Shaw, G.B. (1916) *Pygmalion*. Harmondsworth: Penguin, 1960.

Sigal, J.J. (1971) 'Second-generation effects of massive psychic trauma', in Krystal and Niederland (1971), pp. 55–65.

——, Silver, D., Rakoff, V. and Ellin, B. (1973) 'Some second-generation effects of survival of the Nazi persecution', *American Journal of Orthopsychiatry* 43(3): 320–7.

Sinason, V. (1985) 'Face values', *Free Assns* 2: 75–93.

—— and Kirtchuk, K. (1985) 'The function of the new member in an adolescent group', *Psychoanalytic Psychotherapy* 1(2): 63–78.

Skura, M.A. (1981) *The Literary Use of the Psychoanalytic Process*. New Haven and London: Yale University Press.

Spillius, E.B. (1988a) *Melanie Klein Today: Developments in Theory and Practice*, Vol. 1, *Mainly Theory*. Routledge.

—— (1988b) *Melanie Klein Today: Developments in Theory and Practice*, Vol. 2, *Mainly Practice*. Routledge.

Stern, D.N. (1985) *The Interpersonal World of the Infant: A View from Psychoanalysis and Developmental Psychology*. New York: Basic.

Sugar, M., ed. (1975) *The Adolescent in Group and Family Therapy*. New York. Brunner/Mazel.

Sutherland, J.D. (1985) 'Bion revisited: group dynamics and group psychotherapy', in Pines (1985), pp. 47–86.

Tchaikovsky, P. and Shilovsky, K. (1879) Opera libretto, *Eugene Onegin*, Opera Guide 38, ed. N. John. Calder, 1988.

Turquet, P. (1974) 'Leadership, the individual and the group', in Gibbard, G.S. *et al.* (eds.) *Analysis of Groups: Contributions to Theory, Research and Practice*. San Francisco and London: Jossey-Bass, pp. 349–51.

—— (1975) 'Threats to identity in the large group', in L. Kreeger, ed. *The Large Group*. Constable, pp. 87–144.

Waddell, M. and Williams, G. (1991) 'Reflections on perverse states of mind', *Free Assns* 22(2): 203–13.

Wagner, G. (1988) *Residential Care: A Positive Choice*. HMSO.

West, D.J. (1982) *Delinquency: Its Roots, Careers and Prospects*. Heinemann.

Wilde, O. (1891) *Lady Windermere's Fan*. Ernest Benn. 1980.

Williams, A.H. (1975a) 'Puberty and phases of adolescence', in Myerson (1975a), pp. 27–40.

—— (1975b) 'Problems of adolescence', in Myerson (1975b), pp. 11–24.

—— (1981) 'The micro environment', in Box *et al.* (1981), pp. 105–19.

Williams, M.H. and Waddell, M. (1991) *The Chamber of Maiden Thought*. Routledge.

Wilson Knight, G. (1961) *The Wheel of Fire*. Methuen.

Winnicott, D.W. (1946) 'Some psychological aspects of juvenile delinquency', in Winnicott (1984), pp. 113–19.

—— (1955) 'The depressive position in normal emotional development', *B. J. Med. Psychol.* XXVIII (II & III): 89–100, and in Winnicott (1958), pp. 262–77.

—— (1956a) 'Primary maternal preoccupation', in Winnicott (1958), pp. 300–5.

—— (1956b) 'The antisocial tendency', in Winnicott (1958), pp. 306–15.

—— (1958) *Collected Papers: Through Paediatrics to Psychoanalysis*. Tavistock.

—— (1960) 'Ego distortion in terms of true and false self', in Winnicott (1965b), pp. 140–52.

—— (1961) 'Adolescence: struggling through the doldrums', in Winnicott (1965a), pp. 79–87.

—— (1963a) 'From dependence towards independence in the development of the individual', in Winnicott (1965b), pp. 83–92.

—— (1963b) 'Hospital care supplementing intensive psychotherapy in adolescence', in Winnicott (1965b), pp. 242–8.

—— (1964) *The Child, the Family and the Outside World*. Harmondsworth: Penguin.

—— (1965a) *The Family and Individual Development*. Tavistock. Routledge 1989.

—— (1965b) *The Maturational Processes and the Facilitating Environment*. Hogarth.

—— (1984) (ed. C. Winnicott, R. Shephard and M. Davis) *Deprivation and Delinquency*. Tavistock.

Woods, M.Z. (1988) 'Bisexual conflict in the analysis of an adolescent boy', *Journal of Child Psychotherapy* 14(1): 33–49.

INDEX

This first edition of
The World of Adolescence:
Literature, Society and Psychoanalytic Psychotherapy
was finished in October 1993

The book was edited by Ann Scott,
copy-edited by Gillian Beaumont,
proofread by Alecks Sierz,
indexed by Ruth Levitt,
and produced by Ann Scott and Chase Production Services
for Free Association Books